MEDIATE, *Don't* LITIGATE

Peter Lovenheim

Mediate, Don't Litigate

How to Resolve Disputes Quickly, Privately, and Inexpensively— Without Going to Court

McGRAW-HILL PUBLISHING COMPANY

New York   St. Louis   San Francisco   Bogotá
Hamburg   Madrid   Mexico   Milan   Montreal
Paris   São Paulo   Tokyo   Toronto

3 4 5 6 7 8 9 DOC DOC 8 9 2 1 0 9

ISBN 0-07-038832-6

Library of Congress Cataloging-in-Publication Data
Lovenheim, Peter.
  Mediate, don't litigate.
  Bibliography: p.
  Includes index.
  1. Dispute resolution (Law)—United States.
2. Mediation—United States. I. Title.
KF9084.L68 1989   347.73'9   89-12088
ISBN 0-07-038832-6   347.3079

Book design by Patrice Fodero.

Contents

Part Four. Appendixes

For my parents,
and especially for Marie

Acknowledgements

I appreciate the help of many people who shared information and ideas with me for this book: Madeleine Crohn, Edith Primm, Andrew Thomas, Elsje H. van Munster, Janet Coyle, Dave Scheffer, Guy Kettlehack, Ruth C. Wolfe, Shannon Mock, Joseph H. Gordon, Anita Miller, Jack Heister, Pattie Allred Taylor, Glenn Powell, Barbara Ashley Phillips, Don Reder, Bill Logue, William Hartgering, Megan Sylvester, Kenneth Cloke, Michael S. Gillie, Janice Roehl, Nadim Saleeby, Joan B. Kelly, and Bill Lincoln. Thanks also, for their research assistance, to Lara Badain and Michael Lipman.

I am especially grateful to those who took the time to read all or part of the manuscript and make valuable suggestions: Ron Kraus, Joan Semrau, Rabbi David Katz, Mona Miller, Amy Mantell, Arthur Posner, and Michael Venditto.

To my family I owe special and important thanks: to my parents, June and Andrew Lovenheim, for the education and opportunity to write this book; to Robert and Jane, for making sure I kept at it; to my wife, Marie, for her encouragement, confidence, and patience; and to Sarah and Valerie—may all your disputes be little ones.

PART
ONE

Why Mediation?

CHAPTER
1

Why Mediate?

In 1850, Abraham Lincoln made some notes for what historians think was a lecture on law he intended to give to a group of fellow lawyers. We don't know whether Lincoln ever gave that lecture, but his notes survive. This, in part, is what he wrote:

> Discourage litigation. Persuade your neighbors to compromise whenever you can. Point out to them how the nominal winner is often a real loser—in fees, expenses, and waste of time.[1]

As a nation, we have not followed very well Lincoln's advice. Indeed, ours has been called "the litigious society." Today, we have more lawyers (713,000) and file more lawsuits (15 million per year), than any other country in the world. To the slightest point of conflict, our conditioned battle cry seems to be "See you in court!"

From 1964 to 1984, the per capita rate at which lawsuits are filed has nearly tripled.[2] Each year, 40,000 law graduates are admitted to the bar.

As one observer noted, "we call our lawyers to sue before we call our opponents to talk."[3] Some of the lawsuits people bring might be amusing if they were not so pathetic: the group of parents who sued all the way to federal court over an official's error in a

3

high school football game;[4] the man who sued a restaurant because his pat of butter weighed less than two full ounces.

Many people who rush to file lawsuits soon discover the many inefficiencies of having one's "day in court": high legal fees, months or years of waiting for a case to come to trial, the frustration of being dependent on a system whose practitioners speak a foreign language of *habeas corpus, corpus juris,* and *res ipsa loquitor.*

"There are thousands of clients throughout the United States today," Justice Howard Ryan of the Supreme Court of Illinois has acknowledged, "who are shocked when they realize that they are going to have to wait not a year, but two, three, four, or five years before they can hope to go to trial."[5]

As in Lincoln's time, so in our own: you may "win" your lawsuit only to lose in terms of fees, frustration, and wasted time. In court cases where plaintiffs recover less than $10,000 (a majority of all cases filed), studies show the total fees paid to both parties' lawyers, when billed at an hourly rate, will equal or even exceed the amount received by the "winning" party.[6]

As the French philosopher Voltaire once said, "I was ruined but twice,—once when I won a lawsuit and once when I lost one."[7]

Many people who have spent too many years and too many dollars dragging through the courts might agree with what Judge Learned Hand said in an address to the New York Bar Association in 1926: "As a litigant, I should dread a lawsuit beyond almost anything else short of sickness and death."[8]

There is another important, though less obvious, reason for frustration with the courts. Contrary to what many nonlawyers may think, our legal system is not designed to solve people's problems. Its goal is loftier, more abstract: *to find the truth.* As every first-year law student can recite, "from the clash of able adversaries [that is, lawyers], the truth shall emerge."

Sometimes it works. After pleadings, interrogatories, examinations, depositions, courtroom testimony, evidentiary objections, and deliberations of the jury, the truth may be known: "guilty," or "not guilty"; "breach of contract," or "not breach of contract"; "violation of leash law," or "no violation of leash law."

But truth-finding and problem-solving are not always the same thing. When you have a dispute with someone, truth is not necessarily what you want; what you want is your problem solved—

quickly, fairly, and inexpensively—so that you can get on with your life.

If your dispute is with someone with whom you need or want to have a long-term relationship, for example, a business customer, a neighbor, family member, or friend, an official finding of fault or guilt—not to mention all the nasty things your lawyer said to prove it—can easily destroy what ever might have been left of the relationship.

The Chinese say: "A lawsuit breeds ten years of hatred."[9] The Chinese may be optimistic.

The Mediation Experiment

In the 1970s, in an innovative effort to relieve our overburdened court system, the Department of Justice and the National Institute of Justice conducted an experiment in three American cities— Atlanta, Kansas City, and Los Angeles. The goal was to answer this question: Could disputes involving ordinary citizens be successfully resolved through mediation as an alternative to traditional litigation? In mediation, disputing parties come together for a private, face-to-face meeting with a specially trained and neutral third party, called a "mediator," who helps them work out a solution to their dispute.

In eastern cultures, mediation has long been the preferred method of resolving disputes. In Japan, where there are said to be more flower arrangers than lawyers, mediation has a rich history. In China, it is estimated that 35 times as many disputes are settled through mediation as through the courts; some 800,000 mediation panels operate at local and regional levels, with more than a million people trained as mediators.[10]

Even in the United States, mediation has a long history. More than 350 years ago in 1636, the Puritan founders of Dedham, a community located southwest of Boston, provided in their covenant for a system of informal mediation. In New Netherland, Dutch colonists established a "Board of Nine Men" to serve as "friendly mediators and arbitrators." In colonial Virginia, the legislature noted the "excessive charges and greate delaies" of litigation and encouraged citizens to resolve disputes by other means.[11]

Later, beginning in the 1800s, Chinese immigrants on the west coast, Scandinavian immigrants in the midwest, and Jewish immigrants in New York set up mediation boards to resolve disputes within their own communities. In 1947, the federal government established the Federal Mediation and Conciliation Service to resolve disputes between industry and labor, and in 1964 the Justice Department formed the Community Relations Service to mediate racial disputes arising under the Civil Rights Act.

Experimental Success

The experiment with local mediation centers succeeded. During a 15-month test period, 3947 disputes were handled by the centers. Of the cases that went to a formal mediation hearing, more than 82 percent were successfully resolved (as many as 95 percent for some types of disputes).[12]

Six-month follow-up interviews with the disputants showed high rates of satisfaction with mediation, as detailed in Table 1-1. (In the following table, "Claimant" refers to the person who initiated mediation and "Respondent" to the other party to the dispute who agreed to come to mediation.)

In telephone interviews, disputants explained their attitudes about having tried mediation. In Kansas City:

● Mr. S. described his experience with the court as lousy, as opposed to his feeling the people at [the mediation center] were fair . . . also, cooperative and helpful, as opposed to the general lack of cooperation at the court. In court he did not get any say.

● Mr. R. [who had been in matrimonial court one time previously with his wife] said, in comparison to court, he felt the [mediation] people were trying to resolve their difference, whereas the court was a frightening experience. Going to court is a contest between lawyers, not a way of solving problems between people.

Table 1–1 Disputant Satisfaction for Mediated Cases

Question	Response	Claimant	Respondent
Satisfied with overall mediation experience?	Yes	88%	88%
	No	9%	8%
	Somewhat	4%	4%
Satisfied with mediation process?	Yes	84%	89%
	No	12%	10%
	Somewhat	3%	5%
Satisfied with mediator?	Yes	88%	88%
	No	8%	7%
	Somewhat	4%	5%
Satisfied with terms of agreement?	Yes	80%	83%
	No	15%	13%
	Somewhat	5%	5%

SOURCE: R. F. Cook, J. A. Roehl, and D. Sheppard, "Neighborhood Justice Centers Field Test: Final Evaluation Report, Executive Summary," Government Printing Office, Washington, 1980, p. 15.

In Los Angeles:

• Claimant [a businessman] was very satisfied with the process and the mediator . . . takes less time than courts . . . and he got his money.

• Claimant very positive about the whole experience . . . mediator skillful . . . respondent lived up to terms of agreement. Previous court experience was "scary."[13]

In 1980, Congress, finding that "the inadequacy of dispute resolution mechanisms throughout the United States is contrary to the general welfare of the people," passed the Dispute Resolution Act to help more local communities establish mediation centers like those that had succeeded in Atlanta, Kansas City, and Los Angeles.[14] President Jimmy Carter signed the bill into law on February 12, Lincoln's birthday.

Today's Public Mediation Network

Congress never did fund a nationwide mediation program, but—fortunately—the federal lead was soon followed by state and local governments. In 1975, there were fewer than a dozen public mediation centers around the country offering general mediation services. In the following year, the number doubled to 21, then doubled again by 1978 to 46, and by 1985, quadrupled to 182.[15]

Today, more than 220 public mediation centers operate in 40 states, the District of Columbia, Puerto Rico, and Canada.[16] Some of these are supported entirely with public funds; others rely on foundation support and small administrative fees from users. They serve U.S. communities from coast (Portland, Maine) to coast (San Diego, California), from large communities (major cities, including Boston, New York, Philadelphia, Washington, Atlanta, Miami, Chicago, Houston, Denver, San Francisco, and Los Angeles), to small ones (Bartow, Florida, pop. 15,000); from college towns (Amherst, Massachusetts), to retirement towns (Fort Myers, Florida). In New York State, mediation centers now serve all 62 countries, giving 100 percent of state residents access to mediation services. Wherever you live in the United States today, there is likely to be a mediation center in or near your community. This national mediation network, still small compared with the country's 17,000 courthouses, already handles an estimated 250,000 disputes per year involving about one-half million people.

Though mediation is not yet a household word, when people hear about it, they seem eager to learn more. In 1986, Ann Landers printed a letter in her advice column saying, "there are now [hundreds of] Dispute Settlement Centers throughout the United States . . . offering professional mediation services—the better way to quick and fair settlement." The column advised readers to write to the American Bar Association for information on local mediation centers. In the following weeks, the Bar Association received 5000 letters and 6000 telephone calls.

The cases mediation centers hear include most types of disputes that normally would go to court, such as:

- consumer vs. merchant
- landlord vs. tenant

- employer vs. employee
- homeowner vs. contractor
- minor, nonviolent criminal cases

They also hear—and are particularly good at resolving—interpersonal disputes that may not rise to the level of a legal claim but are nonetheless vitally important to the parties involved, such as

- neighbor vs. neighbor
- ex-boyfriend vs. ex-girlfriend
- roommate vs. roommate
- business partner vs. business partner
- spouse vs. spouse

Private Dispute Resolution Services

A second and growing part of the national mediation network is made up of private, for-profit dispute resolution services. Some serve local communities; others are regional or national in scope. These services are especially good at mediating divorce, business, and environmental disputes, as well as multiparty community disputes that raise important issues of public policy. Some examples follow:

In St. Paul, Minnesota, a company called The Mediation Alternative has resolved discrimination and wrongful termination cases among non-union employees at local companies.

In Oakland, California, the Lemmon Mediation Institute specializes in divorces and disputes within family businesses.

In Washington, D.C., Endispute, Inc., (with offices also in Chicago, New York and Boston) uses mediation and related techniques to resolve construction, anti-trust, product liability, and other business disputes.

As private companies, these firms charge higher fees for their services than do public mediation centers, but the fees are nearly always far lower than the cost of litigation. In Chapter 4, we will have more to say about the difference between public mediation centers and private dispute resolution services, and how to choose the appropriate one for your case.

Motivation to Mediate

Of course, people don't agree to mediate simply because "it's nice to make peace with your neighbors," as Ray Shonholtz, president of the Community Boards of San Francisco mediation center has observed.[17] People involved in disputes try mediation because they perceive an advantage in doing so.

By and large, people who use mediation generally find plenty of advantages in it. Mediation, they discover, can be:

QUICK: most disputes at public mediation centers can be sched-uled for a hearing within two to three weeks; average time per hearing is about one and one-half hours.

CONFIDENTIAL: everything said in the hearing is confidential; there is no "public docket"; no press coverage.

INEXPENSIVE: most public mediation centers provide quality services for free or for a nominal charge; lawyers are not nec-essary.

FAIR: the solution to a dispute can be tailored to the needs of each party; legal precedents will not dictate the solution in your case.

SUCCESSFUL: in more than four out of five cases that reach the mediation stage, both parties attain a successful result.

Certainly some of these factors, such as speed and low cost, also may apply to small claims court, a forum well-known thanks to the popular television program, *People's Court.* In the next chap-ter, we will consider which disputes should go to small claims court, but—for now—consider: What happens in small claims after Judge Wapner takes a recess? Does the hapless hairdresser who acciden-tally burned her customer's hair actually pay the plaintiff 35 dollars, as the judge ordered?

According to a surprising study, the hairdresser would be much more likely to pay if the customer had taken her to mediation instead. In an experimental program in Maine, small claims judges were able to have some disputants try mediation before coming to trial. Researchers Craig McEwen and Richard Maiman then compared results of the mediated cases with those that went straight to trial. Their results indicate that defendants in the mediated cases (71 percent) were more than twice as likely as defendants in the litigated cases (34 percent) actually to make payment in full to the plaintiffs. "People are more likely to feel bound by an obligation they have undertaken voluntarily . . . than one imposed upon them in a court of law," the researchers concluded.[18]

Interestingly, even the defendants who took part in unsuccessful mediation and later went to trial were still more likely to make payment in full than were defendants who had not participated in mediation at all. As McEwen and Maiman suggest, "Perhaps merely facing one's opponent for a time, having the opportunity to speak with and to hear him or her, humanizes and personalizes the process enough to affect the defendant's attitude toward payment."[19]

Mediation may also offer a better chance of changing your opponent's behavior toward you. In a study of disputes in Brooklyn involving personal harassment, 62 percent of people who took their case to mediation said the defendant's behavior had improved following a hearing, as against only 40 percent of people who took their case to court.[20]

Mediation's ability to deal effectively with harassment cases may explain why at some public mediation centers a majority of claimants are female, while a majority of respondents are male. "The male-female ratio we see may correspond to an increase in the number of women who are victims of sexual or other types of harassment and who try to resolve those disputes through mediation," explains Andrew Thomas, past president of the New York State Association of Community Dispute Resolution Centers.[21]

Some people who go through mediation and have a successful outcome are not just satisfied, they are amazed. They cannot believe that two hours of sitting in a room with "the enemy" has produced not only a fair and workable solution to their problem, but has neutralized the hostility and anger they felt, and in some cases transformed it, if not into friendship, at least into a peaceful truce. For example:

In Delaware County, Pennsylvania, an elderly woman was at the end of her rope when she called the Community Dispute Settlement Center. She complained of the young couple next door who came and went at all hours of the night in a high-performance Porsche, with motor roaring and radio blaring. So intimidated was she by her neighbors that she asked for police protection at the mediation hearing.

After the hearing, she told the dispute center's staff, "I didn't believe in miracles until the night of my mediation."[22]

What Is Mediation?

"I still spend time at dinner parties explaining that mediation is neither arbitration nor meditation," writes David Matz, director of the dispute resolution program at the University of Massachusetts in Boston.[23] People often do confuse mediation and arbitration, but the words themselves sound more alike than do the procedures they describe.

Of the two, arbitration is more widely known. It has long been used to resolve commercial and labor disputes (including, more recently, labor disputes in professional sports). In arbitration, a neutral third party called the "arbitrator" conducts a hearing between the disputants and then, acting as a judge, renders a legally binding decision. Arbitration is less formal than litigation, and—in most hearings—strict rules of evidence will not be followed.

In mediation, on the other hand, the neutral mediator does not act as a judge; he or she has no authority to impose a decision. Instead, the mediator conducts a face-to-face hearing with the disputants and, using special skills of listening, questioning, negotiating, and creating options, helps the parties work out *their own* solution to their dispute. In effect, the mediator acts as a catalyst; it is his or her special skill acting on both parties that helps them resolve their dispute. Compromise, as Lincoln urged, is often involved, but not in the sense merely of splitting the difference. The goal is to find a "win-win" solution, where both sides achieve something they want. Rules of evidence and other formal procedures are not normally used in mediation, but the agreement reached can be made legally binding when drafted in the form of a contract.

Table 1-2 lists some of the differences among mediation, arbitration, and litigation.

Table 1–2 Comparison of Mediation with Arbitration and Litigation*

Process	Mediation	Arbitration	Litigation
Who decides?	Parties	Arbitrator	Judge
Who controls?	Parties	Usually attorneys	Attorneys
Procedure	Informal	Somewhat formal	Formal
Time to hearing	3–6 weeks	3–6 months	2 years or more
Cost to party	Nominal or low	Moderate	Substantial
Rules of evidence	None	Informal	Technical
Publicity	Private	Usually private	Public
Relations of parties	Cooperative	Antagonistic	Antagonistic
Focus	Future	Past	Past
Method of negotiation	Compromise	Hard bargaining	Hard bargaining
Communication	Improved	Blocked	Blocked
Result	Win/Win	Win/Lose	Win/Lose
Compliance	Generally honored	Often resisted or appealed	Often resisted or appealed
Emotional result	Release of tension	Tension continued	Tension continued

*The above is adapted from the referenced table and includes material not appearing in the original.

SOURCE: Kenneth Cloke and Angus Strachan, "Mediation and Prepaid Legal Plans," *Mediation Quarterly*, no. 18, 1987, p. 94.

Flexible and Forward-Looking

Courts often are limited in the kinds of disputes they can hear: bankruptcy courts hear bankruptcy cases; family courts hear family disputes. Mediation, however, is not a court; it is a process and, as such, it can be applied to nearly all kinds of disputes. It can be used to decide who will own the Sinai Peninsula or who will park their car on weekends in the driveway you share with your next-door neighbor. It can be used to determine how Fujitsu will compensate IBM for infringing its operating system software, or how your dry cleaner will compensate you for fraying the collars of your dress shirts. It can be used to determine if a shelter for the homeless can be operated by a church in a residential neighborhood in Atlanta, or in whose home your children should live after you and your spouse divorce.

For these and so many other types of disputes, mediation works so well because it is forward-looking, not backward-looking. The law looks back to find who was right and who was wrong; mediation looks ahead to find a solution both parties can live with. In law, the court uses its power to dictate a decision; in mediation, you *empower yourself* to find your own solution.

Empowering

This issue of "empowerment" may be a key to understanding why mediation has taken hold in the United States today and why it is gaining so much in popularity. Many people rightly wonder why it should take two to three years to get a result in a simple legal claim for $10,000. Indeed, why should you tolerate an experience that may resemble, to paraphrase author Jerold S. Auerbach, a "sudden regression to childhood," where you can understand neither the procedures nor the language, where your attorney assumes the role of a parent and you become the dependent child, and where "the judge looms as a menacing authority figure," empowered to divest you of property or liberty?[24]

Why not, as an educated and reasonable adult, meet face-to-face with the person with whom you have a dispute and, with the aid of the skilled mediator, give *yourself* the power to work out a solution to your own problem? "Mediation," notes Paul Wahrhaftig, president of the Conflict Resolution Center International, Inc. in Pittsburgh, is an "attempt by everyday people to wrestle back control over their own problems."[25]

On a practical level, mediation also makes good sense today simply because, as a nation, we can no longer afford to spend so much of our resources in litigation. In 1985, all the people who brought lawsuits in the United States received in total judgments an estimated 14 to 16 billion dollars. But it cost an estimated 16 to 19 billion dollars in lawyers' fees and court costs for our legal system to deliver that money.[26] That is not an efficient way for us as a nation to resolve disputes.

"We have a lot to learn from Asian cultures about resolving disputes," says attorney Bowie Kuhn, former commissioner of major league baseball. He warns that the Asian tradition of mediation gives Japanese businesses an advantage over American firms because they divert far less money and attention from production to lawsuits.[27]

Kuhn serves as a director of the New York-based Center for Public Resources, an organization that encourages businesses to use mediation and other alternatives to litigation. To date, chief executive officers and general counsel of more than 400 of the nation's largest companies—including AT&T, Coca-Cola, IBM, and Xerox—have signed a document known as the ADR (Alternative Dispute Resolution) Corporate Policy Statement. This statement pledges them to explore mediation or other techniques before pursuing full-scale litigation in the event of a business dispute with any other company that also has signed the pledge. In one case, for example, American Can settled a 40-million-dollar fuel contract dispute with Wisconsin Electric.

Mediation As a First Resort

Mediation is not a cure-all, of course. There are some cases that should be litigated. Threats to individual rights, serious crimes, defamation of character—these and other cases should be taken to court and kept in court until personal liberties are protected, malevolent acts punished, and the truth disclosed.

Yet mediation, if we can learn to consider it as a first resort when disputes arise, can help resolve perhaps a majority of our interpersonal disputes and a large portion of other types of disputes without litigation. As writers Kenneth Cloke and Angus Strachan have observed: "To proceed from complaint to lawsuit without attempting settlement through the auspices of a trained mediator no longer makes sense, either for individuals or groups."[28]

Wider use of mediation would, in turn, help free our judges and court personnel to concentrate on those cases that do require what Justice Holmes called, "the magnificent deliberateness" of a trial.[29] In the next chapter, we will consider which disputes are most appropriate for mediation and which for litigation.

But, to appreciate mediation's potential to help resolve even the most complex of cases, consider the recent tragedy of L'Ambiance Plaza.

In April, 1987, L'Ambiance Plaza, a 13-story apartment building, collapsed while under construction in Bridgeport, Connecticut. Twenty-eight workers were killed and sixteen others were injured. In the following months, two retired judges, acting as mediators, met with nearly 100 lawyers representing contractors, subcontractors, and the victims' families.

In November, 1988, in what has been called "a remarkable breakthrough in the use of mediation" which "eliminated years of potential litigation," it was announced that a settlement had been reached through mediation, resolving all legal claims for a total of $41 million.

Speaking of the victims' families, Judge Robert C. Zampano, who acted as one of the mediators, said, "There was not a greedy person among them. These were honest, hardworking people who just got caught up in a horrible tragedy."

Relatives of the victims told a reporter for *The New York Times* that they were relieved at not having to relive the tragedy in months or years of court testimony. "We're glad to have it behind us and get on with what's left of our lives," said a man whose son was killed when the building collapsed.

"I've been involved in a lot of mass disaster cases," said the lead attorney for the workers' families, "but I think never before has one been brought to a close so quickly and in a way that has so satisfied all the parties."[30]

Most of us are unlikely ever to be involved in disputes as large and complex as the disaster at L'Ambiance Plaza. Yet, if that mammoth case can be successfully resolved through mediation, it stands to reason that many more common disputes can, too.

Support from the Bar

It is encouraging that some of the most respected members of the legal community agree. Indeed, the American Bar Association's Standing Committee on Dispute Resolution has been among the strongest and most effective supporters of public mediation centers. And there has been no more ardent supporter of mediation and related techniques of dispute resolution than Warren Burger, former Chief Justice of the United States Supreme Court. Chief Justice Burger has said:

> The notion that ordinary people want black-robed judges, well dressed lawyers and fine courtrooms as settings to resolve their disputes is not correct. People with problems, like people with pains, want relief, and they want it as quickly and inexpensively as possible.[31]

Nevertheless, you may find in your community that some lawyers are less than enthusiastic about mediation. In part, this may be because until very recently, law schools did not teach about mediation and, as a result, many practicing lawyers still have scant understanding of the field. In some cases, it may be a matter of turf. "Lawyers," write Jay Folberg and Alison Taylor, "consider dispute resolution to be the business of lawyers."[32]

If you find that your own lawyer is uninformed about mediation or even contemptuous of it, you might point out that when lawyers have disputes with other lawyers, it is to mediation that they increasingly turn. In Pennsylvania, for example, when law partnerships break up or when law partners quarrel over division of fees, the Bar Association now offers a program to resolve such disputes through mediation.[33] Bradford Hildebrandt, who mediates 30 to 40 law firm disputes a year, told the *Wall Street Journal* that, "without mediation most law firms let their emotions run away and end up in court. It's very expensive and very unnecessary."[34]

Opening Closed Doors

Mediation can save you from wasting time and money; it can free you from lawyers and the foreign language of the law; it can empower you to work out solutions to your own problems—quickly, fairly, and inexpensively—so that you can get on with your life; it can protect your privacy and dignity from exposure of your problems in newspapers and on TV; it can help you solve your problems without destroying your important personal, family, and business relationships.

Mediation can be, to borrow a phrase from President George Bush, a "kinder, gentler" way to resolve your disputes. As a nation, we can no longer afford to expend so much energy, talent, and time on litigation. As individuals, we are reasonable and capable enough, given the aid of a skilled mediator, to resolve many of our disputes ourselves.

"Mediation is like making love," professor Jay Folberg has observed, "there is much literature about it but it's done behind closed doors."[35]

This book is designed to open the door of the mediation hearing room for you to help you understand how mediation works, how to do it well, and how to use our country's growing network of public and private mediation centers for your own advantage.

CHAPTER
2

Which Disputes Should You Mediate?

Some types of common disputes are well-suited to mediation:

- disputes between neighbors over noise, trash, landscaping, children, etc.
- disputes between consumers and local merchants over quality of goods and services
- disputes between coworkers over personal matters that interfere with work performance

And then there are some disputes that even the strongest advocates of mediation would cringe to see mediated. Consider, for example, how history might have been changed had Rosa Parks, in 1955, chosen to take her dispute over seating with the Montgomery, Alabama, bus company to mediation. Mediation of that historic case might have resulted in an agreement like this:

This Agreement made today between Rosa Parks and the Montgomery Bus Lines Co., Inc., provides as follows:

1. Rosa Parks shall be entitled to ride in the forward section of buses operated by Montgomery Bus Lines on weekdays between the hours of 9 a.m. and 5 p.m.

2. If Montgomery Bus Lines is unable due to heavy ridership to provide Rosa Parks a forward seat on a regularly scheduled bus, it shall provide such a seat on the next available bus on that line.

If establishing a legal precedent is more important to you than quietly resolving the dispute, then mediation is not appropriate. If Rosa Parks had taken her dispute with the bus company to mediation, she might have emerged with a front seat on the bus for herself, but she and the civil rights movement—indeed the whole nation—would have lost an historic opportunity. (This example, of course, is fictitious. Mediation was not an option available in Montgomery in the 1950s and, at any rate, Ms. Parks and other civil rights leaders did seek to establish a legal precedent.)

In theory, nearly all disputes can be mediated. But whether or not you should try to mediate any particular dispute will depend on a variety of practical considerations: what you want, what your opponent wants, and the facts of your case.

To illustrate a dispute where the facts clearly favored mediation, consider the following actual case:

Mr. K., a suburban homeowner in the northeast, was upset to discover large brown streaks running the length of his driveway. They apparently were caused by a local contractor's poor sealing job. When he discovered the problem, Mr. K called the contractor. The two men had done business before, but—as they discussed the streaking—they got into a shouting match because it seemed to Mr. K. that the contractor was blaming the problem on Mr. K's wife.

Neighbors encouraged Mr. K. to sue, but Mr. K., who was concerned that the driveway be fixed before the warm weather ended, decided to try mediation. He submitted the dispute to a public mediation center and was somewhat surprised when the contractor agreed to participate.

At the mediation hearing, Mr. K. complained that the streaking was the contractor's fault and insisted that it be corrected without delay and at no additional cost. For his part, the contractor explained that the streaking had been caused by sealing components mixing with rain water on the driveway. He said he had not wanted to do the job on the day scheduled because it was raining, but when he came to the house to suggest the work be postponed, Mr. K was out and Mrs. K insisted he go ahead and seal the driveway as scheduled. The contractor said he was willing to repair the driveway but not at his own expense.

In a mediated settlement, Mr. K. agreed to pay for nine gallons of new sealant and the contractor agreed to do the repairs within two weeks with no charge for labor.

Here, homeowner and contractor had done business together in the past and presumably would like to continue doing business in the future. This particular job was not worth more than a few hundred dollars; it would hardly pay for Mr. K. to file a lawsuit, except possibly in small claims court but the prospect of standing up in a public court and complaining to a judge about streaks on his driveway did not much appeal to Mr. K. Also, timing was of importance; Mr. K. wanted the driveway resealed, if not by the original contractor then by someone else, before the summer ended.

The wisdom of Mr. K's choice to use mediation was borne out by the fact that he got what he most wanted: the contractor satisfactorily resealed the driveway on schedule.

Factors Favoring and Opposing Mediation

In most disputes, if you can work things out by negotiating directly with your opponent, then that is the quickest, least expensive, and most private way to resolve your problem. If, however, direct talks would be impractical, or have been tried and have failed, then you will want to consider whether mediation might be appropriate.

Following are ten factors to consider in deciding whether a particular dispute is one that should be mediated: five factors tend to favor mediation; five do not. These categories, which are adapted from those outlined by authors Nancy H. Rogers and Richard A. Salem, should be useful in helping you evaluate your dispute and come to a reasoned decision about whether to try mediation.[1]

Factors Favoring Mediation

1.   When the Law Cannot Provide the Remedy You Want

Though there are thousands of laws on the books, many common disputes raise no legal claims that you could take to court. Disputes between family members and between neighbors are often of this type. For example, two sisters who owned and ran a jewelry store disagreed about who should control different aspects of the business. If they could not come to terms, the business might fail. Yet there were no legal claims involved, just a dispute between partners that mediation could help settle. Similarly, when a suburban homeowner found that lights around his neighbor's pool shone in his window at night, the law offered no solution because no local ordinance regulated residential lighting. In mediation, however, the neighbors could sit down and work out an agreement.

If you do not know whether the law might provide a remedy for your dispute, then you should consult a lawyer about this question.

2.   When You Want to End a Problem, Not a Relationship

Does your dispute involve another person with whom—either by choice or circumstance—you need to remain on good terms? This may include family members, coworkers, your landlord, neighbors, or others with whom you have a continuing personal or business relationship. One of the advantages of mediation is its ability to resolve a dispute without destroying a relationship.

"If the parties are going to be in a continuing relationship after the dispute, then anything other than mediation is a mistake," observes Arno Denecke, retired Chief Justice of the Oregon Supreme Court. "Litigation can leave lasting scars, and arbitration is still confrontational." With mediation, he notes, the resolution the parties hammer out is theirs and not something imposed by a third party.[2]

Filing a lawsuit can indeed be a hostile act. Our expression "to be slapped with a lawsuit" or "hit with a lawsuit" conveys the sense of combat and agressiveness inherent in legal action. If you are the one doing the suing, you can be sure that whatever relationship you had with your adversary before papers were served will be worse afterwards. Your attorney, motivated by the need to prove your opponent's guilt or liability, will use every means possible to show your opponent in the worst possible light. Even if you and your opponent want to keep on speaking terms, your lawyers will likely forbid it lest you reveal something to jeopardize your case.

In this regard, Professor Jack Ethridge of Emory University Law School has written:

> Litigation paralyzes people. It makes them enemies. It pits them not only against one another, but against the other's employed combatant. Often disputants lose control of the situation, finding themselves virtually powerless. They attach allegiance to their lawyer rather than to the fading recollection of a perhaps once worthwhile relationship.[3]

In mediation it would be inappropriate for one side to call a witness merely to discuss the bad character of the other party. Similarly, in the written mediation agreement, there is no place for stating who was right and who was wrong; the agreement speaks only of who will do what and when in order to remedy the problem. It is this absence of fault-finding—plus the experience of working cooperatively with your opponent toward settlement—that helps parties in mediation save face and thus preserve a relationship.

(Disputes between strangers can also be mediated. In Columbus, Ohio, for example, the Night Prosecutor's Mediation Program reports an 85 percent success rate mediating such stranger-to-stranger disputes as worthless check cases, animal complaints filed by a city agency against a citizen, and health code violations.[4])

3. When Your Dispute Is No One Else's Business—and You Want to Keep It That Way

As noted earlier, one of the drawbacks to having your dispute settled in court is that, by and large, everything said or submitted to a court in connection with a lawsuit becomes publicly available. Only by a special order of a judge can information be "sealed" from public exposure.

If, for example, you were involved in a lawsuit against your employer, all the information collected for that lawsuit would be available to the public. This would include not only what was said in court, but also what was revealed before trial in "discovery" proceedings during which you may have had to answer questions about your wages, your work performance, your associates, and your personal habits on the job. Your employer may have had to answer questions about the company's structure, ownership, profitability, and employee relations—just to name a few topics likely to come up.

Newspaper and television reporters who cover the courts know where to find the information that will make an otherwise boring legal story come alive with interesting personal details.

For our democratic system, open courts are important because they give the public a chance to see if prosecutors and judges are doing their jobs well. But from the point of view of individual litigants, public exposure usually is undesired.

Mediation, in contrast, is a strictly private affair. Mediators take an oath to protect the confidences entrusted to them during the hearing. In many states, the confidentiality of mediation proceedings is expressly protected by statute. At your mediation hearing, there will be no stenographer or tape recorder; your mediator will even throw away his or her notes after the hearing.

Whether your desire is to protect trade secrets or just to avoid washing your dirty laundry in public, your privacy will be substantially increased by resolving a dispute through mediation rather than through litigation.

4. When You Want to Minimize Costs

About 99 percent of your costs in bringing a civil (noncriminal) lawsuit will be your lawyer's fees.[5] In most major cities today, lawyers' fees range from 75 to 300 dollars per hour and up. The median time lawyers spend on a typical civil case, whether in state or federal court, has been found to be about 30.4 hours, according to one study.[6] At 150 dollars per hour, that comes to more than 4500 dollars.

In contrast, fees for using mediation services range from zero at nonprofit mediation centers (their operations are supported by tax dollars), to a few hundred dollars per hearing at private mediation services handling business cases. For example, Endispute, Inc., in Chicago, charges each party to a half-day hearing a basic minimum fee of 350 dollars. The American Arbitration Association, which now offers mediation as well as arbitration, charges for business mediation services based on the amount of the claim: 150 dollars per party for claims up to 50,000 dollars; 250 dollars per party for claims up to 100,000 dollars, etc.

Most people do not have a lawyer accompany them to the mediation hearing, although you are entitled to do so if you wish. But even if your lawyer does attend or if she later reviews an agreement you have conditioned on her approval, your cost for her fee plus the fee, if any, of the mediation service will probably still be much less than if you had pursued the case in court or had your lawyer do all the negotiations from the start. (In some cases, such as those involving personal injury, lawyers will charge on a contingency fee basis rather than by the hour and will take a percentage—usually about 30 percent—of any amount you recover. Here, too, you might save money through mediation, because if you can settle without your lawyer's full participation, you will not have to give up the 30 percent.)

Former Texas Chief Justice Joseph R. Greenhill has observed, "A Chinese proverb says, 'Going to the law is losing a cow for the sake of a cat.' When it costs a cow to gain a cat, alternative action is appropriate."[7]

5. *When You Want to Settle Your Dispute Promptly*

"Our civil courts can be described as parking lots for civil litigation," says Robert Coulson, president of the American Arbitration Association.[8] A litigated case may be pending for two, three, four, or five years before trial. Recently, some 75,000 personal-injury cases backlogged in Chicago's Cook County Circuit Court took an average of 69 months to come to trial.[9] While more than 90 percent of litigated disputes are settled before trial, settlement discussions often do not get serious until a trial date is near. This aspect of the law has not changed much since 1759 when the British statesman Edmund Burke observed, "The contending parties find themselves more effectively ruined by the delay than they could have been by the injustice of any decision."

At most public mediation centers, a hearing can be scheduled in your case within a couple of weeks, and most cases require just one session to reach agreement. In New York State, where nearly 20,000 cases were resolved in fiscal year 1987–1988 by public mediation centers, the average time from intake to final disposition was 13.7 days.[10] Private dispute resolution services take a bit longer because the business and public policy disputes they handle tend to be more complex—a few months from intake to disposition, for most cases.

Factors Opposing Mediation

1. When You Want to Prove the Truth or Set a Legal Precedent

There are no "test cases" in mediation. Mediation may resolve your problem, but it will not establish a legal precedent. That is why, as noted at the beginning of this chapter, it would have been inappropriate and a great national loss for someone like Rosa Parks to have taken an important civil rights dispute to mediation.

Winning test cases or proving the truth of something cannot be done through mediation because mediation agreements do not establish "right" and "wrong" and they are binding, if at all, only on the parties to that particular dispute. Mediation does not establish a precedent because what is agreed between parties in one dispute does not affect the parties to any other dispute.

If there is a bad law that you want overturned, or if you need publicly to prove the truth of something—for example, if you have been unfairly maligned in the local newspaper and want to clear your name—you will have to do this through the courts rather than in mediation.

Additionally, though quite rarely, there are some disputes where the facts and the law make it clear that one side is completely right and the other completely wrong, and if taken to court, the completely right side will surely win. If you are in such a dispute—and on the right side—then as long as you can tolerate the delays, loss of privacy, and other drawbacks of a lawsuit, litigation will be your best recourse because you will probably win a bigger verdict than you could settle for in mediation.

2. When You Want to Go for the Jackpot

It seems at times to have become an American sport: sue a giant corporation for a huge amount of money, have your lawyer take the case on a contingency fee basis, and hope a sympathetic jury will award you a jackpot.

In point of fact, not as many people win this legal version of the lottery as it may appear. The press plays it up when a jury awards a plaintiff millions of dollars, but often the judge or an appeals court later substantially reduces the award. The reduction seldom gets as much publicity as the original award.

If you are in the situation where you want to go for a jackpot against a big company (or even a small company with plenty of insurance), your choice should be litigation, not mediation. If you were to mediate such a claim, you might get a settlement more quickly and therefore get your money sooner, but because of the tendency of disputants in mediation to compromise, you would be unlikely to get as much money as if you litigated the claim and carried it all the way to a jury trial. Of course, you could also lose in court and recover nothing. Your lawyer can advise you in advance of what your chances might be in court.

You might come out of mediation with a fair settlement, but there are no jackpots in mediation.

3. When One Party Is Absent or Incompetent

Mediation requires all parties to a dispute to be present for face-to-face discussion. If one or more parties to your dispute is physically unable to attend a hearing, then mediation cannot take place. For example, in one case a party could not attend the hearing because he was already in jail. More typical is the situation where one party leaves town.

Mediation also assumes that both parties are rational and can participate in reasoned discussion and negotiation. If one party is mentally impaired or affected by alcohol or drug abuse, mediation will not work.

Physical impairment, however, usually is no bar to mediation. A speech problem should not deter anyone from participating. In one case, for example, an elderly man had great difficulty speaking clearly due to throat surgery. Fortunately, he brought his lawyer with him to act, literally, as his mouthpiece. Similarly, the fact that someone does not speak English should not be a deterrent. Many public mediation centers have staff who are bilingual in English and Spanish, and also keep a roster of mediators who speak other languages. In Des Moines, Iowa, an area hosting many Vietnamese, Cambodian, and other Indochinese refugees, the Polk County Attorney's Neighborhood Mediation Center is able to conduct mediations in 11 different languages.

4. When One Party Is Unwilling to Mediate

You may find that your opponent, though available to mediate, has no interest in doing so. He may genuinely prefer litigation because he thinks he has a good chance to win in court; or he may not perceive enough of an advantage in mediation to consider trying it, or he may just enjoy the dispute and not be in a hurry to end it.

Nationally, about 30 percent of cases referred to mediation never reach a hearing because one party declines to participate. Some ways to try to overcome an opponent's reluctance to mediate are discussed in Chapter 4. Often the mediation center or service will actively work to bring the reluctant party into mediation. But if your opponent persists in refusing to participate, there is little you can do about it. Perhaps at a later stage of the dispute, if his circumstances have changed so that mediation looks more attractive (his legal fees are getting too high, a court decision is inconclusive, he needs to end the dispute quickly), you can try to interest him in mediation again.

5. When the Dispute Involves a Serious Crime

Cases involving spouse or child abuse, for example, do not belong in mediation. These are serious crimes and should be prosecuted by the authorities. Mediation requires that both parties be able to engage in rational and effective negotiation. If one party has been the victim of abuse, that party may be too intimidated or fearful of reprisal to participate freely. Also, mediation requires the assistance of a neutral third party. But mediators are human beings, and faced with evidence at a hearing of child abuse, for example, few mediators would be able to maintain their neutrality because they would be prejudiced against the abusive party. In many centers, mediators in such cases are taught to excuse themselves from the case if they do not feel they could continue in their neutral roles.

If new evidence of spouse or child abuse is disclosed at a hearing, the mediator may be required by state law or the rules of the particular mediation center to stop the hearing and disclose this to authorities. This is one of the few exceptions to the general rule that everything said in mediation is confidential.

Other types of major crime, such as those involving serious personal injury or extreme property damage, also do not belong in mediation. In Massachusetts, for example, district attorneys are instructed that no crime for which the state would normally recommend a jail sentence should go to mediation.[11]

Minor criminal cases, on the other hand, make up a large part of the caseload at many public mediation centers. These are cases involving assault, personal harassment, and minor property damage, for example, where no serious injury or damage has occurred and the major issue is how much money the offender should pay the victim. These cases usually are referred to the centers by prosecutors before they issue an arrest warrant or by judges who adjourn a court hearing temporarily to see if the parties can reach an agreement.

AT A GLANCE
Should I Mediate?

Factors Favoring Mediation	Factors Opposing Mediation
No legal remedy	Wanting test case
Preserving a relationship	Wanting jackpot
Maintaining privacy	Party absent or incompetent
Avoiding high fees	Party doesn't want to settle
Avoiding delays	Serious crime

The Question of Power Imbalance

Sitting down for face-to-face mediation with the contractor who sealed your driveway would not be very intimidating for most people, but what if your opponent was your landlord, or a vice-president of the gas and electric company, or Sears Roebuck?

Should you mediate a dispute where your opponent is far more powerful than you are?

This problem of power imbalance is of concern to mediation professionals. There are different opinions as to how to handle it. Some advise not to attempt mediation with a too powerful opponent on the theory that it is like taking a lamb to slaughter (with you as the lamb). Others say fears about lambs being slaughtered are greatly exaggerated by opponents of mediation and that mediation has ample protections for the weaker party.

Indeed, there are protections built into the mediation process, and there are other steps you can take as well, which should keep you from being overwhelmed by a powerful opponent. First, your opponent must have some desire to settle, else he would not take the time to come to mediation. You need to figure out what motivates that desire: is it the administrative cost of continuing to handle your dispute, or a concern about bad publicity, or maybe you have threatened to file a lawsuit (or actually filed one) and your opponent wants to avoid the cost of defending it. If you can understand what motivates your opponent, you can use this understanding to your advantage during negotiations to help even up the balance of power.

Secondly, there are indeed checks built into the mediation system to protect the weaker party. Some mediators will take an active, interventionist approach and do their best to ensure that any agreement they oversee is not blatantly unfair. (This practice is especially common in the area of divorce mediation, discussed in Chapter 10.) Recall, too, that mediation is voluntary. It is voluntary going in, and it is voluntary going out. If you don't like the way your mediation is shaping up, you can stand up and walk out. If you reach an agreement and then find, after it is typed and ready for signing, that you don't like it, you don't have to sign it. You can also insist that a clause be put in the agreement making it conditional on your lawyer's approval within, say, five days. (For a sample of such a clause, see Chapter 7.)

A related example of power imbalance occurs when your opponent is someone who, for one reason or another, intimidates you to the point where you cannot effectively represent yourself. There may be some people—a former spouse or boss, for example—in whose presence you just feel you cannot speak intelligently, cannot put two thoughts together. In some cases like this, it might be best not to attempt mediation. But again there are ways to try to make mediation work even in this type of dispute. You can bring a lawyer or friend to the hearing to help present your case, or—as noted earlier—if you don't like the agreement, you can decline to sign it or make it conditional upon your lawyer's review.

Power imbalance is definitely something to consider in deciding whether to try mediation, but in most cases it should not be decisive, because there are enough steps you can take to compensate.

A Note on Small Claims Court

In some cases, you may be better off taking a dispute to small claims court rather than mediation. The time it takes to get to small claims court and the token fees involved are about the same as with mediation. And, as with mediation, you do not need a lawyer. Small claims courts are particularly good at handling cases where the facts and the law are clear, and where each party's legal rights are plainly spelled out in writing, as in a lease or other contract. Many disputes between landlords and tenants involving nonpayment of rent or return of security deposits, for example, are routinely handled in small claims court. (All small claims courts have limitations on the size of cases they can hear. Upper limits range from about 1000 dollars to 5000 dollars.)

But small claims judges—like most other judges—have neither the time nor the authority to help disputing parties resolve differences stemming from nonlegal factors, such as interpersonal disputes, or from complicated fact situations that take a long time to discuss. As Judge William H. Bristol of the city court of Rochester, New York, has observed, courts are not designed to solve angry feelings. "It's like Joe Friday says, 'the facts ma'am, just the facts,' " explains the judge. [12]

Unlike mediation, small claims court offers no privacy from the public or the press. And, though it may take only a few weeks to schedule a hearing for your case, you may have to sit in court all morning or all afternoon or all evening waiting for your case to be called. Finally, even if you may get a judgment in your favor, there is no guarantee your opponent actually will pay what he owes. In fact, as noted in Chapter 1, one study has shown that parties in mediation pay what they owe more than twice as often as parties in small claims.[13]

If your dispute is one that could be heard in small claims, you should weigh these factors, as well as those discussed earlier, in deciding whether small claims or mediation would be most appropriate.

CHAPTER
3

What Your Mediator Does

"I mediate because I believe in helping people stay out of the courts. The work can be depressing and draining; during a hearing I'm sometimes annoyed and frustrated. But if I've helped people find a solution, it gives me a lift and a sense of accomplishment."

Female mediator, 46 years old

"When I'm in the middle of a mediation, I feel like the director of a powerful drama where I can help influence the plot to come out with a happy ending."

Female mediator, 35 years old

"It's an ego trip and a challenge, and when I help the parties reach an agreement, I feel very good inside—and also exhausted from the release of tension when it's over."

Male mediator, 38 years old

As the testimonies above relate, a mediator's work can be uplifting, a powerful "ego trip." Yet, for this, the mediator also pays a price. Labor mediator and professor Jerome T. Barrett, in his paper "The Psychology of a Mediator," identifies some aspects of the mediator's work that can exact a "pyschic cost":

Isolation: most of the mediator's work is done in isolation from colleagues and supervisors.

Helper Role: the mediator's power is limited to that of a helper; without the will of the disputing parties, the mediator is powerless to make things happen.

Limited Positive Feedback: the very human needs of the mediator for recognition, appreciation, and respect generally are unfulfilled by the parties as they focus on their own disputes.

Confidential Information: the absolute requirement of confidentiality places on the mediator the same pressures that a priest has regarding confession and a lawyer has with a client.

Filtered Reaction Role: to maintain their impartial role and retain their effectiveness, mediators must suppress such normal reactions as frustration, hostility, and anger and replace them by neutral or opposite reactions.

In summary, observes Barrett, the mediator is "an outside intervenor, working under high stress on the problems of others . . . in isolation from any support groups, and bound by a strict code of confidentiality. The mediator's opportunities for positive feedback are limited, the success of his performance is difficult to measure, and he is subjected to the manipulations" of the parties.

Yet, "in spite of the pyschic costs," concludes Barrett, "there is no shortage of candidates for the job, and incumbents talk glowingly about a 'high' from achieving a difficult settlement."[1]

There are about 22,000 mediators working in the United States today. Some of these are full-time, career mediators who work in the well-established labor-management field. A few others work full-time in the growing fields of divorce, business, and environmental mediation. Most, however, are nonprofessional mediators who have been trained to serve as volunteers at the expanding network of public mediation centers. (Some centers pay their mediators a small stipend. At the Community Mediation Center in Coram, New York, for example, mediators are paid $12.50 per hearing.)

At public mediation centers, mediators bring a healthy diversity of experience to their work. In New York, for example, the 1450 citizens who have been trained to serve at the state's network of 61 public mediation centers come from a variety of professional and work backgrounds: teaching, social work, law, business, parenting and homemaking, and journalism, among others. Surveys show most mediators are college educated with an average of three and one-half years of mediation experience. Their median age is 46 years.[2]

In Massachusetts, about 700 mediators serve the state's 29 community mediation programs. A statewide study found them to be, on average, "more white, more female, somewhat better off financially, (with) more formal education and somewhat older" than the general population.[3]

The Mediator's Role

"To mediate" means "to go between" or "to be in the middle." This, literally, is what your mediator does. He or she "goes between" you and your opponent to help you find a solution to your dispute.

Your mediator's role is not to be a judge, deciding who is innocent and who is guilty. Neither is it to give legal advice (even if the mediator happens to be a lawyer); nor to be a counselor or therapist. The mediator's sole function is to bring you and your opponent together to help *the two of you* find a solution *of your own making*.[4]

Exactly how the mediator does this will be puzzling to those not familiar with the process. After all, each of us is at times a mediator: department heads mediate between workers, parents mediate between children, friends mediate between friends. Yet most people would not presume themselves capable of sitting down in a room with total strangers and in the course of an hour and a half successfully help them find a solution to a problem that may have vexed them for months or years.

Formal mediation involves a lot more than just "getting folks together to talk about their problem." It involves the mediator, who is trained in conflict resolution, and it involves the mediation hearing, a highly ritualized, multistage proceeding. Employing his or her special skills through the different stages of the hearing, the mediator attempts to unfreeze the parties from their fixed positions and open them to the possibilities of creative solutions. The mediator works to help the parties:

- discover the true issues involved in their dispute
- understand the difference between what they want and what they need
- understand the wants and needs of the other side
- and realistically consider the possible options

How the Mediator Changes the Parties

The mediator must motivate without manipulating, cajole without coercing. The mediator must try to create doubt in each party's mind so that person can see the weaknesses in his own position and thus open himself to compromise.

The mediator, writes Professor Susan J. Rogers of City University of New York, "attempts to modify the disputants' relationship by enhancing and controlling communication, altering their perceptions, balancing their power positions, and proposing and defending specific agreements."[5]

To try to measure how the presence of a mediator changes the behavior of disputants from the beginning of a mediation session to the end, Professor Rogers studied the conflict styles of 82 disputants in 41 landlord-tenant mediations at a mediation project in Colorado. Each hearing lasted about two hours.

Professor Rogers' findings would not surprise anyone who has served as a mediator. Her study was able to measure significant changes in each disputant's conflict style: disputants generally becoming less competitive and more accommodative (defined as "trying to soothe the other person's feelings"), more compromising (willing "to give up some points in exchange for others"), and more collaborative (attempting to "get all the issues out in the open" and trying to "deal with the other person's concerns as well as his or her own").

In Table 3-1, Professor Rogers' results appear in tabulated form.

Table 3–1 Mean Conflict Styles of Disputants
at Beginning and End of Mediation*

Style	Beginning	End	Significant Difference?
Competitive	1.35	1.14	−0.21 ≤ .05 Yes
Avoidant	0.48	0.56	+0.08 No
Accommodative	0.45	0.59	0.14 Yes
Compromising	1.12	1.51	0.39 Yes
Collaborative	1.20	1.35	0.15 Yes

*Scoring of style was from 0.0, the lowest degree, to 2.0, the highest degree.
SOURCE: Susan J. Rogers, "The Dynamics of Conflict Behavior in a Mediated Dispute," *Mediation Quarterly*, no. 18, 1987, p. 66.

"The results of this study indicated that the conflict approach of a disputant during a mediated session changes significantly from the beginning of the mediation to the end," concluded Professor Rogers, "with the competitive orientation reduced and the cooperative orientations, especially the compromise approach, increased."[6]

How the mediator uses various techniques to help change the disputants' approach to conflict at different stages of the hearing will be examined more closely in Chapter 6: "Inside the Hearing Room."

How to Evaluate Your Mediator

When you enter the hearing room to meet and shake hands with your mediator, you will naturally wonder whether this stranger to whom you are about to entrust many confidential matters—and a couple of hours of your time—is any good at what he or she does.

As we will see in the following section, any mediator who has completed a training and apprenticeship program, and who has successfully mediated even a few cases, will be competent enough to handle most routine disputes. It is simply not possible to keep mediating for very long if you do not have the basic ability. Still, some doctors are better than others; some judges, lawyers, and teachers are better than others. How can you tell if your mediator is any good?

Some people make the mistake of judging style over substance. For example, as your hearing begins, your mediator may open with an aggressive, "take charge" style, stating in a grave and authoritative voice the rules of the hearing, telling you when you can talk and when you must be silent, warning against interruptions and use of uncivil language. Or, your mediator may use a more passive style, quietly introducing herself or himself and offering a few ground rules for behavior during the hearing.

Later on, if your hearing has progressed to where a settlement is within reach, your mediator may become like an orchestra conductor, subtly cuing each party when a shift in negotiating position would be helpful. Or, your mediator may become a shuttle diplomat, working hard in private meetings with each side to formulate and win agreement on a settlement plan.

There is no "right" style of mediation. Different mediators use different styles. Their choice of styles depends on their own personalities, the nature of the dispute, and their assessment of the parties' relative strengths and weaknesses.[7] Thus, you cannot tell very much about a mediator by the style in which he or she conducts a hearing.

Nonetheless, if he or she is to be effective, then in each hearing—regardless of the style employed—the mediator must demonstrate to the parties through words and behavior that he or she is:

- an expert listener
- able to speak in clear, neutral language
- able to defuse hostility
- able to control his or her own prejudice and bias
- respectful toward the parties and sensitive to their strongly felt values, including gender, ethnic, and cultural differences
- able to see issues on multiple levels
- able to deal with complex factual materials and to analyze problems

- able to think on his or her feet
- able to control the hearing without being overbearing
- able to direct the dramatic flow of the hearing
- trustworthy to keep confidences

Mediators must do all of the above in order to inspire confidence in themselves and in the mediation process, and to foster a cooperative attitude. For, unlike a courtroom, where the flag of the United States and other trappings of authority hang over the proceedings to inspire a sense of confidence, duty, and authority, in mediation it is only the mediator—and the good-faith efforts of the parties—that can make the process work.

If you perceive during the hearing that your mediator can do all of the above, then you are in good hands. Your mediator probably has an impressive record of achieving settlements that last.

Of course, no mediator succeeds all the time. As noted, one of the frustrations of being a mediator is that one has no control over the facts in dispute or the attitudes of the disputants. There are some cases that, due to especially thorny issues or especially thorny people, just cannot be successfully mediated even with the finest mediator doing a first-rate job. In such cases, the good mediator will close the hearing without a settlement rather than try to force the parties into a settlement that will not last.

How Is Your Mediator Trained?

Even people with natural ability to mediate must work to focus their skills towards the demands of formal mediation and master the special rules and procedures involved.

Consequently, nobody becomes a mediator at any public mediation center without completing a program of training and apprenticeship. In some states, including California, Florida, Michigan, New York, and Texas, legislation or court rules set minimum training requirements for those mediating in state-funded centers.

There is no standardized curriculum for training; the discipline of mediation in this country is still too new. Consequently, mediator training varies from state to state and city to city. The actual training is done either by staff of the local center or by private firms that specialize in training mediators.

The Training Program

In most training programs, mediators will complete 30–40 hours of classroom work over a period of one to three weeks. The number of hours depends on local rules and whether state law sets a minimum. Mediation trainees will be lectured on the laws of mediation and confidentiality, the rules of the local mediation center, and mediator ethics. Other subjects often covered include the psychology of human conflict and conflict resolution, and negotiation theory.

Role-Playing

The trainee will also study and practice mediation techniques. Often this will take the form of role-playing, in which the trainee will play the part of one of the participants in a simulated mediation hearing:

- the mediator
- the claimant (the person who first brings the dispute to a mediation center)
- the respondent (the person with whom the claimant has a dispute)
- a witness (brought to the hearing by either side)

Some of the role-plays will be designed to improve listening and negotiating skills, to reveal personal prejudices, or to develop an ability to detect hidden interpersonal conflicts among the parties. A typical training exercise, for example, will cast the trainee in the role of mediator in a mock case. Before the hearing starts, he or she is told that the case involves a property-line dispute between two neighbors, a man and a woman. Two other trainees play the roles of the neighbors.

What the trainee is not told, however, is that, in this fictional case, the two neighbors many years ago were close friends but then had a falling out when the wife of one quarreled with the husband of the other over attitudes about child rearing. The dispute about the property-line, while real, is just the latest expression of continuing anger between the neighbors because of the earlier break in their friendship. In the mock hearing, the "disputants" know this, but the trainee does not. The trainee's task is to discover it through careful listening and questioning. The goal is not to make the neighbors friends again, but to help them come to terms with the break in their relationship so they can resolve not only this property-line dispute, but can agree to live as neighbors without further disputes erupting. This type of role-play is typical and helps sharpen important skills a mediator will need to resolve real cases.

Revealing Prejudices

In another typical exercise, this one designed to reveal to trainees their own prejudices, the trainer will describe a fictitious third person: her looks, clothes, occupation, manner of speech. Trainees are then required to answer a series of questions about the personal habits, family life, political beliefs, and financial situation of the person described. When trainees compare their answers, they find that what they have described are their own assumptions and prejudices about people. The exercise can be helpful in teaching the trainee how to be aware of his or her own prejudices, particularly during the important opening stages of mediation when a mediator may be tempted to judge disputants based on outward appearance or superficial information.

Apprenticeship

Once the trainee successfully completes the classroom part of the training, it is time to begin an apprenticeship. The first step is to observe experienced mediators as they conduct hearings in real cases. Usually, the trainee will sit in the back of the hearing room, saying nothing, taking no notes. The trainee's job is to sit quietly and try to understand the techniques the mediator is using. (In this situation, of course, the trainee attends the hearing with the permission of the disputants and is bound by the same rules of confidentiality as the mediator.) This experience exposes the trainee to different styles of mediation and to some of the issues that come up in real cases.

The next step is co-mediation. During an actual mediation, the trainee will sit next to the experienced mediator and practice conducting various parts of the hearing. The trainee may, for example, deliver the opening statement, the first stage of formal mediation in which the purpose and rules of the hearing are explained to the parties.

The final step of the apprenticeship comes when trainees are allowed to "solo," to mediate cases on their own. An experienced mediator will observe the hearing from the back of the room and step in if the trainee falters. The observer will take notes on the trainee's technique to review with him or her afterwards. Several "solo" mediations may be scheduled until both the trainee and the staff of the mediation center feel confident that the trainee can handle cases alone. (Lawyers, in contrast, may go into court alone on the first day after being admitted to the bar without ever having observed or participated in a courtroom hearing under the supervision of an experienced attorney.)

Certification

Trainees who successfully complete the entire training program are eligible for certification by the local mediation center. Official certification usually comes at a ceremony presided over by a judge or other local civic leader. In some communities, the new mediators are required to swear an oath to abide by the rules of the mediation center, to be impartial, and to protect the disputants' confidentiality.

Your mediator's education and training does not end with certification, however. At most centers, mediators are required to attend continuing education programs several times a year. These advanced training sessions cover special topics in depth, such as updates on state law affecting confidentiality, techniques for drafting agreements, issues in family disputes, etc.

Though mediators are certified as having successfully completed a training program, they are not licensed as are doctors, lawyers, and other professionals. Some people would like mediators to be licensed as a way to protect consumers against unqualified practitioners. Florida, for example, recently enacted a law prohibiting people from mediating in certain court-sponsored programs unless they have advanced degrees in social work or related fields or unless they are lawyers or former judges. Leaders of the mediation field generally oppose the idea of minimum educational requirements because, they say, it will squeeze out of the field some of the most talented people who, though they may lack advanced degrees, have intuitive skills as mediators.

Speaking recently to a gathering of mediators in Syracuse, New York, George Nicolau, president of the Society of Professionals in Dispute Resolution, an organization that represents many mediators, said, "Every one of us in this room and everyone in this field knows first-rate mediators who are not lawyers, who are not psychiatrists, who are not MSW's or MA's [holders of master's degrees in social work or arts]."[8]

In the future, some kind of statewide or national program to license mediators may be enacted. For the time being, however, you can be confident that anyone assigned to mediate your case at a public mediation center has successfully completed a training program similar to the one described above. You can also inquire as to whether a particular mediator is a member of any professional organizations in this field. While membership in such an organization does not by itself tell you how good your mediator is, it may indicate how experienced she is and perhaps how significant her work in mediation is to her. For example, if your mediator is a full member of the Society of Professionals in Dispute Resolution, a national organization that as of 1987 had 2000 members, it means she has had at least three years' substantial experience as a mediator or arbitrator (or as a teacher of these disciplines). Associate members have less than three years' experience.

Confidentiality in Mediation

One of the most important topics covered in your mediator's training is the question of confidentiality. There is no duty of the mediator greater than the duty to preserve the confidentiality of everything revealed to him or her during the hearing. That is why no recordings or stenographic records are made during a hearing, and why mediators usually are instructed to destroy their notes when it concludes. Indeed, without the sure knowledge that everything said during the hearing will remain private, mediation would not work because the parties would not feel free to explore honestly all aspects of their dispute and possible avenues to settlement.

The need for confidentiality can arise in at least three circumstances:

First, if you meet with the mediator in a private "caucus," you will want to be assured he will not reveal what you say to your opponent without your permission.

Second, after the hearing you will want to be sure that the mediator will say nothing about your case to anyone, including his family and friends, and the press.

And third, you will want to know that nothing you said or did during mediation will later be used against you in court. This might occur, for example, if your opponent later sued you and called you or the mediator to testify.

Mediators understand that they are required to protect your confidence in each of the above situations. They are bound to that duty by the oath of office and by the rules of the particular center where they work. Though the specific language of different centers' oaths and rules may vary, all should include the same broad requirements as to confidentiality.

Your mediator is also bound by the standards of the profession. Ethical standards of the Society of Professionals in Dispute Resolution, for example, state:

Maintaining confidentiality is critical to the dispute resolution process . . . (T)he neutral must resist all attempts to cause him or her to reveal any information outside the process. A commitment by the neutral to hold information in confidence within the process also must be honored.[9]

The only exception to the above requirement is where child abuse or other serious crimes are revealed during a hearing. In that event, the mediator is required to "advise the parties . . . that the confidentiality of the proceedings cannot necessarily be maintained" and give the parties the option of terminating the hearing.[10] If the information disclosed concerns a crime not previously reported or one planned for the future, the mediator may be obligated to notify authorities.

An increasing number of states have passed laws that impose on mediators a duty of confidentiality, except where information on serious crimes is revealed. These states include New York, Oklahoma, Colorado, and California. In Texas, one of the more recent states to enact such a law, the Alternative Dispute Resolution Procedures Act states:

> (The mediator) may not disclose to either party information given in confidence by the other and shall at all times maintain confidentiality with respect to communications relating to the subject matter of the dispute.[11]

When—if ever—a mediator or a party could later be forced to reveal in a court hearing what had been learned during a mediation session, is an unsettled question. The law does not now recognize a "mediator-client" privilege in the same way it does the doctor-patient, lawyer-client, and priest-penitent privileges that give a person the absolute right to prevent a doctor, lawyer, or member of the clergy from testifying in court. Yet, this is the direction in which we may be headed. Some states have passed laws that create something like a mediator-client privilege. The Texas statute, for example, provides:

> Any record made at an alternative dispute resolution procedure is confidential, and the participants or the third party

facilitating the procedure may not be required to testify in any proceedings relating to or arising out of the matter in dispute or be subject to process requiring disclosure of confidential information or data relating to or arising out of the matter in dispute.[12]

One federal court recently has considered this question. In 1987, when Mack Trucks, Inc., and the United Auto Workers reached an impasse in collective bargaining, they hired two mediators to try to help them settle. No agreement was reached, however, and later Mack Trucks went to court seeking a subpoena for "all notes and memoranda" made by the mediators during the hearing. (In the labor-management field, mediators would not necessarily destroy their notes after a hearing as they typically do at public mediation centers.) The mediators resisted the subpoena, arguing they had a duty to keep all matters revealed during the mediation confidential. Judge Thomas F. Hogan called it a "case of first impression." Though he said he was not going so far as to establish a mediator's privilege, he did grant an order protecting the mediator's notes. Otherwise, he said, the "whole mediation process could be brought into question."[13]

These new laws and recent court decisions add important legal safeguards to your mediator's ability to preserve the confidentiality of your mediation hearing.

PART TWO

The Mediation Process

CHAPTER
4

How to Start Your Case

"He who avoids entering into litigation [and seeks a friendly settlement] rids himself of hatred, robbery and perjury."

Pirke Avot (Ethics of the Fathers), 4.9.

Starting your mediation case is easy. Usually it will involve no more than completing a simple, one-page form with some blank spaces in which to describe briefly your dispute. The mediation center will do the rest. There are, however, some strategic choices to make that can affect the outcome of your case, or whether your case is heard at all.

Choosing a Mediation Center or Service

Once you have determined that your dispute is appropriate for mediation, your next step is to decide where to have your case mediated. Following is a brief look at the various types of mediation centers and services operating today in many communities.

Public Mediation Centers

What we have been referring to as "public mediation centers" are, for the most part, independent, nonprofit organizations that receive funds from state and local governments, foundations, and modest user fees. They are called by various names: "dispute resolution center," "neighborhood justice center," "community mediation center."

By and large, public mediation centers do not have a lot of frills. You will not see in them the internal winding stairways and expensive art you might find in a major midtown law office. The centers have more of a "public service" look, but that is okay because all you need for a successful mediation is a quiet room, a table with three chairs, and a good mediator. These, even the most humble public mediation center can provide.

These centers' caseloads vary greatly in size, from just a few dozen to more than five thousand cases per year. Annual budgets vary, too, from under 100,000 dollars for the Dispute Settlement Center in Chapel Hill, North Carolina, to over one million dollars for the Institute for Mediation and Conflict Resolution in New York City. A caseload of 100 to 500 disputes per year would be typical for an average center.[1] About one-fourth of such centers were founded within the past five years.[2]

Most cases heard at the centers are referred there by judges, police, and social service agencies. But, these days, the centers are also seeing more cases brought to them directly by disputants, so-called "walk-ins."

Indeed, you can walk into a public mediation center with nearly any kind of dispute and they will be able to accommodate you. This is one of the most impressive aspects of their work. Regardless of how large or small their budget, most centers are prepared to handle an extraordinarily broad range of cases, from charges of assault and harassment to consumer claims, housing disputes, multiparty neighborhood disputes, and disputes among coworkers at a factory or between spouses.

As if this were not a full enough agenda to keep the centers busy, some have also developed special programs to meet local needs: homeowners vs. remodeling contractors, farmers vs. bankers, disputes between roommates, and disputes involving bad checks, overdue library books, and barking dogs.

As most centers receive the bulk of their funds from state and local governments, their services are generally provided for free or at nominal cost (perhaps five dollars). Several states, including Florida, Illinois, and Texas, raise funds for their centers by assessing an extra filing fee on civil court lawsuits.[3]

Court-Connected "Justice Centers"

In an effort to resolve minor criminal complaints without prosecution, some cities have established a kind of mediation center inside the public prosecutor's office. These are sometimes referred to as "court-connected justice centers."

In Cleveland, for example, when a citizen files a criminal complaint against someone, if the complaint is not about a serious crime, the complainant may be encouraged to take the dispute to the Cleveland Prosecutor's Mediation Program. The program is voluntary, but as its director, Andre A. Craig, acknowledges, "The prosecutor can refuse to prosecute until mediation is tried, so while mediation is always optional, it could be your only option." About 6000 cases are mediated a year; local law students serve as mediators, often hearing two cases a night. Hearings last about 45 minutes. When successful, agreements often call for parties to pay damages, or return property, or avoid seeing each other.

These court-connected programs serve a useful function, but most are limited to hearing criminal matters and do not offer the truly voluntary, diversified, formal mediation we have been discussing.

Christian Conciliation Service

If you would like your dispute mediated or arbitrated based on Christian biblical principles of conflict resolution, you may want to use one of 35 local centers around the country established by the Christian Conciliation Service. Information on these centers can be obtained by contacting Christian Legal Society, P.O. Box 1492, Merrifield, 22116, (telephone: 703-642-1070).

Private Dispute Resolution Services

In 1987, when actress Valerie Harper and Lorimar Productions filed breach-of-contract suits against each other over Harper's role in the TV series *Valerie*, it looked as if the case might drag on until 1992 before it went to trial, according to *Time* magazine. Instead, both sides got together and hired a private judge who began hearing the case in mid-1988. "I'm very happy to have my day in court so quickly," Harper told *Time*.[4]

Private judging, mini-trials, mediation—these and other techniques are available to you, for a price, by an increasing number of companies in the growing field of private dispute resolution. These firms handle contract disputes between business corporations, construction disputes, employment cases involving wrongful termination, and disputed insurance claims, among others.

Fees generally start at a minimum of about 350 dollars per party for a half-day mediation session. Costs can rise to 20,000 dollars, or more, depending on the complexity of the case and the length of time needed to resolve it.

Private dispute resolution firms operating at the national level have organized themselves in various ways:

Endispute, Inc., headquartered in Washington, D.C., is a privately owned corporation.

Judicate, Inc., the Philadelphia-based firm that specializes in private judging, is a public company whose stock trades over-the-counter.

U.S. Arbitration and Mediation, Inc., based in Seattle, is a franchise operation with locations in more than two dozen cities.

A "second tier" of private dispute resolution services includes companies that operate primarily at the local or regional level. Their fees generally start at about 250 dollars per party. In Chicago, for example, Resolve, Inc., handles personal injury claims and disputes within closely held businesses. In St. Paul, the Mediation Alternative handles employment disputes, insurance claims, and business contract disputes. The American Arbitration Association also has begun offering mediation services through its 32 local and regional offices.

Where to Take Your Dispute

For most categories of dispute, your public mediation center will provide services quickly and at low cost. With some kinds of disputes, however, such as large consumer or employment claims, you may want to use a private dispute resolution service. The following guide considers various categories of dispute and where, as a general rule, you should go for mediation:

ASSAULT, HARASSMENT: For these and other minor criminal matters, your best forum is the local public mediation center, which will have experience handling these cases. If your community has a court-connected justice program, however, the local prosecutor may prefer you take the case there.

NEIGHBOR vs. NEIGHBOR: Nationally, nearly one-fourth of cases at public mediation centers involve neighborhood disputes such as those concerning property, noise, shared driveways, barking dogs, behavior of young people, etc. The public center is the best place to take such a case.

CONSUMER COMPLAINTS: These include demands for reimbursement due to unacceptable goods or services. Complaints against auto repair shops and dry cleaners are common, as well as against in-home services such as roofing, plumbing, and carpentry. If the amount of money you are seeking is under 5000 dollars, the public mediation center is your best choice. Above that, a private mediation service might be cost-effective and offer greater expertise.

INTERPERSONAL FEUD BETWEEN FRIENDS/ACQUAINTANCES: This subject includes disputes involving current or former girlfriend-boyfriends, roommates, over money, property, relationships, etc. Public mediation centers are most experienced at handling these.

INTRA-FAMILY DISPUTES: This subject includes disputes between spouses, siblings, or relatives concerning behavior, money, inheritances, etc. Best heard at public mediation centers. However, if the dispute affects the running of a family-owned business and if the amount at risk is enough to justify the cost, then private service may be preferable because of greater sophistication in handling business and financial matters.

LANDLORD/TENANT: This subject includes failure to make repairs, nonreturn of security deposit, adherence to building rules, etc. Public mediation center is experienced in hearing these cases, including multiparty disputes involving many tenants. If dispute involves condominium owners, however, where matters such as capital assessments are involved, private service will offer more financial expertise.

EMPLOYER/EMPLOYEE: This subject includes money owed in salary, unused vacation, sick leave; discrimination and discharge; employee theft. Where amount of dispute is under 5000 dollars, public mediation center is best. Above that, private service may be cost-effective, with greater business expertise.

DIVORCE MEDIATION: This subject is discussed in Chapter 10.

BUSINESS MEDIATION: This subject is discussed in Chapter 11.

COMMUNITY-WIDE DISPUTES, ENVIRONMENTAL DISPUTES: These subjects are discussed in Chapter 12.

In deciding where to take your case for mediation, your first consideration will have to be: What is available in my community? To locate the choices in your city or town, check local telephone directory listings under "mediation" or "dispute resolution" or "arbitration." Local bar association and social service offices may also be able to refer you to mediation providers. Appendix A lists many of the public mediation centers throughout the country, and Appendix B lists many of the leading private dispute resolution services.

Your "Submission to Mediation"

Once you have selected which mediation service to use, it is up to you to start the process. The rest of this chapter assumes you will take your dispute to a public mediation center, although the procedures discussed here would not be very different at most private dispute services.

Under ideal circumstances, you could approach your opponent directly and suggest you both try mediation. In practice, this happens only rarely, because usually by the time one side is thinking about the need for mediation, the relationship is so strained that neither is talking to the other. Common procedure, therefore, is for one side to initiate mediation by contacting a mediation center, and the center takes over from there.

You begin your mediation case by going to the center and completing a one-page form called "Submission to Mediation" (or sometimes "Consent to Mediation"). A typical example of such a form is reproduced on the following page. The form is simple enough. It asks for basic information such as your name and address and the name and address of your opponent.

"Claimant" and "Respondent"

Most centers designate the person who begins mediation as the "claimant" and the other person as the "respondent." This sometimes creates a problem when both sides feel they have something to complain about. Sometimes the "respondent" takes offense at being cast in what sounds like a defensive role. Unfortunately, we do not have words that mean "the person who initiates mediation" and "the person who agrees subsequently to mediate" without calling them claimant and respondent. Mediation centers might avoid this problem by forgoing the use of "claimant" and "respondent" on their forms and instead just referring to the parties by name.

Describing Your Dispute

The submission form asks only three questions about your case. In answering them, you should bear in mind that your opponent will see your answers when asked to sign his or her own submission form. Consequently, what you write here can affect whether or not

THE CENTER
FOR
DISPUTE SETTLEMENT, INC.

SUBMISSION TO MEDIATION
BEFORE THE CENTER FOR DISPUTE SETTLEMENT, INC.

REFERRING SOURCE _____   CDS CASE NO. _____

TOWN _____   DATE REFERRED _____

ADJOURNED DATE _____   DATE RECEIVED _____

The parties agree to submit the following dispute to mediation under the Rules and Procedures of The Center for Dispute Settlement, Inc., and in accordance with Article 21-A of the New York Judiciary Law.

What is the nature of the claim?

What remedy is sought?

Amount of money being asked for (if any): _____

We agree that we will abide by and perform any Agreement reached and we are aware that our Agreement shall have the same binding force as a contract with the same penalties for failure to honor it.

The failure to honor a Mediation Agreement may entitle the aggrieved party to undertake enforcement proceedings in a court of law, and may cause the non-complying party to be liable for court costs, disbursements, attorney fees, and interest.

Name of Claimants(s) _____   Relation to Respondent _____
Address _____   Phone (H) _____   (W) _____
Claimant's Signature _____
Date _____   or Attorney _____

Name of Respondent(s) _____   Relation to Claimant _____
Address _____   Phone (H) _____   (W) _____
Respondent's Signature _____
Date _____   or Attorney _____

Founded by the American Arbitration Association

CDS Copy 1   Parties Copy 2   Referral Source Copy 3 your opponent agrees to participate. Following are the three questions, and some thoughts on how best to respond:

1. *"What is the nature of the claim?"*

Try to avoid describing your dispute in legal terms, as this may trigger the "litigation response" in your opponent and send him or her to a lawyer rather than to mediation. For example, if your dispute is with your landscape gardener because the shrubbery that was guaranteed for three years died after three months, instead of describing this as "breach of contract," which legally it may be, just say "dissatisfaction with shrubbery plantings." If the landscaper sees the former description, she may go to her lawyer; if she sees the latter, she may view it as a customer relations problem and more readily agree to mediate. Similarly, if you are bothered by noise from your neighbor's air conditioning unit, describe it simply as "noise from air conditioner" rather than "violation of municipal noise ordinance."

Also, your description here can affect whom the center assigns as a mediator for your case. If there are issues involved that concern technical subjects, such as auto mechanics, medicine, finance, etc., be sure your description reflects this fact, so that a mediator with appropriate knowledge of the subject can be assigned.

2. *"What remedy is sought?"*

"Return of property" with itemized descriptions, or "payment for my injuries" are typical answers here, where the dispute involves property or money. But if your case is about how someone is behaving toward you or your family, then you want to be careful what you write. For example, if you are complaining about a neighbor who drives dangerously on your street, you might say "Remedy sought: Mr. Adams to drive more carefully on our street." That would be just fine. However, you would make a mistake if you continued the sentence, to read: ". . . so he doesn't run over my kids."

Imagine being Mr. Adams, getting this form in the mail, and realizing that he has been accused of nearly "running over" someone's kids? That can trigger the litigation response (Mr. Adams:

"Can you believe that that woman is going around telling people I try to run over her kids! I ought to sue her for slander!"). Be as little threatening or accusatory as you can. It will not limit the ultimate agreement, but if stated too strongly, it may keep you from getting into the hearing room.

3. *"Amount of money being asked for (if any)"*

How much money, if any, do you want the other person to pay you? Normal negotiation strategy is to claim much more than you really want—often by a factor of ten or more—in order to appear threatening and start with a "strong" bargaining position.

In mediation, however, this practice can be counter-productive. Again, your first hurdle is to get the other side to agree to mediate. If a demand for money appears too outrageous, your opponent may go straight to a lawyer. In mediation, temper your claim for money to a figure closer to what you really want.

Binding or Not Binding?

Agreements reached in mediation can be either binding or nonbinding. If they are binding, it means they have been written with the requirements of a legal contract, and will be enforceable by a court as would any other contract. Nonbinding agreements, on the other hand, merely express the intentions of the disputants.

As you complete the submission form, this is the time to decide if you want any agreement reached to be binding or not. In most cases, you should opt for the binding agreement. This will create an atmosphere in mediation more conducive to a full airing and working out of all the problems involved. And if your mediation is successful, it means you will have the problem dealt with, once and for all.

Submission forms at some centers routinely state that agreements reached will be binding; others state they will be nonbinding unless otherwise agreed by the parties. Examine the submission form provided by the center and make sure it states your intent. If it does not, a staff person will add language to conform to what you want.

The "Med/Arb" Option

If you and your opponent actually attend a mediation hearing, studies consistently show there is a better than 85 percent chance you will reach an agreement satisfactory to you both. If, however, your case should fall into the minority 15 percent that are not resolved through mediation, you have another option to choose as a kind of insurance.

The option is arbitration. Recall that in arbitration, the arbitrator has authority—much like a judge—to render a decision that will be binding on the parties. Some mediation centers have created an interesting hybrid procedure that combines the best of mediation and arbitration. It is called "med/arb" (pronounced "meed-arb").

In med/arb, you and your opponent proceed with a normal mediation hearing with the intent of working out your own agreement. If, however, after a reasonable effort, one or more aspects of your dispute have not been settled, then the mediator assumes the role of arbitrator and decides the matter for you. In effect, the mediator switches hats and says: "Despite your and my best efforts, no agreement has been reached on points X and Y. Therefore, because you both signed a "Submission to Arbitration" form in addition to the "Submission to Mediation" form, I will now act as arbitrator and make a decision on those two points."

The mediator closes the hearing and later sends the written decision to both parties.

In one study conducted at a mediation center in Buffalo, New York, researchers Neil McGillicuddy, Gary Welton, and Dean Pruitt found that under med/arb, disputants were less hostile toward each other, suggested more novel proposals for settlement, and showed greater motivation to reach agreement, than under straight mediation. The reasons seem to be fear of losing control of one's fate in the event of arbitration, and also greater respect for a mediator who has power to make decisions.[5]

If you think you would like to have the arbitration option, ask the staff at the mediation center if they offer med/arb. Only a minority of centers do, but the number appears to be increasing. If the center does offer this option, you will probably be asked to sign a "Submission to Arbitration" form as well as one for mediation.

Note, however, that, when you submit a dispute to arbitration you do commit to having the matter resolved through arbitration and bind yourself to abide by the arbitrator's decision. Thus, by submitting to arbitration, you give up some legal rights. If the dispute for which you are considering arbitration involves significant money or property or personal rights, you probably should consult your attorney before submitting to arbitration. Arbitration is discussed more fully in Chapter 8.

Conciliation

Some disputes brought to mediation are resolved by the parties even before a hearing can be held. This is called "conciliation," which means, literally, "winning over by goodwill." Conciliation typically occurs at either of two points early in the proceeding.

The first point occurs when the respondent receives notification from the center that you have brought the dispute to mediation. Some respondents will react right away by contacting you directly and offering to settle. They do this either because they genuinely did not realize how seriously you viewed the dispute, or because they do not want to get a third party—the mediation center—involved, and figure it is easier to settle.

The second point occurs when a staff person from the mediation center calls the respondent after the respondent has failed to reply to the center's notice of your desire to mediate. During the conversation, the respondent may make a settlement offer and ask the staff person to convey it to you. If a settlement is reached, the case will be withdrawn.

At many centers, about 15 percent of all disputes are conciliated in this way before a hearing. Rates of conciliation for self-referred or "walk-in" cases are even higher, above 20 percent.[6] Typically, conciliations are not reduced to writing, although if your dispute is conciliated and you would like the settlement in writing, most centers will accommodate you.

Overcoming Resistance to Mediation

After you have completed and signed the submission form, the center will notify your opponent by mail that you have initiated mediation and request that he also complete a submission form. He will be asked to sign and return the form, usually within seven days, so that a hearing can be scheduled.

Though more than four out of five disputes that go to a mediation hearing are settled successfully, nearly one-half of disputes brought to a center never reach the hearing room. In nearly a third of such cases, this is because the respondent refuses to mediate.

Many studies have tried to analyze why people refuse to participate in mediation. Sometimes, of course, the respondents may have good reasons to refuse, if they are likely to win in court and if they have the money and time to see the case through to a verdict.

At other times, however, a person may refuse to mediate simply because mediation is unfamiliar and therefore threatening. "The disputant," write professors Maria R. Volpe and Charles Bahn, "not knowing how mediation works, or perhaps never having even heard of mediation, fears the unknown and balks at taking part in it."[7]

Anne Richan has observed:

> Mediation is an alien concept in our society. We are taught to fight to the finish, and let the best person win. And, if you cannot win on your own, take it to the judge. Sitting down at a table and talking about conflicts is a strange and often frightening prospect, and few people are willing to give it a try.[8]

Another factor inhibiting your opponent may be hostility. After receiving a notice inviting him to mediate, one respondent called the mediation center and said, "I don't want to face that guy (the claimant) because if I do I'm going to go across the table and punch him." Even where there is not personal hostility, there may be, as researchers Merry and Silbey have said, a strong urge for vindication:

By the time a conflict is serious enough to warrant an outsider's intervention, disputants do not want what alternatives have to offer. At this point the grievant wants vindication, protection of his or her rights (as he or she perceives them), an advocate to help in the battle, or a third party who will uncover the "truth" and declare the other party wrong.[9]

Another factor may be contrary advice from a lawyer who is unfamiliar with mediation or who has a negative attitude about it. For example, the lawyer may tell your opponent, "Oh, this mediation business isn't for you. Ignore it. If the guy's serious, let him file suit and then we'll deal with it."

Getting Your Opponent to the Table

You may be tempted to call your opponent to try to convince him or her to join you in mediation. In most cases, this would not be helpful because your opponent is unlikely to trust your judgment, particularly with an unfamiliar process like mediation.

The best way to overcome your opponent's resistance is if the mediation center, not you, extends the invitation. This has been borne out by experience. For example, Travelers Insurance Company, a leader in using mediation in the insurance industry, has found that if the company asks a person to go into mediation, he declines; however, if the mediator asks, the person usually agrees.[10]

The mediation center wants to see your case go to mediation as much as you do. It believes in mediation and, more pragmatically, its funding sources will want to see a large number of hearings to justify continued financial support. Thus, you have a strong ally in wanting to get your opponent to the hearing table.

Consequently, the notice and supporting materials the center sends to your opponent are designed with one purpose in mind: to get him or her to agree to mediate. They will emphasize, for example, the potential benefits of mediation, detailing the center's success rate and outlining mediation's advantages in terms of low cost, privacy, speed, etc.

If your dispute came to the center not on a "walk-in" basis, for example, but on referral from the district attorney, then the notice may recite this fact for its persuasive effect: "District Attorney Sullivan has referred this dispute to our center in hopes it can be mediated." The expectation is that your opponent will think to himself: "The district attorney has my case and is suggesting I go to mediation. I certainly don't want to annoy the district attorney so I better give it a try." Cases referred to mediation by judges, prosecutors, police, and other authorities, have a high probability of making it to the hearing table. In a U.S. Department of Justice study, for example, four out of five cases referred by judges went to hearings.[11]

The mediation center's notice may attempt to exercise a little legal muscle of its own. It may bear, for example, a "case caption" in imitation of court papers:

In the Matter of the Mediation between
   Michael Jones, Claimant
and
   Russell Osgood, Respondent,
Case No. C–177–89

The notice may also employ legal jargon that carries a mild, if ambiguous, threat, for example: "Failure to appear for your hearing may result in the claimant's filing a legal action against you." The implied threat is that, if the respondent does not agree to mediate, the claimant will take him to court.[12]

If your opponent does not respond to the center's notice within a week or so, the center will likely follow up with a phone call. The staff will answer any questions about mediation and review its potential benefits. If your opponent indicates he or she is declining to participate based on a lawyer's advice, the staff may ask permission to call the lawyer directly to be sure the lawyer understands mediation.

If one, or perhaps even two, follow-up phone calls to your opponent do not result in an agreement to mediate, the center will mark your case "respondent refused to mediate" and close the file. You can pursue any other remedies, including litigation, that you want.

A Second-Chance Tactic

There is a tactic that sometimes might offer you a second chance at mediation. It takes advantage of the persuasive authority of the police and courts. Assume, for example, that your dispute involves excessive noise from a neighbor's house. You initiate mediation but, despite the best efforts of the center's staff, your neighbor refuses to participate. At this point, what you can do is file a complaint about the noise with the police, and tell the responding officer, or the prosecutor if you get that far, that you would like to try to mediate. There is a good chance that the police will be glad to get rid of the case in this way, and will notify the mediation center of the referral. Now, when the mediation center contacts your neighbor again, the referral will state that the dispute has been referred to mediation by the police. Your chances of getting your neighbor to a hearing should markedly improve.

CHAPTER
5

Preparing Your Case

You could go into a mediation hearing without any preparation and still come out with a satisfying result, but your chances of being pleased with mediation will be greatly increased by a little preparation. At most mediation centers, your hearing will be scheduled about two to three weeks after you and your opponent have signed "Submission to Mediation" forms. Use this time to prepare.

Rules of the Tribunal

Hearings at most centers are governed by a written set of rules (sometimes called "Rules of the Tribunal"). These rules cover basic operating procedures such as case scheduling, selection of mediators, confidentiality, and fees. They also cover technical procedures such as how you can postpone or adjourn a hearing, request a new mediator, or in the case of arbitration, when and how to appeal an award. You should get a copy of these rules, just in case any situation arises where you might need them. If the center does not send you a copy of its rules when it notifies you in writing of your hearing date, call and request a copy.

Rules of Evidence Do Not Apply

"Objection!" shouts Perry Mason, rising to his feet.

The young lady on the witness stand has just said the defendant was in the victim's apartment on the night of the robbery.

"But, Your Honor—" stammers district attorney Hamilton Burger.

"Mr. Mason," the judge inquires, "on what do you base your objection?"

"The witness's statement is incompetent, irrelevant, and immaterial," Mason intones.

"Objection sustained," rules the judge.

If Perry Mason were at a mediation hearing rather than in a courtroom, he would have a lot less to do. In mediation, the legal rules of evidence do not apply; each of the disputants and their witnesses are competent to speak, and no issue is irrelevant or immaterial if the disputants want to discuss it.

You might think this would make mediation hearings go on endlessly because no evidence is excluded. But just the opposite is true. With no objections to evidence, mediation hearings tend to move right along. The parties say what they want and show what they want, witnesses speak and then leave.

In mediation, you are free to bring to the table almost anything and anybody that will help you present your case. This can include:

- witnesses
- photographs
- drawings
- maps
- tape recordings

- medical bills
- pay stubs
- receipts
- apartment rules
- letters from friends and
  neighbors, and more

You can be creative in what you bring to a hearing.

At a California mediation program that hears disputes about noise from barking dogs, owners often bring in their dogs.

A man who wanted to show that his basement was damaged by water pouring off his neighbor's roof brought photographs, taken during a rainstorm, of the neighbor's gutter angled at his house and water running onto his basement wall.

When the owner of an auto repair shop wanted to show why a customer was expected to pay a storage fee for unclaimed engine parts, he took an 8-foot by 4-foot sign off the front of his building and brought it into the mediation hearing. The sign said, "Storage Fee: $1 per day after 30 days."

In deciding what evidence to prepare for your case, the question to ask is not, "Will it be admissable under the rules of evidence," but "Will it help me tell my side of the story in a clear and persuasive way?" Evidence can also be useful to show your opponent where her position on an issue is based on a mistake or misperception. It can also establish the extent of any losses or injuries for which you seek compensation.

On a strategic level, bringing evidence to the hearing can increase your bargaining strength by showing your opponent you have a strong case. It says, in effect, "you should settle with me in mediation, because if I am forced to take you to court, I may win."

The best time to present your evidence is during your "opening statement," that stage at the beginning of the hearing when both disputants have a turn to tell, without interruption, their side of the story. How to make your opening statement is discussed in the next chapter.

Four Kinds of Evidence

Your mediator will have been trained to evaluate the credibility of different types of evidence. Much of this is just common sense. A bill of sale, for example, is given more weight than someone's handwritten notes recounting the transaction. The mediator, of course, does not "rule" on how much weight any piece of evidence should be given. (Although, if the mediator ends up arbitrating, he or she would base the decision, in part, on the evidence submitted.) However, since you are trying to present your position in a clear, persuasive way, you should try to bring the types of evidence generally considered most persuasive.

Following are examples of four types of evidence ranked according to the relative weight they normally are given:

1. *Real or demonstrative evidence:* sometimes called "the thing itself," this refers to the actual thing in dispute. For example, the BB gun you claim your neighbor's child used to shoot your dog; the shutter with bubbled paint you claim the painter forgot to prime; the suit from the cleaners, with bleach stains. If you can bring in the physical item that the dispute is about, it has a powerful way of getting others to understand a problem from your point of view.

2. *Live testimony by a witness with knowledge of the facts:* sometimes called "viva voce" (the living voice); live testimony of a person who saw, or heard, or otherwise knows something firsthand about your dispute.

3. *Documentary evidence:* there are four important kinds of documentary (that is, written or printed) evidence.

   a. *Public records:* government documents carry much weight because of their official status. They include, for example, the report the police wrote about your accident or complaint; copies of your town ordinance (usually available from the town library) showing allowable noise levels in your community; the brochure distributed by the city explaining rules for putting trash in front of your house.

b. *Business records:* a record made "in the ordinary course of business," such as a hospital's or doctor's medical report; your receipt for a purchase at a hardware store; the organization chart drawn by your company's personnel office showing who is supposed to report to whom; the rules of your apartment building issued by the building manager when you signed your lease, and the lease itself.

c. *Photographs, maps, etc.:* nonofficial written or printed materials that have a high likelihood of authenticity. These are more believable if the maps come from reputable companies, and if the photos have a date of printing on the back (ask the developer to date the paper on the back so you can prove they are current photos).

Take photographs from the point of view that matters most to you. In one case, for example, a homeowner complained of a junked car parked on his neighbor's lot. He brought to the mediation hearing color photos of the old, rusted car which he had taken from the angle from which he was forced to see the car every day from his kitchen window.

d. *Private writings:* these include written statements from family, colleagues, or neighbors about your dispute, such as a neighbor's written statement that, "Yes, the Gallagher's dog barks at all hours of the night." These writings do not carry much weight because the writers are not present to be questioned by the mediator or your opponent to check their stories. You can make private writings more persuasive if the writers will have them notarized.

4. *Opinion testimony:* this includes the "expert witness" such as a doctor, auto mechanic, or carpenter—anyone who, by training or experience, has special knowledge in a field. When the mediator has no special knowledge of the subject in dispute, this kind of witness can be helpful.

AT A GLANCE
Four Kinds of Evidence

1. Real or demonstrative ("the thing itself")
2. Live testimony by a witness

3. Documentary (written or printed)
   a. Public records
   b. Business records
   c. Photographs, maps, etc.
   d. Private writings
4. Opinion testimony ("experts")

Checklist of Evidence

Below are five common kinds of disputes and examples of the types of evidence that would be helpful to bring to a hearing:

HARASSMENT: police report on incident where ex-boyfriend grabbed, pushed, and threatened you in public; notarized statement from friend who was with you and who saw incident; notarized statement from current roommate who has heard ex-boyfriend telephone repeatedly, late at night; letter from your doctor stating effects on you (loss of sleep, anxiety, difficulty concentrating at work) due to past incidents of harassment and fear of future ones.

PERSONAL INJURY: photograph of your injury (assuming your injury has already healed); doctor's report describing extent of injuries, medical bills, written statement from employer showing wages lost due to absence from work; copy of insurance company statements showing medical expenses not covered by insurance.

PROPERTY DAMAGE: photograph of damaged area of your home or car; actual repair bill or estimates from two contractors or auto repair shops; statement from insurance carrier stating or affirming cost of repairs.

NEIGHBORHOOD NOISE: tape recording of rock band or barking dog; written, notarized statement from neighbors confirming disturbance; copy of page of town ordinance stating limits of acceptable noise in residential area during evening hours; report on decibel level reading from acoustics expert.

LANDLORD/TENANT: photograph showing dangerous condition caused by rotted boards on stairs; sample of rotted board; copy of your lease stating landlord's duty to repair; copy of report by city housing inspector responding to your complaint.

Witness or Party?

In preparing for a hearing, you may ask various people to be witnesses for you. In some cases, however, it might be better to ask those people to join you as co-claimants. For example, if you were a tenant in an apartment building and had agreed to mediate a dispute with your landlord over poor trash collection in the parking lot, your first impulse might be to bring other tenants to your hearing as witnesses to confirm your story about the trash problem.

A mediated agreement, however, only applies to the parties in a dispute, not the witnesses. Thus, if your mediation agreement said, in effect, "The landlord agrees that rent can be withheld unless parking lot dumpsters are emptied once a week," this might be a good agreement for you, but it would not let the other tenants withhold their rent because they were not parties in the case. Instead of bringing the other tenants to the hearing as witnesses, it might be better to sign them on to the case as "co-claimants." Then they could come to the hearing as parties (or, if the group was too large, they could designate you to represent them) and share in the benefits of the mediated agreement. Their participation as co-claimants would also give you added bargaining power at the hearing, and possibly help you achieve more favorable settlement terms.

Character Witnesses Not Needed

In a courtroom, a witness may be called to testify about a party's character. The purpose of this is to show, by evidence of past acts or reputation, that the other person is likely either to be telling the truth or to be lying.

In mediation, where the goal is not to find the truth but to find a solution, character witnesses are not needed. Your virtues and fine reputation, and your opponent's vices and bad reputation, are not at issue. Furthermore, there is in mediation an underlying assumption that both sides have come to the table in good faith to work together toward finding a fair and workable solution. To bring in a witness with no knowledge of the dispute but merely to speak ill of your opponent or to show that your opponent has a reputation for lying would, in effect, challenge your opponent's good faith. This could poison the cooperative atmosphere necessary for mediation to succeed.

Similarly, you do not need to round up your sister or friend or teacher to come and tell the mediator what a good person you are. Your reputation is not at issue, and the mediator will not want to waste time hearing from someone with no knowledge of the matter in dispute.

Should You Bring Your Lawyer?

You have an absolute right to bring your lawyer to your hearing. Usually, however, disputants are discouraged from bringing their lawyers and, in fact, lawyers probably attend fewer than 10 percent of all hearings held at public mediation centers.

As Linda Hack has written:

> Lawyers are wholeheartedly encouraged to be part of the process by doing their job—that is, to give legal advice to their clients—but not within the confines of the mediation room. The more parties participating in (mediation), the more dynamics involved, and the less likelihood that a resolution of the problem will be produced. Only the mediator and the clients should be in the room and involved in the (mediation) process.[1]

For mediation to be most effective, disputants need to deal with each other directly, to air their differences, learn to perceive the dispute from each other's point of view, and work together to find a resolution. Many people who would bring a lawyer to a hearing would have a tendency to let the lawyer do the talking for them, thus defeating the purpose of mediation. This is not so great a problem in disputes between strangers over money or property, but it can be self-defeating in interpersonal disputes involving family, friends, neighbors, or business colleagues where preservation of the underlying relationship is a goal.

As a practical matter, many lawyers are so accustomed to the adversary system of litigation, and so unaccustomed to the cooperative system of mediation that they often do not know how to act in mediation. A lawyer unfamiliar with the principles and rules of mediation, for example, may find it difficult to sit quietly without objecting while your opponent cites hearsay evidence against you; or may chafe when you and he or she are asked to leave the room so that the mediator can meet privately with your opponent.

To many lawyers, conducting a hearing under these procedures might seem as absurd as playing bridge with your cards showing. But in mediation, it works. And if your lawyer, through education or experience, doesn't have confidence in that fact, then your lawyer's presence at the hearing may do your case more harm than good.

Another reason that lawyers are seldom needed is that there just is not much for them to do. With no need to object to evidence, or lead witnesses through testimony, or give a closing summation to a jury, most disputants can handle a mediation quite well on their own. If your lawyer were present, all you might want him or her to do would be to sit quietly and be sure all the points about which you are concerned get discussed, and later see that the agreement is drafted with the required formalities of a contract, if that is what you and your opponent wish (although this is also a role of the mediator).

How Best to Use Your Lawyer

The best way to use your lawyer in connection with mediation may be to meet with him or her before or after your hearing, or both, for legal advice.

Before the hearing: Consult with your lawyer about the issues in dispute; discuss your bottom-line position and the legal consequences of various options for settlement you may want to propose during the hearing.

After the hearing: You can condition your agreement on your lawyer's approval. One way in which this often is done is by having the mediator insert a clause stating that the agreement will take effect one week after it is signed, unless either party objects in writing before that date. During that week, have your lawyer review the agreement to be sure it says what you want it to say and that it does not impair your legal rights in any way you did not intend.

As a practical matter, you would probably not want to bother conditioning your agreement on your lawyer's approval unless significant amounts of money, property, or important legal rights were involved. This device is often used in business mediation and divorce mediation. (In divorce mediation, good mediators today insist that each spouse have his or her own lawyer review the mediated "Memorandum of Understanding" before it is signed. This practice is discussed more fully in Chapter 10.)

Some Cases When You *Should* Bring a Lawyer

There are some circumstances in which you probably should have your lawyer accompany you to a mediation hearing. These would include:

When, due to a speech problem or lack of fluency in the language, you need someone to speak for you at the hearing (although, in many cases, an articulate friend or relative could do the same).

When your opponent intimidates you so much that only the presence of your lawyer will give you enough confidence to participate effectively in the hearing.

When some of the issues in dispute touch on legal issues, such as how local building codes may affect terms of settlement, so that it would be impractical to conduct the hearing without a ready source of legal advice present.

When significant amounts of money or property, or important legal rights are involved, and you will not have time to have your lawyer review the mediated agreement after the hearing.

If you do decide to bring your lawyer, work out in advance what the fee will be, because you probably will not need to pay him or her as much for accompanying you to a mediation hearing as you would if you were being represented in court.

Planning Your Bottom Line

Perhaps the most important way to prepare for your hearing is simply to take time to think carefully about what you want out of mediation.

In mediation, there is no need to pound the table and demand 100,000 dollars for an 8000-dollar injury "just to get the other side's attention." In mediation, you have the other side's attention. In fact, you are going to be sitting face-to-face with plenty of time to talk about anything and everything that is important to you.

But unlike litigation, where you would not have to decide for months or years what your bottom-line settlement position is, in mediation you know that before you leave the hearing room you are going to be asked—if not by your opponent, then by the mediator in private caucus—what exactly it is that you want. Not what you are asking, but what it is you really need. How much money would you settle for? Which items do you want returned and which can you let go?

In other words, you are going to need to know your bottom line very soon—within a short time after you go into the hearing room. It is worth giving it some thought beforehand.

Of course, when you enter the hearing room, you enter a fluid situation. Your opponent's position may change; your position may change. One thing mediation does very well is help "unstick" disputants from preconceived positions. You may be prompted to think of solutions that never occurred to you before. Giving some thought ahead of time to what you really want out of mediation will help you evaluate any new ideas for settlement that emerge during the hearing.

How a Mediator Is Assigned to Your Case

After you and your opponent have both signed submission forms, and while you are preparing for your hearing, the mediation center will assign a mediator to your case.

Most public mediation centers use just one mediator per hearing. Some use a team of two; a few use panels of three or five. For the following discussion, we will assume that just one mediator will be hearing your case.

Your mediation center, depending on its size, will maintain a panel of trained and certified mediators, ranging in number from as few as a dozen to a hundred or more. It is from this panel that the center will select a mediator for you.

When the center contacts a mediator to whom it would like to assign your case, it will tell him the names of the parties and the nature of the dispute, for example, "bad check," "neighborhood disturbance," "quality of goods sold." This is the mediator's opportunity to consider whether he can be unbiased in the case. Does he know either of the parties? Does he own stock in a company involved, and could the outcome of the dispute affect the company's fortunes? He may also decline the assignment if he lacks substantive knowledge of the matter in dispute (such as finance) or if he is uncomfortable with the kind of dispute. For example, some mediators like hearing consumer disputes but feel uncomfortable hearing family disputes, with their greater degree of interpersonal conflict.

Requesting a Special Mediator

If your case involves a simple matter of the dry cleaner fraying your shirt collars, you do not need a chemist to be your mediator. But if your dispute concerns a matter of some technical complexity, in fields such as construction, medicine, or finance, then you should consider requesting a mediator with the relevant specialty. For example, if your dispute is with a contractor about an addition to your home, it would be helpful to have a mediator who understands something about carpentry, masonry, and other aspects of home remodeling.

Having a knowledgeable mediator means you and your opponent will not have to spend much time during the hearing educating him about the technical side of your dispute. Also, the knowledgeable mediator may be better able to suggest new ideas for settlement than would one who is dependent on what you and the other disputant tell him. Your hearing can succeed without a mediator with subject-matter knowledge, but it is likely to go more quickly and smoothly with one. Make your request, if possible, when you sign your submission form so that the center has plenty of time to arrange for the type of mediator you want.

You can also request that your mediator fit a particular demographic profile. You may, for example, feel most comfortable with a woman rather than a man, an older person rather than a younger one, or a member of your own ethnic or religious group. This is a matter of personal preference only; mediators are trained to handle all cases impartially, regardless of the sex, age, or background of the disputants. Nevertheless, most centers will accommodate your request if they can, and as long as your opponent does not object.

Checking on Your Assigned Mediator

You can be confident a mediator will disqualify himself if there is any reason to think he could not be impartial in your case. On the other hand, if you want to take an extra step to be sure there is no potential conflict of interest, you do have the right to contact the center and ask about the mediator they have tentatively assigned, what his background is, and what experience he has in hearing cases like your own. This may give you some added peace of mind as you await your hearing.

If you do learn who your mediator will be, however, do not contact him, as this might be seen as compromising his neutrality.

He might have to disqualify himself, and the process of assigning a mediator would have to start all over.

Scheduling Your Hearing

Most public mediation centers schedule hearings at the convenience of the disputants and the mediator (who, after all, usually works as a volunteer). To accommodate work schedules, hearings can be held either during the day, in the evening, or on weekends. While most centers work out of downtown offices, many also can schedule hearings in surrounding suburbs and towns. These "satellite" hearings are usually held in schools, libraries, court offices, or other public buildings.

Be sure to tell the center what times and locations will be most convenient for you. And remember that no one can tell in advance how long your hearing will last. Although a typical hearing runs about one-and-a-half to two hours, some may last as long as five hours at a stretch. Be sure to clear your calendar so that if your hearing is going well, you can stick with it as long as it takes. Once a hearing is interrupted, even if it is later reconvened, it can take a long time to reestablish the same productive levels of energy and cooperation.

With the mediator assigned, the place and time for the hearing set, and your own preparation completed, your case is ready to proceed.

CHAPTER
6

Inside the Hearing Room

(Bailiff bangs three times on courtroom door) "All Rise! This Court is now in session, The Honorable Thomas A. Watson presiding!"

That is how a typical courtroom hearing begins. Mediation begins differently.

"Hello. Are you Elizabeth Fields? I'm Tom Watson, the mediator. Will you follow me to the hearing room, please?"

Mediation's low-key opening is deceiving because it is really just the overture to a compelling drama about to unfold. What happens most days in court, by comparison, could be considered boring. Remember, mediation is not combat by hired gun; in a mediation hearing, it is the disputants themselves—the ex-lovers, the feuding neighbors, the boss and the fired employee—who in a few minutes will be nose-to-nose across the hearing table, with the chance at last to say what is on their minds.

As mediation sessions begin, the mediator has no need to get the disputants' attention because, typically, no one is speaking. Usually it is the first time they have seen each other in weeks or months. Now they sit, silently, across the table, staring at the mediator, waiting for him to explain the mystery of this place and this proceeding.

In this chapter, we will look inside the hearing room at the six stages of a typical mediation hearing. We will consider what is happening, and what you should be doing, during each of those stages in order to make your mediation as successful as possible.

Preliminaries

Where You Sit

After your mediator greets you in the waiting area and escorts you to the hearing room, he will invite you to take a seat at the table.

Exactly what *is* the perfect shape for a mediation table? This is a subject that mediators debate vigorously in the pages of professional journals. Some prefer a rectangular table because they believe its resemblance to a typical boardroom table inspires confidence in the mediation process; others dislike the rectangular, because they think the hard lines encourage hard and inflexible bargaining positions. Some like a square table on the theory that its four equal sides suggest equality among the parties. Still others prefer no table at all, and instead like to have the disputants sit in upholstered armchairs around a coffee table or on a comfortable sofa facing the mediator.

Often, a mediation center will have several hearing rooms arranged differently. The mediator can choose which he or she prefers to use in a particular case.

There is no strategic advantage in jockeying for position; the mediator knows where he wants you to sit and, much like a host at a dinner party, will direct you to a seat. Do not balk or insist on another seat; this one is the mediator's call, and you should sit where he suggests.

A typical seating arrangement would place you at one side of a rectangular table, your opponent directly across, and the mediator at the head. If a lawyer or witnesses are with you, they will be seated next to you, along your side of the table.

What the Mediator Knows About You

As your hearing opens, your mediator has only sketchy information about you and your dispute. He knows your name and address, the "nature of the dispute" as you stated it on the submission form, and the referral source, if any (such as City Court Judge, district attorney, etc.). If your dispute at some time involved a call to the police, a copy of the police report will probably be in the file, and the mediator would have glanced at it. But the mediator knows this information is only part of the story and forms no fixed opinions before the hearing begins.

Stage 1: Mediator's Opening Statement

The first lines in this drama are the mediator's, and they are known as the "opening statement." It is a short speech, usually delivered without notes, through which the mediator will try to demystify the proceeding for you by describing in simple terms the procedures and rules of the hearing. The mediator knows from memory the half-dozen or so key points that must be covered.

Sample Opening Statement by Mediator

The opening statement below is typical of the kind you will hear at any public mediation center. In the left-hand column are the key points the mediator wants to make.

Introduces self	Good morning, my name is Tom Watson. I'm the mediator who has been assigned to your case.
Introduces claimant	Before we go any further, I want to make sure I have everyone's correct name and address. On my left is Elizabeth Fields of 225½

Bristol Ave. Ms. Fields, you are the claimant in this hearing.

Introduces respondent and witness

And on my right is Mr. Richard Powell, 644 Eastbrooke Drive. Mr. Powell, you are the respondent. The witness you have brought with you is Mr. Robert Medden of 206 Savannah Boulevard.

Commends parties

I would like to start by commending each of you for choosing mediation as a way to resolve your dispute. By doing so, you have given yourselves the opportunity to solve this problem in a cooperative rather than an adversarial way and with greater flexibility, speed, and privacy than you would likely have in court.

States goal

The Center for Dispute Settlement is a nonprofit organization set up to help people in our community resolve their disputes through mediation. Our goal in this hearing is to find a solution to your problem that will be fair to both of you and workable in the long run. Our experience is that disputants who work in good faith during the mediation hearing have a very high success rate in reaching an agreement. My job is to help you do that.

Explains mediator's role

As a mediator, I have been trained and certified by the center to hear disputes such as yours. I have no authority to render a decision, and I can't send anyone to jail or impose any fines. My only job is to help you find your own solution to this dispute. I am completely neutral. I don't know either of you, and I know nothing about your case except its general nature as you described it on your submission forms.

No time pressure

One of the advantages of mediation is that we are under no time pressure. This hearing room is available to us for as long as we want it, and I am prepared to stay here as long as the hearing appears to be productive. If, as we go along, you want to take a break for a cold drink or a stretch, just let me know and we'll do that.

Explains procedure We'll begin today by having each of you make an opening statement to tell us what this dispute is all about from your point of view. Ms. Fields, as the claimant, will go first, and then Mr. Powell, as the respondent, will have his turn. While one of you is speaking, the other one will absolutely not be allowed to interrupt. If you need to make notes to remind yourself of comments you want to make later, there are pads and pencils on the table for you to use.

While each of you is speaking, you may notice me taking notes. If I write something, it doesn't mean I agree or disagree with what has been said. I am taking notes just to help keep track of the facts of the case.

Use of evidence While you are speaking, you can show us anything in the way of evidence you have brought with you, such as bills, letters, photographs, or whatever. The purpose of evidence is to help us understand your side of this dispute. The rules of evidence followed in court are not followed here, so I am willing to look at anything you want to show me. The other party will be able to look at it, too.

Discussion stage After the opening statements, we will begin to discuss the issues in dispute, and hear from any witnesses you have brought today. During this discussion phase, you can each say whatever you like, but I will not allow any uncivil language or swearing.

Caucusing At some point during the hearing, I may want to talk to each of you separately in what is called a "caucus." If that happens, I will ask one of you to leave the room while I speak with the other party. Everything you tell me in a caucus I will keep confidential and not tell the other side, unless you give me specific permission to do so. If I spend longer in caucus with one of you than the other, it doesn't mean I am partial to one side, it just means it may be taking me a little longer to understand all the facts and the options available.

Confidentiality You have both signed a pledge to keep everything said and revealed in mediation confidential. I have taken a similar pledge to keep secret everything you say or show me. In fact, when the hearing is over, I will even throw away my notes. The Center considers this rule of confidentiality the most important rule of mediation and expects each of you to uphold it strictly.

Consent agreement As I said, our goal today is to find a solution to your dispute which both of you feel is fair and workable in the long run. If we can find such a solution, I will help you write it up in the form of what we call a "Consent Agreement." This will be an official document you both will sign and which we will have notarized. It will be a binding contract and may be legally enforceable in court.

Questions? Now, before we begin with your opening statements, are there any questions? If not, then Ms. Fields, you are the claimant, so let's begin with you. Please tell us what this case is all about.

What the Mediator Is Trying to Do

Besides explaining how the hearing works, your mediator will use his opening statement to help achieve his first and perhaps most important goal: to gain control of the hearing.

He has temporary control at the start, of course, but that is not earned and soon can be lost. The first time your opponent calls you a liar and a disgrace to your profession, things quickly can get out of hand. What is to prevent one of you from leaving, or taking a swing at the other, or more likely, from the hearing degenerating into a shouting match or, worse yet, an endless gripe session where nothing is accomplished?

Only by earning and keeping control can the mediator keep the hearing on track and moving forward. Yet, he cannot dominate or be too authoritative; if he were to do so, it would inhibit the disputants from taking the initiative to find their own solutions. Instead, your mediator attempts to gain control by earning your trust, respect, and confidence.

From first meeting you in the waiting room, everything your mediator says and does is designed with this goal in mind. He did it when he met you in the waiting room, by presenting a neat appearance and speaking politely and respectfully to you. And he will try to do it during his opening statement by speaking confidently, answering your questions fully, and otherwise demonstrating that he is intelligent, knowledgeable, unbiased, and of potential help—in short, someone in whom you can and should place your trust.

What You Should Do

Listen carefully to the mediator's opening statement for how things will proceed and for any variations on normal rules, and then ask any questions that occur. Also, use the few minutes it takes for the mediator to make his statement to relax and become comfortable in the hearing room. It will soon be your turn to speak.

Weapons Check

At some centers, particularly those that hear many disputes involving assault and harassment, the mediator will follow his opening
statement with a "weapons check." He will ask if you are carrying
any weapons and, if you are, instruct you to remove them from the
hearing room and check them with the receptionist or other staff
member. Both parties will then be required to sign a statement
affirming they are unarmed.

Stage 2: Disputants' Opening Statements

After the mediator's opening statement, witnesses are asked to
leave the room. You may recall them later to confirm parts of your
story, but the principal source of information about your story will
be you, and it starts with your opening statement.

This is your chance, finally and without interruption, to tell
your opponent and the mediator your view of the dispute. Consider
how delicious this opportunity is: even if you had tried before
mediation to negotiate a settlement directly with your opponent,
you probably never had the chance to tell your side of the story
without being interrupted or having to shout. Even if you were to
go to court, you probably would not get such a chance until the
case came to trial and your attorney called you to testify—but even
then you would be interrupted by objections from opposing counsel
and constrained to limit your testimony to the narrow legal issues
in dispute.

But now in mediation, the floor is yours. No one will stop you.
No one will object or try to twist your words. If your opponent
interrupts to shout, "No, he's lying!" the mediator will quickly
remind him he may not interrupt while you are speaking.

What You Should Do

Address your opening statement to the mediator. Later on—if your
hearing is going well—you should be speaking directly to your

opponent, but at this early stage speak to the mediator and look at him as you talk. This should help you keep calm by avoiding having to look directly at your opponent and also help establish a rapport between you and the mediator.

Unless the mediator invites you to use first names, address the mediator and your opponent as Mr. or Ms. Here are some other guidelines that may be helpful:

1. Tell Your Story Chronologically

Your task in your opening statement is to tell the mediator and your opponent what the dispute looks like from your point of view and how it has affected you. The best and simplest way to do this is to tell about your dispute in the order it developed.

Start by briefly describing the situation before the dispute began. In this way, you paint a picture of how the dispute has affected you by changing a good situation to a bad one. For example:

> *Ms. Fields (the claimant)*: "The trouble began in July of 1988. That's when I started being woken up at night by noise from parties that Mr. Powell had at his backyard pool. Our houses back up to each other. Before then, the neighborhood was very quiet; I could sleep with the windows open and never be disturbed by noise."

2. Use Dates Carefully

As you tell your story, be sure to have in mind the dates as closely as possible when events occurred. Your mediator will be working hard while you speak to place in historical order all that has transpired. Exact dates will help him do this.

> *Ms. Fields*: "The first time I was woken up by noise from a pool party was the night of July 15 at about 2 a.m. I remember the date because the next morning I had to be up at 6 a.m. for an early flight to Chicago for business."

Showing the mediator you can be accurate with dates is also a good way of demonstrating to the mediator and your opponent that you are reliable when relating other information.

3.   Display Evidence as You Tell Your Story

Display your evidence as it comes up in your story, rather than all at once at the beginning or at the end. For example:

> *Ms. Fields*: "As I mentioned, later that night some of Mr. Powell's party guests climbed over the fence into my yard and purposely damaged my car. I took the car for repair to Irwin's Garage on North Street. They did some body work on the hood and also had to replace the radio antenna. The bill was 432 dollars, and here is the receipt (shows receipt from auto shop).
>
> "I also took a photo of the car to show the damage (shows photo of dents in hood)."

The mediator will look at your photos and other evidence and then pass it to your opponent to view, but your opponent will not be allowed at this time to comment on it or ask any questions because the floor is still yours. The mediator, too, will likely hold any major questions or comments about your evidence until later in the hearing. He doesn't want to disturb your train of thought in telling your story.

4.   Do Not Conclude with a Demand

You may have the urge to wind up your opening statement with a strong demand, such as "I insist Mr. Powell pay me the 432 dollars for the damage his guests did to my car and also pay for repairs to my backyard fence." But to do this would be a mistake. Nearly everyone who goes through mediation decides during the hearing that they should change their settlement position from what it was initially. For example, you may think you know what your opponent wants and what he is willing to give up, but your assumption may be wrong. You may learn during your opponent's opening statement that you could have asked for more and gotten it in exchange for something you would not mind giving up. But if you lock yourself into a settlement position during your own opening statement, it makes it that much harder to change your position later without losing face.

What Your Mediator Is Doing

While you are making your opening statement, you may have the feeling that no one outside family and closest friends has ever listened to you quite as attentively or with as much understanding as your mediator is listening to you now. This is the way it is supposed to be.

Earlier, your mediator used his greeting to you in the waiting room and his opening statement to show he is intelligent, reliable, and respectful, and thus to build trust. Now, he uses your opening statement—not only to grasp the facts of the dispute—but also to show he is a good listener, that he cares about your problem, and not only understands it but understands your emotional reaction to it. This is called "empathic listening," an important skill your mediator uses to help build your trust in him and thus help him earn control of the hearing.

Professors Nancy H. Rogers and Richard A. Salem have written:

> Empathic listening means listening for how the parties feel as well as to what they are saying, and providing verbal and nonverbal (eye contact, facial expression, body position) feedback that lets them know the mediator understands and cares about both. An empathic mediator conveys respect to the parties, doesn't register approval or disapproval of what is being said, refrains from providing unsolicited advice and does not interrupt.[1]

Though the mediator's primary job is to listen while you speak, he will also help you out as the situation may require. Few disputants are able to tell their story smoothly from beinning to end without a little help. Without interrupting the flow of your opening statement, the mediator may use a few devices to assist you, as needed:

- *Helping questions:* these are sort of "stage prompts" the mediator may use to help you get the facts straight. For example, "Excuse me, Ms. Fields, let me be sure I understand, that event happened in August, before you called the police?"

- *Open-ended questions:* the mediator may interrupt to ask a neutral, "open-ended" question designed to remind you of a part of your story that may prove important but which you may have forgotten to tell. For example, "Ms. Fields, do you often need to get up for work very early in the morning?" These questions can also be used to probe for underlying issues. For example, "Did you and Mr. Powell ever have any conversation that was not about the noise problem?"

- *Venting:* your mediator knows how much frustration or anger you may feel toward your opponent and during the opening statements may waive the usual rule against uncivil language in order to let you vent some of your anger.

- *Echoing and summarizing:* by repeating back to you in his own words what he has heard you say, the mediator both assures himself he has understood the facts of your story and gives you the chance to correct any misstatements you may have made.

> *Mediator*: "Ok, Ms. Fields, let me see if I understand what you are telling us about your dispute with Mr. Powell. Since he opened his backyard pool last July, you have been disturbed from your sleep at least once each week by loud noise from parties held at his home." (The mediator summarizes the major facts of her story.)
> *Ms. Fields*: "Yes, that's the situation."

Your Opponent's Opening Statement

Along with the mediator, you have a primary task—while your opponent makes his opening statement—of listening carefully. In most cases, you will hear things about your dispute you never heard before, such as your opponent's emotional reaction to it, his perception of how you responded to settlement overtures he made, or a statement of what he really wants out of the case. You may also hear things that upset you:

> *Mr. Powell*: "Ms. Fields has a reputation around the neighborhood as a real complainer."

If he embellishes the truth or insults you, try not to interrupt; doing so will only annoy the mediator. Make a note of the statement that upset you and raise it later if it still seems important.

Listen, as the mediator will be doing, for clues to what it is that is important to your opponent:

> *Mr. Powell*: "You know, I would like to feel I can enjoy my own yard without having neighbors listening to my guests or rushing to call the police the second things get a little loud. I like my privacy, too."

You might also discover a few bargaining chips you didn't know you had:

> *Mr. Powell*: "If she's so concerned about being a good neighbor, why doesn't she keep her dog on a leash like she's supposed to, and out of everyone's trash?"

Stage 3: Discussion

After opening statements are concluded, it is time for you and your opponent to start talking directly to each other. The take-off point for the discussion is often a comment one disputant wants to make on something the other party said during the opening statement.

> *Ms. Fields*: "Mr. Powell, I don't know where you got the idea that I have a reputation in the neighborhood for being a complainer, but I can tell you that is just not true. Since I moved into my house five years ago, you are the first person who has given me any reason to complain about anything."

There is a tendency for things to get out of hand during these early stages of discussion, and so the mediator will normally try to stay in control. He will remind disputants about not using uncivil language and will discourage character attacks. Instead, he will try to help the disputants discuss in general terms the various issues in dispute.

The first thing your mediator may do is attempt to put the issues in some kind of order. A common practice is to tackle the easiest ones first in order to build up the disputants' confidence in the mediation process and in their own ability to address their dispute in a reasonable and productive way.

> *Mediator*: "I can see from your opening statements we have several issues to talk about. There is the damage to Ms. Field's car which she believes was caused by Mr. Powell's pool guests, then the more general question of noise from the pool parties, and then some concern about Ms. Fields' dog running loose and getting into trash. Let's start with the specific problem of damage to Ms. Fields' car."

What the Mediator Is Doing

This is a time for narrowing and broadening. On the one hand, your mediator will try to narrow the number of issues in dispute: Can any complaints discussed in the opening statements be dismissed because they are no longer relevant or were simply based on misinformation? If so, it will be easier now to focus on the other issues. On the other hand, the mediator will probe to see if any of the issues raised need to be broadened to include underlying issues—such as hidden interpersonal conflicts—not disclosed by the parties.

Beginning with this stage of the hearing and continuing through to its conclusion, your mediator will be engaging in several types of activity. Mediator Christopher Honeyman has observed five activities performed by mediators in labor disputes, and these seem to apply as well to the more general kinds of mediation with which we are concerned. Honeyman's five categories of mediator activity are:

1. *Investigation:* in searching for the facts behind the dispute, sometimes the mediator finds information the disputant did

not want to give, or demonstrates potential holes in a disputant's point of view.

2. *Demonstration of empathy:* by showing a willingness to hear and discuss matters of concern to the disputants, even if not technically relevant to the dispute, the mediator builds trust and helps engender a cooperative attitude.

3. *Persuasion:* slowly at the beginning, and then more intensively as the hearing progresses, the mediator may encourage disputants to embrace one or more possible terms for settlement.

4. *Invention:* if no workable options for settlement emerge from the disputants, then during the later stages of the hearing the mediator may propose some of his own creation.

5. *Distraction:* the mediator will often try to relieve tension during the hearing by use of humor, anecdotes, or just switching to other issues (one mediator described this as the "vaudeville element" of mediation).[2]

During the discussion stage, the mediator will try to help you and your opponent begin to approach your dispute in a cooperative, rather than competitive, way. On a very simple level, for example, instead of asking, "Ms. Fields, what would you settle for on this damage issue?" the mediator may ask, "Ms. Fields, can you think of some ways this issue possibly could be resolved?"

What You Should Do

Primarily, this is the "research" part of your hearing. Your opponent told his story the way he wanted to during his opening statement, but undoubtedly he failed to answer some questions that have been troubling you. Ask the questions now; this is the time to explore what went wrong between you.

> *Ms. Fields*: "One thing I don't understand, Mr. Powell. When I called your home to complain about the noise, why didn't you show me the courtesy of taking the call yourself and talking with me about the problem? Instead, you let one of your guests handle it. Why?"

In the later stages of the hearing, you will be constrained by the mediator to put aside the past and focus on the future. Thus, if you have questions about your opponent's past behavior, ask it of him directly now.

Explore all the possible issues. Like the mediator, you will need to understand as much as you can about the facts and the players in this dispute to help you formulate realistic settlement ideas. Though you are, obviously, very close to the dispute, there may be facets of it about which you have little information.

> *Ms. Fields*: "Tell me, Mr. Powell, what kind of schedule do you generally keep at your house? How often do you use the pool in the summer? Are these social gatherings, or do you entertain business guests, too?"

Try to make your opponent see how the problem has affected you. You may have done some of this in your opening statement, but this is a good time to reemphasize, as needed.

> *Ms. Fields*: "Do you know what it is like to go to work on three hour's sleep, Mr. Powell? Let me tell you something about the kind of work I do. Three mornings a week at 8:15 a.m. I have to chair a meeting of 12 department heads," etc.

Finally, listen carefully to your opponent. As you did during his opening statement, try to discern from the discussion what his real needs are and what he is seeking from mediation.

Calling of Witnesses

Early in the discussion stage, the mediator may suggest that it would be useful to hear from the witnesses. He will call them, one at a time, back into the hearing room and ask them to tell what they know about the dispute. As the disputants were allowed to make their opening statements without interruption, so the witnesses are given a chance to say what they came to say:

Mr. Powell's Witness: "I was at the party in July where Mr. Powell's neighbor says she called to complain about the noise and we were rude to her and then climbed over into her yard and damaged her car. But you should have heard how nasty she was when she called and some of the language she used. I wouldn't even repeat it here. If she'd asked us nicely to turn down the music we would have. Anyway, I didn't see anyone go over into her yard. Most of the people at the party—we all work together—they're not the kind of guys who would purposely smash someone's car. She's got the wrong idea about us."

If you have any questions of the witness, you can ask them directly. The mediator may ask a few questions, too. After that, the witness is dismissed and told he can go home. Witnesses in mediation hearings are seldom recalled because the rest of the hearing focuses exclusively on the two disputants.

Stage 4: The Caucus

At this point in the hearing, your mediator will likely take advantage of one of mediation's most innovative features: the caucus.

Mediator: "I would like to meet now with Ms. Fields for a private caucus. Mr. Powell, would you mind sitting in the waiting room and I'll come and get you when we're done." (Respondent, Mr. Powell, leaves the hearing room.)

The caucus, which is a private meeting between you and the mediator, gives the mediator a chance to talk with you more informally and more candidly than he could in the presence of your opponent. He may assume a more relaxed posture, taking off his jacket and rolling up his shirt sleeves. And he may step over the line of strict impartiality just a little to tell you he genuinely sympathizes with your predicament and hopes a solution can be found.

Mediator to Ms. Fields: "Well, I can see you've been under tremendous stress because of this situation. I really hope we can find a way out of this for you so that you can get some sleep."

In caucus, you may be probed, cajoled, and challenged by your mediator. He may probe to find additional facts about your story that may reveal underlying interests. He may want to know what your bottom line really is. He may point out some weaknesses or holes in your story in order to create some doubt in your mind and help you bring your expectations in line with reality. He will not, however, ridicule or find fault with your past behavior. He may "translate" for you what he thinks your opponent is trying to tell you. And he will certainly challenge you to think of new options for settlement that might satisfy both you and your opponent.

Dr. Vivian Einstein, author of *Conflict Resolution*, lists the following as among the questions a mediator is likely to ask a disputant during caucus. "All these questions," Dr. Einstein writes, "will help the mediator get at the parties' real interests and may generate some excellent solutions."

- What do you really want to happen?
- What do you think is the proposal to which both of you most likely would agree?
- If you were in the other person's shoes, how would you feel?
- What would you do?
- What will you do, if both of you do not reach an agreement?
- How much will not agreeing cost you?
- How would it feel to walk away just now, with the whole matter settled satisfactorily?
- What are some fair ways of settling this problem, fair to you and to the other side?[3]

Perhaps the most important questions the mediator may ask during caucus are those beginning with "What if. . . ?" In other words, posing to you the terms of a hypothetical settlement: What if your opponent did X, would you do Y?

Mediator: "Ms. Fields, what if Mr. Powell agreed to pay you for half the damage to your car and also agreed in writing to move all his parties indoors after midnight? How would you react to that?"

What You Should Do

To take full advantage of the opportunities caucusing presents, you need to be open and honest with your mediator. If there is some matter about which you have not been able to be entirely truthful in the presence of your opponent, tell your mediator the full story during caucus.

Ms. Fields: "Look, I'm not 100 percent sure the damage to my car hood was caused by the people at Mr. Powell's party; it might have been there already. If he would just pay me for the cost of replacing the antenna—I think it was about 200 dollars—I'd be satisfied."

Ask questions. If there is any aspect of the hearing you are not understanding, or you are not sure about something the mediator or your opponent said, bring this up during caucus.

Float some trial balloons. Pose your own "What if . . ." questions. You may not have wanted to suggest an idea for settlement during the hearing for fear of looking weak or too eager to settle, but the caucus is the time to try the idea out on your mediator. If it holds any promise, and if you want him to do so, the mediator will be glad to present it to your opponent as if he, and not you, thought of it.

Stage 5: Negotiations

If your mediation is working, it should begin to show now. After the initial, generalized discussion of Stage 3, and the honest exchange with the mediator during caucus, disputants now are focused on a narrow range of issues. They are forward-looking, searching for workable settlement terms that will satisfy their own and their opponent's real interests.

Often, the relationship between disputants has begun to change, too. Not only has their negotiation style changed from competitive to more collaborative, their perceptions of each other is more realistic. Mediator Anne Richan has compared this stage of the hearing to "watching a wall come down brick by brick, as the disputants confront each other with all the things that have been bothering them and discover that the other is not an inhuman tormentor."[4]

What the Mediator Is Doing

If you and your opponent are able to conduct your own negotiations, the mediator at this point will be glad to take a back seat. If not, he may be an active orchestrator of your negotiations, proposing new ideas for settlement and using information he learned in caucus to cue you when changes in bargaining positions might be helpful. If needed, he may call another round of caucuses, or perhaps caucus with just one disputant again. All the while, your mediator is listening carefully to be sure that:

- negotiations stay focused on the real issues in dispute
- negotiations are not starting down a path that may lead, in his assessment, to an unfair or unworkable settlement
- there are not any new issues emerging that may need to be addressed more fully before negotiations can proceed

What You Should Do

This is the time to reorient yourself to problem solving the "mediation way." This means you need to:

1.   Let Go of the Past and Look to the Future

Shift your concern from who is to blame to how you and your opponent are going to reorder the future so that the problem is solved and does not recur. In the dispute we have been discussing, for example, Ms. Fields' anger over past incidents is far less important than her need for some assurance that she will be able to sleep undisturbed in the future. This is what she should be most concerned about during negotiations.

Shifting your concern in this way will help you redirect your priorities so that you know where to concentrate your energies while negotiating. It will help you let go of nonproductive issues that are backward-looking, such as insisting that your opponent admit he was wrong. You could insist that your opponent do so before continuing with negotiations, but if you do, your mediation session is likely to collapse because your opponent will prefer to walk away than admit guilt. Mediation and fault-finding are just not compatible.

2. Be Prepared to Share Responsibility

In most (but not all) disputes there is some shared responsibility for the problem; rarely is one party 100 percent right and the other all wrong. In some cases, for example, though one side is at fault for the initial act (Mr. Powell's noisy pool parties), the other side's response (Ms. Fields' abusive telephone call) exacerbates the problem and itself becomes part of the dispute.

3. Focus on Your Interests, Not Your Rights

You go to court to insist on your rights; in mediation, you try to protect your interests. These are not necessarily the same thing. Again, to use our illustration, Ms. Fields may have a legal right under the local noise code to insist that her neighbor be quiet after 11 p.m. Even if the police would enforce the code (which they probably lack the manpower to do), the 50-dollar fine that may be levied against Mr. Powell would do little to assure Ms. Fields of a good night's rest. All it might do, in fact, would be to push Mr. Powell to insist on his rights under the leash law and seek a fine against Ms. Fields for letting her dog run free.

In this case, as in many others, the parties' interests are broader than their rights. Here, both have an interest in enjoying their homes—whether by sleeping undisturbed or by entertaining guests without harassment. Both should be willing to give up a little of their "rights" in favor of protecting their overriding interests.

4. Be Flexible

Let go of preconceived ideas about how the dispute should be resolved and instead be open to creative solutions that may satisfy your needs just as well. This means giving some consideration to your opponent's needs as well as your own.

If you need to change your position in front of your opponent and feel that by doing so you will lose face, blame it on the mediator. In fact, use the mediator in whatever way you need to adopt the positions that will get you the settlement you want. Use him as a scapegoat; put words in his mouth. Don't worry about incurring his anger or hurting his feelings. He can take it; it's part of the job.

> *Ms. Fields*: "I honestly feel you owe me the money for the damage to my car hood, but I'm tired of the way the mediator is pushing me on this, so if you agree to pay me for the antenna, I'll accept it as payment in full."

More positively, you can also simply attribute your change in position to the persuasiveness of the mediator.

Finally, if your dispute is one where you and your opponent are going to have some kind of continuing relationship—as family members, business associates, or neighbors—now is the beginning of that new relationship. This is probably the first time since your dispute began that you are dealing together in a positive and constructive way. Take advantage of this opportunity. Show your opponent that dealing directly and honestly with you will pay off. Though the circumstances may make it difficult, try to be respectful, polite, and as far as possible, accommodating to the needs of your opponent.

Stage 6: Closure

"Closure" occurs at the moment when you and your opponent say "yes" to a proposed agreement. Mediation hearings tend to speed up as this point nears. Disputants are speaking directly to each other. The mediator is also more direct in proposing refinements to possible terms of settlement. Everyone is intimately familiar with the issues, and so a kind of shorthand language develops that helps the discussion speed along to conclusion.

Your mediator will be listening carefully to detect the first instance when a package of terms for settlement emerges from your negotiations.

> *Mediator*: "Ms. Fields, Mr. Powell, if I'm hearing you both correctly, I think you have reached agreement on all the major issues. I've tried to write them down in a very rough format. Let me read them to you and you tell me if I have it straight:
>
> "On the issue of car damage, Mr. Powell would be willing to pay Ms. Fields 200 dollars, plus 15 dollars for the cost of cabs she had to take on two days when her car was being repaired.
>
> "On the noise issue, Mr. Powell is willing to turn off any amplified sound, including stereos and radios, in his backyard by 11 p.m. on weeknights and by midnight on weekends, and will be responsible for keeping his guests quiet if they continue to use the pool after those hours.
>
> "Ms. Fields, you will agree to call Mr. Powell directly, before calling the police, if you are disturbed again at night.
>
> "On the dog issue, Mr. Powell would agree to call Ms. Fields directly, before calling police or dog control officers, if he thinks her dog has disturbed his trash barrels, soiled his lawn, or in any other way disturbed his property."

What the Mediator Is Doing

As he did during the negotiation phase, the mediator is testing the tentative terms of settlement against his sense of whether they are fair to the parties and hold reasonable promise of being workable in the long run. He is also trying to recall everything said during the hearing to be sure there were no underlying issues that he may have forgotten that would threaten the agreement. Also, he is helping the parties strike a good balance between a set of terms that are specific enough to handle reasonably foreseeable problems while not being so overly detailed that they would become too cumbersome to be workable.

What You Should Do

You, too, should be testing in your mind how satisfied you would be with these tentative terms of settlement. Remember that it is a package; you may have to give up a little, here, in exchange for something else, there. If you want, you can request a caucus with the mediator to give yourself a chance to talk over the proposed terms and get his assessment of how they would affect you.

You should consider as well how realistic this proposed settlement would be. If you are Ms. Fields, for example, are you really willing to tolerate some noise from Mr. Powell's home until 11 p.m. in exchange for quiet thereafter? If awakened at 2 a.m., are you willing to take the trouble of reaching Mr. Powell on the phone rather than just calling the police? And if your dog does disturb Mr. Powell's trash, are you willing to clean it up as intimated by the agreement?

Also, don't agree to things you are not really willing to do or that would be impossible to perform. This would include agreeing to pay more money than you can afford, controlling the behavior of your relatives, etc.

If the proposed terms don't look favorable enough or realistic, this is the time to say so. Do not wait until the agreement is in writing and everyone is standing around waiting for you to sign your name. At that point, the compulsion to sign will be too great and you will end up signing an agreement you don't believe in.

When the mediator hears you and your opponent both say "OK," he will seize the moment.

"Then we have agreement," he says.

Closure.

AT A GLANCE
Six Stages of a Mediation Hearing

1. Mediator's opening statement
2. Disputants' opening statements
3. Discussion
4. Caucus
5. Negotiation
6. Closure

CHAPTER
7

Writing an Agreement That Works

At the point in your hearing when closure has been reached, you are probably going to be worn out. There is one more important thing to do, however: committing your agreement to writing.

It is important that you leave your mediation hearing with a written agreement that spells out the decisions, intentions, and future behavior of the disputants. Studies show that a written agreement will aid significantly in assuring that terms of the settlement are adhered to over time. As Ernie Odom, executive director of the Community Mediation Center in Coram, New York, has written:

> An important reason for written agreements is that once a person commits himself or herself on paper, that commitment cannot be easily ignored. *The psychological effect of a written agreement is one of the main reasons why mediation works.* The parties cannot "forget" what they have agreed to, and have a permanent reminder which tends to hold them responsible to their word.[1]

How the Agreement Gets Written

Your written agreement does not appear from on high, as does a judge's decision in court. Instead, like the settlement itself, the written agreement is the work product of the disputants and the mediator. In practice, it is common for the mediator to draft each provision and then read it aloud so the disputants can consider the ordering and phrasing of each term of settlement. Sometimes several drafts may be needed before the language is to everyone's satisfaction.

Following are some useful guidelines to keep in mind as you work on writing your agreement.

1. Use Plain English

In a mediation agreement, there should be no "parties of the first part stipulating and heretofore abrogating the stipulation of the parties annexed hereto as exhibit A in the attachment to the amended answer." Legal gobbledygook has no place in a mediation agreement. Your mediation hearing was easy to understand, and your agreement should be, too. Vague words and dense prose will only serve to confuse you and your opponent later, when you both try to remember what was agreed to at mediation.

Here are some examples of formal, legalistic terms often used in mediation agreements that can be replaced by simpler words that are easier to understand.[2]

Instead of	*Use*
apprise	inform
cease	stop
commitment	promise
communicate	write, telephone
demonstrate	show
desire	wish
effectuate	bring about
eliminate	remove, strike out

Instead of	*Use*
employment	work
endeavor	try
expiration	end
locality, location	place
locate	find
objective	aim
prior to	before
remuneration	pay, wages, salary, fee
reside	live
terminate	end
utilize	use
afford an opportunity	allow

2. Identify People by Full Names

In writing the agreement, always use full names (first and last) rather than referring to the parties as just "Ms. Smith" or "the Claimant." Also, when naming a business corporation, use the business's full name; if a store has branches, name the specific branch with which you are concerned. In this way, each provision of the agreement will be clearly understandable, if you ever need to discuss it separately from the other provisions.

WRONG WAY: The Respondent piano store will let the Claimant exchange his piano . . .

RIGHT WAY: Stwertka's Pianos and Organs, Inc., will allow Mr. Richard Goldberg to exchange . . .

3. Specify Dates

Be sure your agreement specifies precise dates when things should happen.

WRONG WAY: The respondent, Mr. Frank Taylor, agrees to remove the rusted Chevy from his front lawn as soon as possible.

RIGHT WAY: Mr. Frank Taylor will remove the rusted Chevy from his front lawn by July 1, 1990.

4. Specify Method of Payment

Many mediation agreements call for one party to pay money to the other. Do not allow anything about money transactions to be left vague. Your agreement should state exactly who is to pay how much to whom, when, and in what form. It is always a good idea, especially when the party doing the paying is an individual rather than a business corporation, to require that debts be paid by money-order or certified check. Personal checks can bounce, and cash leaves no record of payment.

WRONG WAY: Mr. Ralph Edwards agrees to pay Mr. Frank Richardson the sum of 845 dollars.

RIGHT WAY: Mr. Ralph Edwards will pay to Mr. Frank Richardson the sum of 845 dollars by money order or certified bank check and sent by U.S. mail to Mr. Richardson at 35 Eulalia Way, Coniston, South Dakota 57453, by February 3, 1990.

5. Answer: Who, What, When, Where, and How

Your mediation agreement should answer the five key questions of "who, what, when, where, and how."

EXAMPLE   [WHO] Stwertka's Pianos and Organs, Inc., will allow Mr. Richard Goldberg [WHAT] to exchange his Yamaha U-131 model console piano for any piano currently in stock of equal or greater value. The exchange can be made [WHEN] during regular business hours until March 31, 1990, [WHERE] at Stwertka's main showroom, 1330 Washington Street, Clinton, Pennsylvania. [HOW] Stwertka's store manager, Ms. Barbara Peters, will make herself available to accommodate the exchange.

6. List Each Provision Separately

Your agreement will probably require certain actions of each disputant. To keep the agreement clear and understandable, state each requirement in a separate, numbered paragraph. An agreement organized in this way is more easily discussed and dealt with, if questions of interpretation or noncompliance arise.

EXAMPLE   1. The Respondents, Glen and Elinor Sidely, agree to keep their dog, Tammy, confined to the house after 6 p.m. if they are not at home.

2. Glen and Elinor Sidely agree to enroll their dog, Tammy, in the Canine Obedience School of the Livingston County Humane Society for the next available program beginning September 1, 1990, and to take the dog to each class of the program.

3. The Claimants, Frank and Katherine Fields, agree to instruct their children, Tricia and Melissa, not to tease the Sidely's dog, Tammy, and particularly not to throw any items into the dog's enclosed run.

7.   *Omit Any Mention of Blame, Fault, or Guilt*

One of the nicest things about a mediation agreement is its total absence of any faultfinding. Agreements *never* include statements, for example, that a party is "guilty of the charge." By omitting statements of fault or blame, the parties save face and, if they need to have an ongoing relationship, they can move ahead without the burden of an official finding of past wrongdoing.

For example, even if it became clear during the hearing that the landlord let the plumbing break down and refused to fix it, the agreement will not state that the landlord was at fault. Instead, the agreement will merely spell out what the landlord now agrees to do. As such, the agreement is entirely forward looking; it states not what happened, but what the parties intend to happen from this time forward. Studies show that these kinds of agreements have a better chance of being complied with in the long run than those that label one side or the other as "guilty."

WRONG WAY: "Whereas Mr. Francis Riley, manager of the Seneca Tower Apartments, failed to keep the piping to the apartment of Mr. and Mrs. Lester Aggazis adequately insulated against freezing temperatures . . ."

RIGHT WAY: "Mr. Francis Riley, manager of the Seneca Tower Apartments, agrees to repair by 5 p.m., March 4, 1990, all piping necessary to the proper functioning of the bathtub, shower, sink, and toilet in the master bathroom of Apartment 7-C, occupied by Mr. and Mrs. Lester Aggazis."

8. Do Not Involve Third Parties in the Agreement

An error often made in drafting mediation agreements is to have one disputant pay money—not to the other disputant—but to some third party not involved in the hearing. The reason this happens so often is because, at the time of the hearing, it seems to the parties a good way to have debts paid off without their having to do business with each other. Do not make this mistake.

If money is owed you, do not agree to have the debt paid to a third party. If you do, the money may never get paid; at best, you will have extra work trying to verify payment. Avoid these complications. If someone owes you money, make sure your agreement calls for him to pay you directly. If there is still so much animosity between you and your opponent that you suspect he would never actually write a check to you, then have the agreement state that he should write a check to the mediation center on your behalf. The center will deposit the check and, when it clears, will write a check to you for the same amount.

WRONG WAY: Garden Way Landscape Company agrees to pay the 650 dollars originally paid to it by Mr. Gerald Secor to any other landscape company Mr. Secor selects to do the work on his lawn.

RIGHT WAY: Garden Way Landscape Company agrees to return to Mr. Gerald Secor the sum of 650 dollars paid by Mr. Secor.

ANOTHER RIGHT WAY: Garden Way Landscape Co. agrees to pay Mr. Frank Secor the sum of 650 dollars. This provision shall be satisfied by issuance of a corporate check, made payable to The Center for Dispute Settlement, Inc., and sent by U.S. mail to the Center, 87 North Clinton Ave., Rochester, N.Y. 14604, by August 15, 1990.

AT A GLANCE

Guidelines for Writing an Effective Agreement

1. Use plain English
2. Identify people by full names
3. Specify dates
4. Specify method of payment

5. Answer: Who, What, When, Where, and How
6. List each provision separately
7. Omit any mention of blame, fault, or guilt
8. Do not involve third parties

On the following pages are reproduced three actual agreements reached at mediation hearings at the Center for Dispute Settlement, Inc. in Rochester, New York. (Disputants' names and other identifying information have been deleted or changed to protect confidentiality.) The form and content of these agreements are typical of cases heard at public mediation centers. The first concerns a landlord-tenant dispute in which the landlord sought return of property and payment for missing items. The second concerns a dispute between neighbors involving children, and the third a consumer dispute between the owner of a race car and an auto repair shop. (Two other actual mediation agreements, from a divorce case and an environmental dispute, are reproduced in Appendices C and F, respectively.)

Making Your Agreement Legally Enforceable

Studies show the vast majority of mediation agreements are still in effect more than one year after settlement. Indeed, as was discussed in Chapter 1, people have been found more likely to uphold the terms of a mediation agreement than to abide by a court order.

Nevertheless, you may want to have the extra protection of knowing that, should your opponent renege on his or her duties under the agreement, you have the option of taking your opponent to court to have the agreement enforced by a judge. To do this, have your agreement written in the form of a legal contract. Then, if your opponent fails to live up to the agreement you can sue for breach of contract and possibly receive any of the following legal remedies:

THE CENTER
FOR
DISPUTE SETTLEMENT, INC.

In the Matter of Mediation Between:

----- S.,   Claimant

VS

----- W.,   Respondent

Case Number: C-111-88

CONSENT AGREEMENT

Under the Rules and Procedures of The Center for Dispute Settlement, Inc., and in accordance with Article 21A of the Judiciary Law and Section 170.55 of the Criminal Procedure Law, the Parties named below have had a full and fair hearing on the issues and willingly agree to the following:

1. Respondent, Ms. S., will return no later than July 22, 1988, to the claimant, Mr. W. (W. Property Management, Inc.), the following articles: two door knobs, door plate, kitchen curtains and rod, bath and back bedroom rods, four draw drape rods, 1 extention cord and two ice trays. Before returning these items, Ms. S. will telephone the claimant at 667-3321 to arrange a convenient time and place for delivery.

2. Ms. S. will pay the following amounts to the claimant for missing articles:

        $26.00 - Security Lock
         48.00 - Kitchen light fixture
         24.00 - Bedroom light fixture
         66.00 - "Mini" blinds from study
         15.00 - Smoke alarm
        $179.00 Total to be paid

Ms. S. will pay to W. Property Management, Inc. $40 per month beginning August, 1988 by money order mailed by the 10th of the month to: Mr. W., 280 S. Hollywood Drive, Apt. 1, Rochester, NY, 14620. The fourth and final monthly payment shall be for the amount of $59.00.

3. Mr. W., on behalf of W. Property Management, Inc., will accept delivery of the items in pragraph 1 and payment of the amounts in paragraph 2 in satisfaction of all claims against Ms. S. arising out of her tenancy during 1987 at the Bedford St. apartment complex owned by W. Property Management, Inc.

The parties to this agreement do hereby acknowledge that the above provisions constitute full and complete satisfaction of all claims submitted to Mediation on _____ July 8, 1988 _____

The failure to comply with the terms and conditions of this Agreement may entitle the aggrieved party to undertake enforcement proceedings in a court of law and may cause the non-complying party or parties to be liable for court costs, disbursements, attorneys fees and interest.

(signature)   (signature)
-----S., Claimant   ------ W., Respondent

(signature)
----- Mediator

STATE OF NEW YORK
COUNTY OF

On this _____ day of _____, 19 _____, the subscriber(s) personally appeared _____ before me and known to me to be the same person(s) described in and who executed the within Instrument, and he/she (they severally) acknowledged to me that they executed the same.

Sworn to before me this _____ day of _____, 19 _____.

THE CENTER
FOR
DISPUTE SETTLEMENT, INC.

In the Matter of Mediation Between:

MELINDA B.,   Claimant

     VS

ALEXANDER AND CAROLYN L., Respondents

Case Number: C-352-88

CONSENT AGREEMENT

Under the Rules and Procedures of The Center for Dispute Settlement, Inc., and in accordance with Article 21A of the Judiciary Law and Section 170.55 of the Criminal Procedure Law, the Parties named below have had a full and fair hearing on the issues and willingly agree to the following:

    1. Respondents, Alexander and Carolyn L. agree that the claimant's children and their friends can play on the swing set and other play equipment in the L.'s backyard.

    2. The Claimant, Melinda B., agrees that her children and their friends will clean up after themselves when they play in the L.'s yard, and that Ms. B. will be responsible for seeing that they do.

    3. Ms. B. further agrees to tell her visitors not to park in or block the L.'s driveway.

    4. Mr. and Mrs. L. agree not to make any verbal threats to Ms. B. or her visitors and to contact her directly in person or by phone if they have any complaints about the conduct of guests at her home.

    5. Mr. B and Mr. and Mrs. L. further agree that if future disputes arise between them they will return to mediation if unable to work them out directly.

The parties to this agreement do hereby acknowledge that the above provisions constitute full and complete satisfaction of all claims submitted to Mediation on __9/12/88__

The failure to comply with the terms and conditions of this Agreement may entitle the aggrieved party to undertake enforcement proceedings in a court of law and may cause the non-complying party or parties to be liable for court costs, disbursements, attorneys fees and interest.

(signature)
_____
Melinda B., Claimant

(signature)
_____
Alexander L., Respondent

(signature)
------ Mediator

(signature)
_____
Carolyn L., Respondent

STATE OF NEW YORK
COUNTY OF

DAVID SCHEFFER
Notary Public in the State of New York
MONROE COUNTY
Commission Expires March 21, 19 , t

David Scheffer.

On this _____ day of _____, 19 _____, the subscriber(s) personally appeared _____ before me and known to me to be the same person(s) described in and who executed the within Instrument, and he/she (they severally) acknowledged to me that they executed the same.

Sworn to before me this _____ day of _____, 19 _____.

THE CENTER
FOR
DISPUTE SETTLEMENT, INC.

In the Matter of Mediation Between:

----- H.,   Claimant

   VS

Z.'s Auto Garage,   Respondent

Case Number: T-18-1988

CONSENT AGREEMENT

Under the Rules and Procedures of The Center for Dispute Settlement, Inc., and in accordance with Article 21A of the Judiciary Law and Section 170.55 of the Criminal Procedure Law, the Parties named below have had a full and fair hearing on the issues and willingly agree to the following:

1. The Claimant, Mr. H., agrees to pay $1,650 and a set of valve springs for work done on his racing car heads in 1987 by the respondent, Z.'s Auto Garage. Mr. Z. agrees to return the cylinder heads and other parts that claimant gave him on October 5, 1987 as collateral for the work to be done.

2. By July 25, 1988, Mr. H., will deliver to the Center for Dispute Settlement (CDS) a check in the amount of $1,650 payable to CDS.

3. CDS will notify Mr. Z. when the check clears, and Mr. Z. will then promptly call Mr. H. at 442-9635 or 244-8897. Mr. H. will go to Z.'s Auto Garage and inspect the heads. If they are satisfactory to him, Mr. Z. will give them to Mr. H., together with his TRW pistons and piston rings. Mr. Z. will keep Mr. H.'s valve springs.

4. When the cylinder heads and pistons and piston rings are returned to Mr. H., Mr. H. and Mr. Z. will call CDS and instruct CDS to send a check for $1,650 to Mr. Z, payable to Z.'s Auto Garage.

The parties to this agreement do hereby acknowledge that the above provisions constitute full and complete satisfaction of all claims submitted to Mediation on _____ July 1, 1988

The failure to comply with the terms and conditions of this Agreement may entitle the aggrieved party to undertake enforcement proceedings in a court of law and may cause the non-complying party or parties to be liable for court costs, disbursements, attorneys fees and interest.

(signature) _____   (signature) _____
----- H., Claimant   ---- Z., for Z.'s Auto Garage,
                                                      Respondent

(signature) _____
----- Mediator   DAVID SCHEFFER
STATE OF NEW YORK   Notary Public in the State of New York
COUNTY OF   MONROE COUNTY
                     Commission Expires March 21, 19 90

On this _____ day of _____, 19 _____, the subscriber(s) personally appeared
_____ before me and known to me to be the same person(s) described
in and who executed the within Instrument, and he/she (they severally) acknowledged to me that they executed
the same.
Sworn to before me this _____ day of _____, 19 _____.

Rescission: the court can void the agreement, releasing you from your obligations under it.

Damages: the court can award you financial compensation for losses due to your opponent's breach.

Specific performance: the court can order your opponent to do what he ought to have done under the agreement.

The decision whether any particular agreement will be enforceable as a contract is up to a judge and may turn on technical factors concerning the facts of the case and the laws of your state. Among other things, the judge will be looking to see if the agreement satisfies the five basic elements of a legal contract. So that you will be aware of these factors, each is discussed briefly below. Of course, the best way to help ensure that your agreement would be enforceable in court is to have your lawyer review it for you.

Five Requirements of a Legal Contract

1. The Parties Have Legal Capacity to Make a Contract

Neither party to your agreement can be a minor (less than 18 years old in most states) or be so mentally impaired that he does not understand he is making a binding agreement.

2. The Subject Matter of the Agreement Is Legal

The terms of your contract must not call for either party to perform an illegal act, nor be so grossly unfair to one side as would seem to a judge or jury that one side was taken advantage of in a morally reprehensible way.

3. The Terms of the Agreement Must be Definite and Complete

If your agreement is too vague, it will not be a contract. Each provision must state clearly who does or pays what to whom, when, and how. If you want the roof of your house ripped off and replaced with a new asphalt roof with a 20-year guarantee, your agreement should say exactly that. An agreement that merely says, "fix the roof," may be too vague to be enforced as a contract.

4. *Consideration*

A lone promise by one party to do something is not a contract. Your agreement must reflect either an exchange of services and money ("Cagney will pay Lacey 200 dollars; Lacey will reseal the driveway") or reciprocal promises ("Smith will keep his dog indoors after 9 p.m.; Jones will call Smith before calling the police").

5. *There is Evidence of Mutual Agreement to the Terms*

Both parties to the agreement must understand and agree to the terms of the agreement, and there must be some evidence of this. The signatures of both parties at the bottom of the form on which the agreement is written will satisfy this requirement.

In some states, even if a mediation agreement satisfies the formalities of a legal contract, it may still not be considered binding unless the parties had explicity stated in writing that they intended it to be binding. This is the custom, for example, among centers in North Carolina. Similarly, Minnesota's Civil Mediation Law states that a mediation agreement is nonbinding "unless it contains a provision stating that it is binding . . ."[3]

Sometimes the printed form onto which your agreement is typed will contain a printed statement that the agreement is intended to be binding. If it does not, you should have your mediator insert such a statement at the end of your agreement. Depending on how important the issue of enforceability is to you, you may want your lawyer to review the clause. The following statement, however, would in most cases be adequate: "The parties understand and accept the terms stated above and intend this agreement to be a legal contract, binding upon them and enforceable by a court of law."

Providing for Lawyer's Review, if Necessary

If your dispute involves significant amounts of money, or property, or limits your legal rights (as a binding contract does), you may wish to consult your lawyer before signing the agreement. You can ask the mediator to insert a clause in the agreement making your signature conditional on your lawyer's review. At the Community Mediation Center in Coram, New York, mediators will add the following clause to agreements when asked to do so: "The terms of the contract will go into effect five business days after signing unless the attorney for either party notifies the Center in writing of objections."[4]

Signing the Agreement

When you and your opponent have read and consented to each provision of your agreement, you are then ready for the last act of the mediation drama: the signing.

If you have adjourned to the waiting room while your agreement was being typed, the mediator will call you and your opponent back into the hearing room. He will hand you both a typed copy of the agreement. He may, once more, read it aloud just to make doubly sure that everyone understands it and that no further changes are needed. He will remind you both of your obligation to uphold its terms. If you have had it written in the form of a contract, he will remind you that it is legally binding and potentially enforceable in court. He will explain that the center will be available to help out if one party violates its terms, or if circumstances change and revisions are needed (see Chapter 9). And he will remind you of your pledge of confidentiality for everything said or revealed during the hearing.

The mediator will then ask each of you to sign the agreement in the space provided. The mediator, too, will sign his name as a witness. At some centers, your signatures will be notarized by a notary on staff.

The Hearing Ends

Mediator Christopher Moore has observed, "Whereas lower animals have devised regularized communication patterns to symbolize when a conflict should or has in fact ceased, human beings have not."[5] Moore's point is well taken. Exactly what do two people who have been engaged in a bitter dispute do when they each sign their names to a paper ending the dispute?

Some mediators have experienced cases, such as those involving estranged relatives or friends, where the parties were reconciled through mediation and concluded the hearing with an embrace. Sometimes disputants are so grateful for the center's help that before they leave the hearing room they offer a financial contribution to the center, though none is required.

Typically, however, the mediator will end the hearing simply by shaking hands with each of the parties as he or she congratulates them on the successful result of their hard work. With a nod to one or both of the parties, the mediator may encourage them to shake hands with each other. Some disputants feel enough relief and understanding of each other's positions to take the cue and end the hearing with a handshake. Others are just glad to have the matter over with, take their copy of the agreement, and go home.

CHAPTER 8

If No Agreement Is Reached: The Arbitration Option

In the film "Little Big Man," the Indian grandfather (played by Chief Dan George) decides it is time to die. He climbs a nearby mountain, wraps himself in a blanket, and lies down to wait for the Spirit to take him away. A little while later, when it begins to rain, he realizes he is still alive. "Sometimes the magic works," he says, "and sometimes it doesn't."

Sometimes mediation works, and sometimes it doesn't. Most often, it does. But if your case is among the few that does not reach agreement, what can you do?

Adjourn and Reconvene

Though in most cases mediated agreements are reached after just one hearing, complex disputes may require additional sessions. There may not be enough time in one hearing to cover all the issues, or disputants may want to consult their spouses or business partners before agreeing to a proposal. In such cases, you can suggest to the mediator and your opponent that the hearing be adjourned and reconvened later. Try not to delay too long before holding the next hearing, however, because the good will and cooperative attitude built during the first session will be likely to diminish between sessions.

Return Dispute to Referral Source

If your dispute was referred to mediation by a judge or other law enforcement agency, then one option if mediation fails is having your dispute sent back to the referral source. The mediation center may do this for you, as part of its normal procedure, by sending a letter to the judge or other referral source, noting that mediation was tried without success.

FOR EXAMPLE: When your ex-boyfriend moved out of your home, he took with him several items of your personal property, including a television set and some valuable photography equipment. He refuses to return them. You called the police and asked that he be arrested. When you talked to the officer who issues arrest warrants, he referred you to mediation. Your "ex" showed up for mediation, but the hearing did not result in an agreement. Now, you go see the warrant officer again. He already has received a letter from the dispute center about your attempt at mediation. You tell him you still want to press charges. Now he issues a warrant for your ex-boyfriend's arrest.

You have given up no legal rights by attempting mediation. In fact, in some ways you may have improved your chances of getting legal action. When judges and warrant officers see you have made a good faith attempt to work out a dispute through mediation, they may be more inclined to exercise their discretion to grant you the legal action you originally requested. In a sense, you are rewarded for having tried mediation as a first option.

CASE IN POINT: The owner of a shopping plaza had gone to court to block a scrap dealer from using a remote area of the shopping center's parking lot to dump unwanted bales of scrap paper. The judge, noting that both parties shared a property line and were likely to encounter the same situation in the future, recommended they try to work out a solution through mediation. After an unsuccessful mediation hearing, the claimant was back in court with his attorney, who told the judge:

"Your Honor, my client made a good faith effort not to burden this Court with this matter by attempting to resolve the dispute through mediation at the Center for Dispute Resolution. A mediation hearing was held on September 22 at the Center, but after nearly four hours of mediation, my client and the defendant were not able to reach a mutually acceptable solution. Now, my client asks this Court to issue the injunction we originally sought to prevent the defendant from unlawfully dumping garbage onto my client's property."

Start a Lawsuit

Even if you did not come to mediation by referral from a judge, you retain your rights to file a lawsuit.

Depending on the type and size of your dispute, you can hire a lawyer to represent you in a regular trial court, or you can represent yourself in small claims court if the amount in dispute is within the small claims jurisdictional limits, usually between 1000 and 5000 dollars in most states.

As noted in Chapter 1, there is some evidence that defendants in court who earlier took part in unsuccessful mediation are more likely to pay a court judgment than defendants who did not participate in mediation at all. Researchers Craig McEwen and Richard Maiman write:

(T)he fact that defendants [in court] who took part in *unsuccessful* mediations had a substantially better compliance record than those who had not participated in mediation at all suggests that the negotiation process itself—independent of its outcome—helps to inculcate a sense of responsibility about payments.[1]

Note, however, that if you do begin a lawsuit, you are bound by the confidentiality rules of mediation not to use in court the information disclosed by your opponent during mediation.

The Arbitration Option

If you tried mediation and "the magic didn't work," arbitration could be your next best option. It will assure you, one way or the other, of a decision in your dispute. The rest of this chapter will discuss how to use arbitration.

Arbitration is more familiar to most people than mediation. Disputes between professional athletes and team owners, for example, often are arbitrated. The concept is simple: both sides tell their story to the arbitrator and the arbitrator renders a decision. Arbitration is popular because, as law professor David Siegel has written, it offers "a private and practical determination with maximum dispatch and minimum expense."[2]

Like mediation, arbitration can be:

- *Quick:* cases are often completed in 60–90 days.
- *Confidential:* hearings are private and there is no public record.
- *Informal:* strict rules of evidence do not apply.
- *Flexible:* an arbitrator is not bound by legal precedent; he or she has broad authority to render a decision that will do justice based on the unique facts of your case.

Though not as inexpensive as mediation, arbitration is still far less costly than litigation. It also offers the advantage of finality; the arbitrator's decision, called an "award," can be made legally binding and is readily enforceable by a judge.

Still, arbitration is a different animal than mediation. It requires you to give up control of your dispute to a third person who takes the place of judge and jury. If you agree to binding arbitration, then your hearing is, in effect, your "day in court"; you are not going to get another.

And arbitration does not strive to help you and your opponent cooperate toward finding a fair and workable solution. In arbitration, your task is to convince the arbitrator that you are right and your opponent is wrong. The arbitrator is free to award one side everything and the other side nothing. The arbitrator's decision—except in unusual circumstances—will not be overturned in court.

Arbitration is better suited to some kinds of disputes than others. It tends to work best with cases that can have a "dollars-and-cents" solution, such as consumer complaints, construction disputes, and insurance claims. Cases involving interpersonal disputes where the parties want to preserve a relationship are usually not well-suited to arbitration.

Automatic Arbitration Through "Med/Arb"

We noted earlier that when you first submitted your dispute to mediation, some centers may have offered as an option the procedure known as "med/arb" (pronounced "meed-arb"). In med/arb, the disputants consent to mediation but with the added provision that if mediation does not produce a settlement, then the mediator can act as arbitrator and make a final, binding decision in your case.

Choosing med/arb gives you the assurance that when you enter the mediation hearing, one way or the other you are going to come out with your dispute resolved. Either you and your opponent will reach a settlement, or the mediator will assume the role of arbitrator and make a decision for you.

At some mediation centers the same person who served as your mediator will also serve as the arbitrator. Other centers offer "sequential med/arb" where the arbitration is conducted by a person other than the one who acted as mediator. This requires an entirely new hearing but does eliminate the possibility that the mediator-turned-arbitrator will be improperly influenced by statements made to him or her in confidence by the parties during caucus. In San José, California, for example, a small-claims mediation project uses this type of "sequential" med/arb process.

If you submitted to med/arb, then at some point in the hearing—after caucuses and negotiation—the mediator may hint she is becoming frustrated and that, if no settlement is reached, she may close the hearing and arbitrate a decision.

> *Mediator* (to the disputants): "I have to tell you candidly that I'm not seeing a lot of progress here. The issues have been raised and you've been over them thoroughly several times, both in joint session and in caucus. Some promising settlement options have been put on the table. I don't see much movement here. Let's give it a little longer, but if nothing develops, say in another hour, I will consider declaring the hearing closed and arbitrating an award as you've given me authority to do."

This kind of statement by the mediator can motivate the parties to move toward settlement. If, in fact, the mediator does close the hearing and assumes the role of arbitrator, she will send her written award to the dispute center within a prescribed amount of time, usually 10 to 30 days, and then the center will forward copies to you and your opponent. Case closed.

Starting Fresh with Arbitration

If you had not originally opted for "med/arb," you can still submit your dispute to arbitration, if both you and your opponent agree in writing to do so. A good time to propose this is at the end of your mediation hearing, while you are both together in the hearing room. The mediator can answer any questions about how arbitration works. It is most convenient if the mediation center also offers arbitration, and you and your opponent can simply complete a "Submission to Arbitration" form before you leave. In some states, such as New York, arbitration is offered at most public mediation centers. If your center does not offer arbitration, however, the mediator or staff should be able to refer you to some organization that does.

Where to Go for Arbitration

There is no shortage of organizations that provide arbitration. The leader in the field is the American Arbitration Association (AAA). This nonprofit group, founded in 1926, operates nationwide through 32 regional offices located in major cities. In Boston, for example, the AAA office heard nearly 6710 cases in 1987, nearly double the number of four years earlier.[3] In 1987, the AAA heard nearly 53,000 cases nationally, and its caseload continues to grow.

In addition to the AAA, most of the private dispute resolution services that cater to business clients also offer arbitration. For information on how to contact some of the major private firms, see Appendix B. Private firms offering arbitration in your community may also be listed in your local telephone directory under "arbitration" or "legal services."

Cost of Arbitration

Arbitration is likely to cost you substantially more than mediation but still a lot less than the typical costs of litigation. Arbitration generally costs more than mediation because, in most cases, the arbitration service is a for-profit business and the arbitrator himself is being paid. Private arbitration fees generally begin at about 250 dollars per party for a one-day hearing.

Even the American Arbitration Association, whose arbitrators in commercial cases often contribute one day's service without pay, charges 3 percent of the first 25,000 dollars in dispute (minimum 300 dollars) plus additional fees for amounts over 25,000 dollars. (These fees are on a "per case" basis and can be paid by one disputant alone or split between the disputants.) Currently, AAA offices in New York City are conducting an experimental program in which they will arbitrate small-claims disputes for a 150-dollar minimum fee.

The only way you could have a dispute arbitrated without a fee would be if your local nonprofit mediation center also offered arbitration as part of it regular tax-supported services.

Starting Arbitration

Arbitration begins when each disputant signs a written "Submission to Arbitration" form. The form will be supplied by the center or service providing arbitration. (An example of such a form appears on the next page.) As in mediation, this form will ask you to describe the nature of your claim, the remedy you seek, and the amount of money, if any, you demand.

(If your dispute is covered by a contract which includes an "arbitration clause," then arbitration is begun by filing a "Demand for Arbitration." Arbitration clauses are commonly found in contracts such as those involving the construction industry, professional sports, and sales of stocks and bonds.)

An arbitrator's power to make an award that is legally binding comes from laws passed by the legislatures in each of the 50 states and by Congress. These laws provide, in essence, that if two people agree in writing to have a dispute resolved by a third party, then the decision of the third party—if it meets all of the legal requirements—will have the same force and effect as the order of a judge. As one commentator observed, it is the disputants who "breathe life" into the arbitrator.

In most states, the law gives an arbitrator great flexibility to make whatever award he or she thinks will be fair to you and your opponent. Some arbitration services, however, limit the amount of money their arbitrators can award to the amount requested in writing in the submission form.

FOR EXAMPLE: You have a dispute over money with your ex-business partner. On the "Submission to Arbitration" form, you state you are seeking 54,000 dollars. During the arbitration hearing, documents reveal that as much as 75,000 dollars may be owed you. Your arbitrator, however, can only award you 54,000 dollars, as that was the highest amount you stated on the submission form.

THE CENTER
FOR
DISPUTE SETTLEMENT, INC.

SUBMISSION TO ARBITRATION
BEFORE THE CENTER FOR DISPUTE SETTLEMENT, INC.

REFERRING SOURCE _____   CDS CASE NO. _____

TOWN _____   DATE REFERRED _____

ADJOURNED DATE _____   DATE RECEIVED _____

The Parties agree to submit the following dispute to Arbitration under the Rules and Procedures of The Center for Dispute Settlement, Inc., and in accordance with Article 75 of the New York Civil Practice Laws and Rules.

What is the nature of the claim?

What remedy is sought?

Amount of money being asked for (if any): _____

We agree that we will abide by and perform any Award rendered and that a judgement may be entered upon the Award. We understand that the decision by the Arbitrator shall have the same binding force as a court order with the same penalties for failure to honor. Failure to appear may result in a default decision to which you will be legally bound.

Failure to honor an Award may result in proceedings in court for confirmation, and the non-complying party will be liable for court costs, disbursements and interest.

Name of Claimants(s)	Relation to Respondent
Address	Phone (H) (W)
Claimant's Signature	or Attorney
Date	
Name of Respondent(s)	Relation to Claimant
Address	Phone (H) (W)
Respondent's Signature	or Attorney
Date	

Founded by the American Arbitration Association

Ask the arbitration service its policy on this question before you state the relief you are seeking, so that you do not risk missing out on a larger recovery than you presently may be able to imagine.

Binding or Nonbinding?

An important choice you will need to make when opting for arbitration is whether to seek a binding or nonbinding decision.

Generally, if your primary goal is to get the dispute behind you as quickly, inexpensively, and privately as possible, you should choose binding arbitration. This will dispose of the case once and for all.

A nonbinding decision, on the other hand, would allow you to see what the arbitrator proposes; if it's acceptable, take it and be done. If not, you retain your option to sue. Remember, however, that if you opt for a nonbinding decision, it is nonbinding on your opponent, too. In that case, the arbitrator can find in your favor, but—if the other side decides not to be bound by the decision— you are no better off than before.

Choosing Your Arbitrator

Given that your arbitrator may have authority to make a final and binding decision in your case, it is important to be sure that the person chosen as arbitrator understands the technical issues of your dispute.

In theory, you and your opponent could select anyone you want to serve as arbitrator. For example, if your dispute involved the quality of a refrigerator purchased from a local appliance dealer, you and the owner of the store could select a person with technical knowledge about refrigerators, perhaps a retired repairman whom you respect for his experience and honesty and who has no financial ties to the store or the manufacturer. Most arbitration services will allow the disputants to pick their own arbitrator as long as the person chosen is willing and able to conduct the arbitration according to the rules of that particular service.

More likely, however, you will use an arbitrator provided by the arbitration service. Most services maintain rosters or "panels" of arbitrators who have expertise in various fields likely to be the subjects of disputes, such as construction, personal injury, labor relations, auto accidents, etc.

To be sure that you and your opponent have confidence in the ability and impartiality of your arbitrator, most services will send you a list naming half a dozen or more qualified arbitrators from their panel, along with a brief biographical sketch of each. From this list, you can cross off the names of anyone you think should not hear your case because of personal, professional, or business conflicts. From the names that remain, the arbitration service will appoint your arbitrator. (In some complex cases, three arbitrators may be used.)

Location of Hearing

Most arbitration services will give you the choice of holding a hearing at their offices or at the offices of either of the disputants. Sometimes it will be helpful to hold the hearing at the site of the dispute. If your dispute involves faulty workmanship, for example, and you want the arbitrator to see the problem firsthand, suggest that the hearing be held at the worksite. (Often the arbitrator is the one who will make this suggestion, after reviewing a preliminary summary of the case prepared by the arbitration service.)

FOR EXAMPLE: A homeowner hired a general contractor to put an addition on his home. Before construction had gone very far, however, cracks appeared in the newly poured foundation. The homeowner refused to pay the contractor his second draw, and, in response, the contractor walked off the job.
   The homeowner suggested, and the arbitrator and contractor agreed, that the hearing should be held at the house so that everyone would be able to inspect the foundation.

Preparing for Your Arbitration Hearing

As there may be no opportunity to appeal the award rendered in arbitration, you will want to prepare for your hearing carefully. This means taking the time to plan a strategy for how you will present your case. What are the points you need to prove? How best can you prove them? Will you call "live witnesses"? Submit documents and photographs? Request the arbitrator to inspect in person the matter in dispute, such as a construction site, an encroaching driveway, a broken doorlock, etc.?

All arbitration services conduct their hearings in accordance with a set of rules that spell out in detail such things as duties of the arbitrator, use of evidence, confidentiality, fees and expenses, and appeals. Be sure to request a copy of these rules if you are not sent one at the time your hearing is scheduled.

As in mediation, strict rules of evidence usually are not followed. Typically, all evidence can be submitted as long as it is relevant to the dispute. The arbitrator decides what is relevant.

In Chapter 5, we discussed the credibility and persuasiveness of different types of evidence used in mediation. This information applies in arbitration as well. As a general guideline, it is worth noting the advice the American Arbitration Association gives disputants preparing for commercial arbitration hearings: "Direct [live] testimony of witnesses is usually more persuasive than hearsay evidence and facts will be better established by documents and exhibits than by arguments only."[4]

Do You Need a Lawyer?

In mediation, the answer to this question is usually "no." In arbitration, however, the answer will more often be "yes."

As noted, by participating in arbitration, you are giving up your right ever to go to court on this particular dispute and the decision of the arbitrator will be just as binding and final as that rendered by a judge. If you have a significant amount of money or property in dispute, or the issues are such that if you lose, it will seriously affect you, then a lawyer should help you prepare for arbitration and go with you to the hearing. For most straightforward cases, arbitration hearings seldom last beyond a half day, or at most a full day, so that the investment in legal fees will not be great compared to those in litigation.

The Arbitration Hearing

One difference between mediation and arbitration is that in arbitration, if you fail to show up for your hearing, the hearing can be held without you. This is called "ex parte" arbitration. In your absence, the arbitrator will hear testimony from the other party, consider the facts as best he or she can determine them, and render a decision just as final and binding as if you were there. Therefore, do not miss your arbitration hearing!

Like a mediation hearing, the arbitration hearing follows set stages: each side makes an opening statement in which he or she tells briefly what the dispute is about, then each submits evidence (photographs, documents, etc.), and calls witnesses, if necessary. It is customary to provide your opponent as well as the arbitrator a copy of any documents submitted as evidence. After both sides present their case, the arbitrator conducts a discussion, posing questions to both sides to elicit more information. Finally, each side makes a closing statement, arguing against the points made by the other and summarizing his or her own position.

Unless the arbitrator decides to adjourn the hearing because more testimony is needed, the hearing will be closed. You can go home. You will be notified by mail of the decision.

The Arbitration Award

The length of time the arbitrator has to make an award will vary according to which arbitration service you use, but the time is generally between 10 and 30 days. The arbitrator has a great deal of freedom to fashion an award that will do justice to the parties. The rules for commercial arbitration by the American Arbitration Association note: "The Arbitrator may grant any remedy or relief which the Arbitrator deems just and equitable and within the scope of the agreement of the parties . . ."[5]

A typical arbitration award is one that requires one party to pay money to the other.

FOR EXAMPLE: It is ordered that the claimant, Ms. Marsha Silver, pay the respondent, Ms. Maya Dale, the sum of $1,485.50 in satisfaction of her claim for breach of contract.

Arbitrators can also award what is called "specific performance," that is, they can order that one party do whatever it was he or she was supposed to do under a contract.

FOR EXAMPLE: It is ordered that the respondent, G & G Landscaping, plant by October 1, 1989, six grapefruit trees along the southeastern border of the property of the claimants, Robert and Jane Peters, at 333 Cyprus Way, Santa Monica, CA 90028. The trees shall meet the specifications stated in the contract for landscaping services signed by the parties on June 12, 1989.

An arbitrator's award usually contains just a statement of who is to do what; it does not give any reasons why the arbitrator decided as he or she did. As the AAA instructs its commercial arbitrators:

[Arbitrators] are not required to explain the reasons for their decisions. As a general rule, the award consists of a brief direction to the parties on a single sheet of paper. One reason for brevity is that written opinions might open avenues for attack on the award by the losing party.[6]

Some arbitration services do ask their arbitrators to complete a separate, longer document called "Findings of Fact and Opinion." It is here that the arbitrator explains what she concluded about the facts of your case, which witnesses or pieces of evidence she found most persuasive, and why she decided as she did. These findings are kept in the files of the arbitration service, and normally not made available to the parties unless one side challenges the award in court. In fact, the main purpose of the findings is to counter any charge of bias or fraud against the arbitrator or the arbitration service. The findings become a record of the hearing and the decision process used by the arbitrator.

If you are curious about why your arbitrator decided your case as she did, it does no harm to ask the staff of the arbitration service if you can see the findings, but be aware that if the staff agrees to let you see them, it will most likely offer a copy to your opponent, as well. In some cases, this might prove embarrassing to you or your opponent.

FOR EXAMPLE: Assessment of Claimant's Testimony: Claimant's statement about his behavior immediately after the accident was not persuasive. From street map examined at hearing, it does not appear credible he could have seen respondent's car in position he claims to have seen it. Claimant's demeanor while testifying was hostile toward arbitrator and respondent and consistent with conclusion he was fabricating this part of story.

With the delivery to you of a copy of the arbitrator's award, your case is concluded. Questions about reopening the hearing, or appealing the decision, are discussed in the next chapter.

CHAPTER
9

*C*ase *C*ompleted: *Assuring Your*
Satisfaction

Your long-term satisfaction with mediation will depend on whether your agreement proves to be both workable and durable. Does it, after all, resolve your dispute? Does the carpenter repaint the hallway and does he do a good job? Does your former business partner pay you the money she owes? Does your neighbor stop harassing your kids?

In this chapter, we will consider some steps you can take to help assure that the time and energy you invested in mediation pays off in the long run.

If Your Agreement Is "O.B.E." (Overtaken by Events)

Even the most thoughtful and well-drafted mediation agreement can be rendered moot by unforeseen events that occur after the hearing closes.

CASE 1: Marcia, 29, was fired from her job as restaurant manager at a hotel. Believing she had been dismissed for inappropriate reasons, she filed an "unfair termination" case against the hotel. The hotel's lawyer and her lawyer agreed to let their clients try to mediate a solution using the local office of a national dispute resolution service. After several sessions, an agreement was reached to reinstate Marcia at her former position.

Three weeks later, however, Marcia's husband was notified that he would be transferred to a new job out of state, thus making Marcia's agreement with the hotel unworkable.

Both sides agreed to another hearing. The result was a new agreement in which the hotel agreed to pay Marcia a sum of cash, to give her a favorable letter of recommendation, and to make available to her its outplacement services to help her find a job in her new town.

At other times, an agreement needs to be adjusted because what seemed like a good solution during the hearing proves to be unworkable in practice, due to a mistaken assumption or wrong information by one of the parties.

CASE 2:   Two teenage boys were arrested and charged with breaking antennas and hood ornaments off cars at an auto dealer's lot. In a mediation hearing, the dealer agreed to drop charges if the boys would perform 40 hours of work without pay at his dealership on weekends. The boys agreed and the hearing was closed.

Soon after, however, the owner called the mediation center and told the staff he just learned that his insurance coverage bars anyone under 18 from working on the lot. He suggested, as an alternative, that the teens could perform 40 hours of community service by working at a local camp for disabled children where he serves on the board of directors. The boys agreed to the change. The center staff circulated a memo to both sides, obtained their signatures, and the agreement was officially amended.

Perhaps the most common reason why agreements need to be modified is that one side agrees to pay a sum of money, but then does not have the cash available.

CASE 3: A general contractor caught a subcontractor stealing lumber from him. In a mediated agreement, the subcontractor agreed to pay back 2150 dollars, in two monthly payments of 1150 and 1000 dollars. The subcontractor made the first payment on time, but then received a notice from the Internal Revenue Service demanding immediate payment of back taxes. The subcontractor told the dispute center he could not make the second payment on time.

After conferring with both sides, the dispute center modified the agreement by means of a letter stating the general contractor "agrees to extend by one month the time by which" the subcontractor "shall make the second payment of 1000 dollars."

In each of the examples above—as in most cases that are "overtaken by events"—the mediation center was available to help the disputants modify the agreement.

Your mediation center has a stake in your long-term satisfaction with agreements reached through its services. To the private dispute resolution service, you are the customer, and the business' ability to attract new clients depends on its reputation for helping foster agreements that work. This holds for the nonprofit public mediation centers, too. Their ability to attract state, local, and foundation funds depends, in part, on the success or failure rate of their operations as measured by client satisfaction.

Many public mediation centers actively monitor closed cases to see if agreements are working well. At some centers, a staff person will call the disputants a month or so after the hearing to see how things are going. Other centers will simply send out a postcard inviting the disputants to call the center if problems occur. The Community Mediation Program in Fair Haven, Connecticut, for example, conducts follow-ups twice: at two weeks, and again at two months, after mediation. At the Neighborhood Justice Center in Honolulu, where more than 600 mediations are held annually, follow-up is done 60 days after a hearing.

If your agreement proves unworkable for any reason, call the center that mediated the agreement. The staff there will be eager to do whatever is possible to see that everyone comes away satisfied.

Modifying the Agreement

If changed circumstances have created a major new issue that needs to be remediated in a face-to-face hearing, the center will contact the other side to obtain their consent to reopen the hearing. Usually a new hearing can be scheduled on an expedited basis, and the center will try to assign the original mediator so that you can skip a long review of the original dispute and get right to the issue that needs to be reworked.

On the other hand, if only a minor point or two needs to be renegotiated, then a new hearing probably can be avoided. Instead, the staff will conduct "telephone shuttle diplomacy" between you and the other side to arrive at the modified terms, and will circulate an amendment to the original agreement for both of you to sign.

If the Other Side Reneges

Even though rates of compliance with mediated agreements are higher even than compliance with court orders, there is little comfort if your case is one of that minority in which the other party reneges.

If your opponent fails to send you a check when due, fails to fix the water heater, or continues to call you at home late at night when he agreed not to do so, your first step is to call the mediation center. Most centers will have a person on staff who handles problems of "noncompliance." They will contact your opponent, usually by telephone, to discuss the situation and remind them of their obligations under the agreement.

COMPLIANCE STAFF TO RESPONDENT: "Mr. Reynolds, I understand from the Claimant in your case, Mr. Barker, that you have not made either of the first two payments of 800 dollars called for under your mediation agreement. Is this true? What exactly is the problem here?"

Persuasive Authority of Mediation Center

In this situation, the center has considerable persuasive authority. In cities and towns where mediation centers are well-established and strongly supported by local government and business, the center often is perceived as representing the "sense of the community." They receive public funds; prominent judges and community leaders sit on their boards of directors. The staff will try to convey to the noncomplying party that the community at large—as represented by the center—expects both parties to live up to the agreement.

If an appeal to civic expectation is not sufficient, the center may try a more direct approach. Staff members will know if the case was originally referred from the police or a judge, and if so, will remind the other party that if he continues to flout the agreement, the center may refer the case back to the police or judge for further legal action.

FOR EXAMPLE: "Hello, Mr. Winters, this is Nancy Lipari from the Center for Dispute Resolution. I'm calling in regard to your case with Amy Gordon. We've been told by Ms. Gordon that you haven't yet paid the amount required in the agreement. (Discussion follows confirming that amount has not been paid.)

"I notice from the file in your case that this dispute came to the Center from Judge Venditto in City Court. He was willing to adjourn the case for six months if it could be settled through mediation. I need to tell you that if you don't make the payment to Ms. Gordon as required by the agreement, the Center will send your case back to Judge Venditto with a recommendation that the original charges be reinstated."

The staff may also remind your opponent she risks being taken to court for breach of contract.

FOR EXAMPLE: "Mr. Winters, you agreed that your mediation agreement would be a binding, legal contract, and the form says that right on it. If Ms. Gordon takes you to court for breach of contract, you could be liable for the full amount you owe her, plus interest, plus damages, plus court costs, as well as whatever it costs you to hire a lawyer. You would risk having a judgment issued against you which would be a matter of public record and available to employers and banks. This might make it difficult for you to get a job or a loan."

Suing on the Contract

Going to court to enforce a mediation agreement is a last resort. Unless you can make use of small claims court, you will endure the costs and delays of the adversary system you tried to avoid by going to mediation in the first place. Nevertheless, if your opponent reneges on the agreement and ignores all the persuasive efforts of the mediation center, then court might be a good place to go.

"I should have sued her in the first place," you might say on the way to the courthouse, "and not wasted time with mediation." After all, you sat down in good faith with your opponent who, now it seems, may never have intended to carry out the agreement. You may feel foolish for having wasted time and for trusting someone who did not deserve your trust.

It is understandable to feel this way, but the attitude overlooks one important point: with a well-drafted, binding mediation agreement in hand, your job (or your lawyer's job) in court is far easier than it would have been without it. Coming into court with the mediation agreement, the only question for the judge is: "Is this a valid contract?" If it is, the judge will enforce it. Had you gone to court without mediation, the questions before the judge would be more difficult: what are the facts, who is right and who is wrong, etc. There is no assurance you would have come out of court with anything resembling what you wanted. At least now, having gone through mediation, you have an agreement that still can be the basis for getting what you want.

In some states—including Texas, Georgia, and Arizona—mediation agreements are assumed under law to be enforceable in court.[1] In other states, you will need to convince a judge that your agreement satisfies the requirements of a contract. If you take your case to a regular trial court, your lawyer will handle this issue for you. If you go to small claims court and represent yourself, the judge will probably ask you about the process that led up to the writing and signing of your agreement. You can prepare by bringing with you a copy of the mediation center's rules, or even a descriptive brochure explaining how mediation is conducted. The judge is looking for assurance that your hearing was conducted fairly, that your opponent was not coerced into making an agreement, and that both of you intended the agreement to be binding.

If a judge finds that your agreement was a contract and that your opponent breached it, she can issue a judgment in your favor for the full amount due, plus court costs and interest from the date the money was supposed to have been paid. She can also order the other party to do whatever he was supposed to do under the agreement, such as fixing the plumbing or resealing the driveway. If you have suffered damages because of your opponent's failure to live up to the agreement, the judge might award you some money for that, too.

Unfortunately, winning in court does not necessarily resolve your dispute. The same opponent who reneged on the mediation agreement may balk at paying a court judgment. You may be facing years of collection proceedings before a wage garnishment or seizure of assets yields the money due you. Thus, while court may ultimately be the only way you can collect, you probably made no mistake by trying mediation first.

Enforcing an Arbitrator's Award

An arbitrator's award is even easier to enforce than a mediation agreement. If an arbitrator has rendered an award in your favor, and if your opponent fails to comply, you can turn the award into a court judgment by a simple procedure known as "confirmation."

In most states, you have one year from the date of the arbitrator's award to go to court to have the award confirmed. In this procedure, your lawyer shows the judge the arbitrator's award, and asks him, in effect, to make it a judgment of his court.

An arbitrator's award is very difficult to oppose in court. Merely because the award strongly favors one side over the other is not grounds to overturn it. Generally, an award can be overturned or modified only if a party can convince a judge of any one of the following:

- There was corruption, fraud, or misconduct in connection with the hearing.
- The arbitrator was biased or prejudiced.
- The arbitrator exceeded his authority or made a serious mistake in calculation.
- Legal procedures were not followed correctly.

Once confirmed, the arbitrator's award like any other court judgments can be enforced by garnishing wages, attaching bank accounts, and seizing personal property such as automobiles.

Starting over in Court

It is possible that you may become so frustrated with your opponent's refusal to live up to a mediation agreement—and so sure that further mediation efforts will be useless—that all you want is to take your opponent to court and sue for all you can.

CASE IN POINT: Two Little League coaches got into a shouting match and fistfight over an umpire's call. One suffered a chipped tooth. At the urging of many of the boys' parents, the two men settled their dispute in mediation with the injured man agreeing to accept 600 dollars as reimbursement for dental bills.

The money was never paid, however, and the injured coach continued to be harassed by the other at subsequent games. Completely frustrated with the situation, he filed a 100,000-dollar lawsuit alleging not only physical injury, but defamation of character.

You may find yourself in the frustrating position of having gone to mediation with someone who, either by changed circumstances or bad faith, cannot or will not live up to an agreement. In such a case, you can, like the injured coach in the above example, ignore the mediation agreement as if it did not exist and press your legal claims for all they are worth. (This would not be possible if the parties had submitted their dispute to arbitration. In arbitration, you do give up your right to sue over the dispute that you submitted.)

Fortunately, these situations occur only rarely. As noted earlier, of disputes that go to mediation, about 85 percent reach agreement and only a small fraction of those, probably fewer than 5 percent, ever face serious problems of noncompliance such that one or both parties needs to consider litigation.

Mediating Special Disputes

CHAPTER
10

Divorce Mediation

Marla and Steven were teenage counselors at a summer camp. There they met and fell in love. In their twenties, they married. He began a dental practice; she became a fund raiser for the local symphony orchestra. When their first child was born, Marla left her job to spend full time raising their son. A second son was born a couple of years later. When the boys reached school age, Marla went back to work.

Eventually, Marla and Steven both knew their marriage was over.

"Steven and I had—and still have—a good relationship," Marla explains. "We care a lot for each other, but our marriage just didn't work. We weren't happy. Divorce seemed like the lesser of two evils."

Each year in the United States more than one million couples divorce. Like an increasing number of them, Marla and Steven (their names have been changed but the case is real) decided they would try a mediated divorce. They hoped this would allow them to work out for themselves the terms of their separation and thus avoid some of the financial and emotional costs of the traditional two-lawyer, adversarial divorce.

Friends of Marla and Steven who lived in another city had gone through an adversarial divorce. It was they who suggested the couple try mediation. Recalls Marla, "My husband's friend was in a terrible battle over who would have custody of their little boy. The husband had his lawyer, the wife had her lawyer, later the judge even appointed a lawyer for the boy. But even with three lawyers and two parents working at it, they couldn't reach an agreement. When it looked as if they would have to go to trial, our friends and their lawyers went to a mediator, and they worked out an agreement they all were pleased with. As a result, when we said we were getting divorced, our friends suggested we try mediation."

Marla's first step was to call a local lawyer who specialized in divorce to ask if she could recommend a good mediator.

"When I told the lawyer I wanted to try mediation," says Marla, "she told me I was in dreamland. 'Wake up and smell the coffee, honey,' she said. 'You can't give away anything to your husband. You've got to grab everything you can.' "

Marla was shocked. "I told the lawyer I had no intention of giving anything away; I just wanted to be fair about it. 'No one has to be penalized,' I told her. 'We were married and it just didn't work. What's wrong if I don't want to add fuel to the fire?' "

Eventually, Marla found a lawyer who thought mediation might work well for her and Steven. He referred her to an experienced divorce mediator and told her to call him when a separation plan was ready, so that he could review it for her.

Marla's husband was at first reluctant to try mediation. He had many friends who were lawyers and who could handle his divorce for him. But Marla urged him to try one session, and he agreed to go.

The mediator Marla chose worked out of a quiet office in a suburban professional building. At the first session, the mediator, a woman in her mid-forties, offered Marla and Steven coffee or tea, and indicated they should sit in two upholstered armchairs set around a central work table.

The first session was "very emotional, very upsetting," recalls Marla. "We told the mediator we had decided to divorce and how concerned we were for our two boys. The mediator explained to us how mediation would work: the different issues we would deal with, the number of sessions, the fact that everything would be confidential, and that we would end up with a memorandum for our lawyers to review and which later would become part of the divorce papers signed by a judge."

Over the weeks, the mediator helped Steven and Marla work through the issues of their divorce, beginning with how to divide their property. She asked them to complete worksheets, listing their assets and debts. The mediator had Steven bring in three years' worth of tax returns for his dental practice.

"I don't think the mediator saw her role as a teacher," says Marla, "but she did give us plenty of time to ask questions and would stop often to ask, 'Steven, do you understand this? Marla, do you understand this?' At one point, she arranged for me to see an accountant to go over some financial questions I had."

One question was how to deal with Steven's pension.

"My husband had a retirement plan and under the law I was entitled to a portion of it," explains Marla. "But Steven also had substantial debts from dental school. We decided he would keep both: he gets the debts now and I gave up my share of the pension later."

Another issue concerned the couple's home.

"There were times during the sessions when I lost it emotionally," Marla remembers. "But soon the mediator learned the areas—such as what we'd do with the house—that I was most sensitive about. Then we didn't waste time with me crying for five minutes, because she'd steer the conversation to a different subject for a while until I could handle it."

They decided to keep joint ownership of the house with Marla having the right to live there with the children.

"I get the house," says Marla, "but if I choose later on to have another man live with me there, then if he's still living there after six months, I agreed to sell the house or to buy Steven's share."

Much discussion concerned the couple's two boys.

"We spent three sessions on child issues," says Marla. "We decided early on that the kids would live with me, but then there were questions about visiting, where the kids go on holidays, grandparents' visits, what will happen if one of us remarries or gets involved with other people."

The mediator spent one session meeting just with the children. Marla recalls:

"My husband and I sat outside while the mediator was in with the boys for a full session. I still don't know what she said exactly, but she gave us a general idea. She made sure they were comfortable with me as the custodial parent and with the visitation plan. She said the boys told her they wanted us to get back together, but, if we couldn't, then they wanted us to be friends.

"Later, I talked about the session with the boys. They said, 'We talked about you and Daddy and how you're separated and how you're going to get a divorce and how we're going to spend more time with Daddy.' "

Marla explains, "At that time, the boys weren't seeing much of their father because he was working a tremendous number of hours, so the visitation plan we worked out would actually have him spend more time with them."

Marla and Steven attended 12 sessions with the mediator before they reached agreement on all issues of their separation. The mediator then drafted a "Memorandum of Understanding," which spelled out in plain, nonlegal terms what the couple had agreed to. She gave each one a copy with instructions to review it and also to have their own lawyers review it.

Marla's lawyer suggested some changes in child support payments that would save money on taxes. Steven's lawyer also advised some minor adjustments. The couple has agreed to the revisions, and the lawyers are now translating the memorandum into "legalese" for later filing in court.

Marla does not mind paying her lawyer's fee on top of the mediator's fee, which she and her husband split.

"The lawyers are making a lot less money this way, because I'm walking in with everything pretty much done. There will be a fee, but it's nothing compared to what we would have faced if my husband and I each had used lawyers for the whole negotiation process. My husband and I would have had to go through all the issues with our own attorneys, and then the two attorneys would have had to argue about them. The worst part would have been that neither my husband nor I would have known what the other one was saying."

Growth of Divorce Mediation

Divorce mediation has grown in sophistication and popularity since the practice began in the early 1970s. Today, an estimated 2000 to 3000 mediators specialize in divorce. They can be found in most cities and towns across the country. In some states, including California, Illinois, Maine, and Oregon, the law requires couples to try to mediate issues—such as support, custody, and visitation—that concern children.

A recent study of divorce mediation conducted by the Northern California Mediation Center tracked 106 couples who chose mediation and 47 couples who chose the adversarial process. Couples who chose mediation gave the following reasons for having done so:

- Reach an overall agreement satisfactory to both me and my spouse (91 percent)
- Reduce or avoid hostility between me and my spouse (83 percent)
- Reduce the cost of obtaining the divorce (82 percent)
- Reduce contact with lawyers and court proceedings (81 percent)
- Want a fair property division agreement (70 percent)
- Retain a friendly relationship with my spouse (65 percent)[1]

Among this important study's many findings is that mediating couples were about three years younger (41 years for men, 38 for women), had significantly higher levels of education, and were more likely to have children under age 18 than couples who chose an adversarial divorce.[2]

Those who chose mediation also "believed their spouses to be significantly more honest than adversarial respondents did and rated their spouses higher on a fairmindedness scale," researchers Joan B. Kelly and Lynn Gigy have written. They continue:

> Thus, despite equally dissatisfying marriages, and equal anger at spouses, the mediation respondents seemed more able to acknowledge certain positive qualities of the spouse,

indicating perhaps an ability to reject the marriage but not the total person.[3]

Despite a good deal of publicity recently about divorce mediation, many people remain unclear about how it works. In this chapter, we will consider some of the most frequently asked questions about divorce mediation.

What Happens in Divorce Mediation?

In divorce mediation, a couple tries to work out an agreement, with the aid of a mediator, on all the essential issues of their separation and divorce. These include:

- Division of property (how will the couple's real estate, stocks, bonds, pension funds, etc., be divided?)
- Spousal maintenance (also called alimony; how much money, if any, will one spouse regularly pay to help cover the other's living expenses?)
- Custody and visitation of children (which parent will have legal control over the couple's children? How often and for how long will the parent without custody be allowed to see the children?)
- Child support (how much money will one parent regularly pay to help cover the cost of raising the children?)

These are the same issues that lawyers would normally negotiate for a couple in an adversarial divorce.

The mediator will also help the couple address issues unique to that couple's circumstances, such as how to care for aging parents or how to deal with relationships involving stepchildren. Finally, the mediator will help the couple develop procedures for joint decision making to avoid any need for future litigation.

When the mediation succeeds, the mediator drafts the terms of the couple's agreement in a document called a "Memorandum of Understanding." A sample of a typical memorandum is reproduced in Appendix C. The memorandum, which usually runs 10 to 20 pages in length, is reviewed by each spouse's own lawyer for any necessary changes. The substance of the memorandum is incorporated into a legal separation agreement, which is filed in court. Later, that separation agreement can be made part of the final divorce decree.

Can I Mediate Just Part of My Divorce?

Yes, this is up to each couple. Some couples, for example, prefer to mediate issues affecting their children, such as custody and visitation, while leaving questions of property for negotiation by their lawyers.

What Is the Role of the Mediator?

The mediator's role in divorce cases is essentially the same as that in other types of mediation. The mediator is a neutral third party whose goal is to help the separating couple find a fair and practical plan for dissolving their marriage and, if necessary, for continuing to parent their children.

Will the Mediator Try to Save My Marriage?

No. Divorce mediation is not therapy aimed at reconciliation; working out a couple's anger and reviewing problems of a marriage are not part of mediation. In fact, most mediators will not consider a couple ready for mediation unless both spouses have accepted the reality that the marriage is over.

"We're not pro-family in the sense of trying to save marriages," says Jack Heister, director of the Mediation Center of Rochester, New York. "On the other hand, we're not out to split up families. At the initial session, I always ask if the couple wants to see a marriage counselor." Even still, says Heister, about one in ten couples who come for mediation do reconcile "because they are in nonadversarial communication for the first time and they also see the economic realities of divorce."

What Does Divorce Mediation Look Like?

Divorce mediators try to give their meeting rooms a private and secure feeling, in order to make the couple feel at ease and in a cooperative, rather than competitive, spirit.

"My consultation room is decorated in blue—a cool color—and the pictures are calming," writes John Haynes, a founder of the divorce mediation movement and author of the book *Structured Mediation*. "Every aspect of the room is designed to enhance co-operation and to promote the mediator's effectiveness."[4]

Tea or coffee typically is offered as each session opens. The seating plan is by careful design. Husband and wife often are directed to sit on a sofa, or around a table, rather than being "squared-off" against each other across a table. The room itself may be soundproofed to add extra assurance of privacy.

How Long Does Mediation Take?

Mediation of all the issues in a divorce will usually take between eight and twelve sessions, each lasting one and one-half to two hours. If there is a special need to quicken the pace of the mediation because, for example, one spouse is planning to move out of state, the sessions can be made longer or held closer together.

Do I Still Need a Lawyer?

Yes. Divorce is a legal proceeding and you still need a lawyer to protect your legal rights. Mediation is not a substitute for the use of lawyers in the separation and divorce process. It is a complement, an enhancement—but it is not a substitute.

Both spouses should have their own lawyer to consult as needed during mediation and to review the Memorandum of Understanding and suggest any changes necessary to protect your legal rights. (Most divorce mediators are not lawyers, but even if the mediator you choose happens to be one, during mediation he or she is not functioning as a lawyer and therefore cannot be your source for legal advice.)

Although your lawyer will not be with you during the mediation session, you may want to consult him or her if questions come up that involve legal issues. For example, you may want an opinion as to whether shares of stock or a piece of real estate should be considered marital property, or whether the Internal Revenue Service would tax the sale of some household property. A phone call to your lawyer between mediation sessions can clear this up and give you peace of mind.

The mediator should be able to refer you to several lawyers in your area who are experienced with divorce mediation and willing to represent you on this basis.

Can Mediation Save Me Money?

Yes. A mediated divorce should cost you and your spouse about half of what a traditional adversarial divorce would cost. In the adversarial divorce, both husband and wife pay their own lawyers to negotiate the issues in dispute. In mediation, husband and wife can share the cost of one mediator. In most communities, a mediator's hourly fee will be about the same or slightly less than the average hourly fee charged by matrimonial lawyers. You will both also have to pay your own lawyers to review the memorandum and to file court papers, but this should be a relatively modest addition to the mediator's fee and, together, the two should still be only about one-half the cost of a two-lawyer adversarial divorce.

Is Mediation Confidential?

Yes. As are other types of mediation, divorce mediation is strictly confidential. Your mediator is obligated—by oath, by the standards of the profession, and, in some states, by law—to keep confidential everything revealed inside the hearing room.[5] And if you and your spouse succeed through mediation in reaching agreement on all the issues of your divorce, you eliminate the risk of ever seeing your case end up in a public court proceeding. In practice, about 10 percent of adversarial divorces do end up going to trial.

John Haynes has observed that the fear of loss of privacy is one of many fears of litigation that encourage people to try mediation. Writes Haynes:

> I do not believe that most clients opt for mediation because of its many positive attributes. Instead, most people choose mediation because they fear the litigation route more. One person may fear that, if the case goes to court, his or her business activities will be exposed to public scrutiny. Another may feel that an earlier affair will become public knowledge. Some people cannot bear the thought of being judged. Others fear the revelation of their private lives. Some relate horror stories of a friend's experience in divorce litigation. Whatever the reason, most people are negative about litigation before they are positive about mediation.[6]

Are There Emotional Advantages to Mediation?

For many couples, the most important advantage of mediation is the emotional benefit that can come from taking and keeping control of their divorce; when it is they, not lawyers or judges or court-appointed experts, who set the terms of their future relationship and their relationships with their children. No divorce is easy, but the emotional benefits of nonadversarial, cooperative problem solving may help make the divorce process easier to bear, and leave fewer scars on the divorcing couple and perhaps also on their children.

Pyschologist Judith S. Wallerstein, reviewing the results of a long-term study of divorced couples and their children, recently has written: "It would be hard to find any other group of children—except, perhaps, the victims of a natural disaster—who suffered such a rate of sudden serious psychological problems." Nevertheless, Wallerstein found, "Children tended to do well if their mothers and fathers, whether or not they remarried, resumed their parenting roles, managed to put their differences aside, and allowed the children a continuing relationship with both parents."[7]

The emotional advantages of a mediated divorce are harder to measure than the amount of money saved, but some recent research offers encouraging evidence.

Post-Divorce Relationship

In 1988, the New Hampshire Mediation Program studied a group of divorced couples, half of whom had been clients of the Mediation Program and half of whom had had a traditional divorce. The two groups were comparable in terms of income, age (30 to 40 years old), and education (most had "some" college). Though this study did not adjust for differences in personality and marital relationships between the two groups, the results nevertheless show some striking contrasts that may reflect the emotional benefits of mediation.

More Stable Agreements: 31 percent of the traditional group had returned to court to relitigate custody or support issues within five years after the divorce; only 12 percent of the mediation group returned for modification.

More Generous Visitation: only 14 percent of the traditional group provided five or more days per month visitation for the non-custodial parent, and 27 percent provided fewer than three days; of the mediation group, 73 percent provided more than six days a month visitation and fewer than 1 percent provided three days or less.

No Missed Payments: 14 percent of the traditional group reported some late payments of child support, and 20 percent never received any payments; of the mediation group, fewer than 1 percent experienced late payments and none had missed a payment.

Better Relations with Former Spouse: 41 percent of the traditional group reported "cordial" relationships between divorced couples, as compared to 71 percent of the mediation group.[8]

Parental Communication and Cooperation

Recent studies also indicate that a mediated divorce may help set the ground for better post-divorce parenting by giving divorcing couples a structured opportunity to improve their communication and cooperation. As noted earlier, in the study by the Northern California Mediation Center, couples choosing mediation were more likely to have children under age 18 than couples who chose an adversarial divorce. Researchers Kelly, Gigy, and Hausman note:

> It appears that divorcing couples with children came into mediation in search of a more amicable forum to resolve their disputes, because they recognized a need for a continued long-term partnership in their parental functioning and roles. Mediation may be viewed by these individuals as a less hostile process than litigation, a process that would allow for the continuation of shared parenting responsibilities and perhaps some longer-term cooperation.[9]

Based on results of the study, the researchers conclude: "The mediation intervention was significantly more effective than the adversarial process in increasing cooperation between the spouses."[10]

And clinical psychologist Jay Finkelstein sought to determine, in another recent study, "whether children whose parents undergo a mediated divorce show less delinquent behavior than those whose parents divorced without mediation." Using names drawn from court records and from records of the Northwest Mediation Service in the Seattle-Puget Sound area of Washington State, researchers produced two groups of families who recently had experienced divorce. The two groups were demographically similar, and showed no differences in pre-divorce relationships between the spouses. Eighty-six percent of the couples had two or more children. The study looked at two factors in the children's behavior: sociability (relations with peers, officials, and parents) and deliquency (problems with police, neighbors, and school).

The findings, though the sample was very small, revealed no pre-divorce differences between the mediated and nonmediated groups, but did find a marked increase in delinquent behavior by the older child in two-child households among the nonmediated group. Reports Finkelstein: "If we look at the nonmediated group pre- and post-divorce we find an increase in deliquency by the older child; there is no such increase within the mediated group."[11]

Regression vs. Empowerment

In considering the emotional aspects of divorce, researchers have noted that separating couples, faced with enormous stress, may regress psychologically. The adversarial divorce, they note, actually can make this problem worse. Explains Howard Yahm, psychotherapist and codirector of the Center for Family and Divorce Mediation in Pearl River, New York:

> The adversarial divorce, with its emphasis on authority dependence, power tactics, winning as much as possible, and defeating the opponent, exacerbates regressive tendencies. By defining the best interests of clients in strictly monetary and legal terms, matrimonial attorneys ignore the

emotional and developmental needs and interests of their clients and their clients' children and unintentionally join with the least mature or most underdeveloped aspects of their clients' personalities.[12]

In contrast, mediation, because it places on both spouses adult responsibilities for rational discourse, learning, and decision making, can have an "empowering" effect, particularly on the weaker spouse. For example, says mediator Jack Heister, a woman with little financial skills because she has worked as a homemaker, who goes into mediation and is required to learn about her financial condition, to make a budget, and to make financial choices, can emerge from the process "a stronger, more informed person with self-esteem and skills to better tackle the new challenges in her life."

A moving testament to this "empowerment" process was expressed by Karen Schneider, author with her former husband, Dr. Myles Schneider, of the book *Divorce Mediation*. She recalls,

> In many ways mediation changed my life. If I had chosen to use the adversarial system, I'm not sure how I would have managed after the divorce. All my married life I had been a shadow behind Myles. If a lawyer had stood up for me, talked for me, substituted for me, I would have gone right on being a shadow . . . Myles would be gone, and I would have been left, just as I was the day he moved out—standing in the kitchen crying. . . . Mediation makes you think. It makes you speak and feel and participate . . . I would advise any woman to consider mediation as a separation/divorce procedure. It is a growth and learning experience that you do not get in the adversarial system.[13]

Results of the recent California study appear to confirm, at least for women, the "empowering" effect of mediation: "Women reported that the mediation process had helped them assume more responsibility in managing their personal affairs than did men, and women had greater confidence in their ability to stand up for themselves as a result of the [mediation] process."[14]

When Is Mediation Appropriate?

As mediator Mona Miller of Divorce Mediation Associates in Rochester, New York, has observed, mediation is appropriate "in any case where both spouses are ready, willing, and able to try it."

"Ready" means that both husband and wife accept the reality that their marriage is ending and are ready to discuss realistically the terms for a fair dissolution.

"Willing" means that husband and wife consent freely to the mediation process and are willing to approach mediation in good faith and with a conscientious effort to attend each session, produce information as required, participate in the negotiations, and retain a lawyer to review the proposed Memorandum of Understanding.

"Able" means both husband and wife can participate effectively in rational discussion. If either one is so impaired psychologically that he or she cannot engage in sustained, rational discussion, then mediation would not be appropriate. Any of the following conditions in either spouse would make mediation inappropriate:

Severe psychological dysfunction: a person is severely depressed or otherwise impaired, and the mediator cannot draw them into a rational mode.

Pathological anger: one spouse is so irrationally angry that he cannot make decisions in his own self-interest nor choose between "getting even" with his spouse and not hurting the children.

Chronic physical spousal abuse: long-term abuse that has continued throughout the marriage.

A good mediator will usually be able to tell if one or both spouses is unsuited for mediation. Sometimes this becomes readily apparent. "I always give the first half-hour of consultation free," says mediator Mona Miller, "because in that amount of time I can sometimes tell if either spouse shouldn't be here due to depression or otherwise not being able to participate. In that case, I terminate the session and refer the couple to an appropriate social service agency or to a professional who can help, such as a therapist or lawyer."

Must a Couple Be Amicable to Use Mediation?

Being "ready, willing, and able" to mediate does not mean the separating couple has to like each other, or even be speaking to each other outside the mediation room. It is not true, as some matrimonial lawyers may tell their clients, that mediation works only for a small number of couples who remain friendly while they are splitting up.

In fact, the evidence suggests that successful mediation is entirely unrelated to the degree of anger a couple feels. In the recent California study, for example, "the common assumption that clients seeking mediation are a less angry group was not supported." Couples who chose mediation were just as dissatisfied with their marriages and just as angry at their spouses as those who did not. Going into mediation, they rated their level of anger at their spouse as follows:

28 percent: very high or extreme levels of anger
30 percent: moderate anger
40 percent: only mild or no anger

And results of that study found no correlation between the degree of anger couples felt coming into mediation and their chances for using mediation successfully.

> Marital conflict and anger toward a spouse at time of entry
> into mediation does not seem to play a role in hindering a
> couple's reaching final written agreement.[15]

As mediator Jack Heister asserts, "Being really angry—short of pathological anger—does not rule out mediation. Everyone at the time of separation is angry."

Can Mediation Work if One Spouse Is Dominant?

Your mediator is not an advocate for you or your spouse. Her job is to help the two of you find a solution to the issues in dispute. Nevertheless, it is possible that in mediation you could strike a deal that, for reasons you do not perceive, is not really in your best interests or in the interests of your children. The question of power imbalance or unequal bargaining strength is raised when one spouse has dominated a marriage, is a much stronger negotiator, or knows a lot more about financial matters than the other. Typically, this might occur where one spouse is a business executive and the other a homemaker. Can the two really sit down in mediation and negotiate a deal that is fair to both? Won't the homemaker always lose out?

Such power imbalances exist in many marriages. Fortunately, there are two important factors in mediation that can protect the weaker spouse.

First, the mediator has a right and a duty to intervene to protect against grossly unfair agreements. The American Bar Association's standards on divorce mediation now *direct* mediators to intervene in settlements in order to ensure fairness:

> The mediator has a duty to suspend or terminate the mediation whenever continuation of the process would harm one or more of the participants.[16]

Professors Joseph P. Folger and Sydney E. Bernard have studied mediators' willingness to intervene and found that:

- 25 percent of mediators are "highly interventionist": very likely to block agreements that do not protect children or weaker spouse

- 10 percent of mediators are "highly non-interventionist": unlikely to block any agreement a couple reaches after being fully informed

- 65 percent of mediators are "interventionist as facts warrant": most likely to intervene when agreements involve children or weaker spouses

These researchers concluded: "(Most mediators) are inclined to . . . intervene on behalf of a broader sense of equity or fairness when they believe such intervention is warranted by the case at hand."[17]

If you are concerned that your spouse may dominate your mediation and that the result may be unfair to you or your children, be sure to select a mediator who states in advance his willingness to block any lopsided agreement. A second check you will have against being stuck with an unfair agreement is that you are going to have your own lawyer and you are not going to sign anything until after your lawyer reviews the proposed Memorandum of Understanding. This double layer of protection—a mediator willing to intervene plus your own private lawyer—should be sufficient to protect you even if your spouse tends to dominate.

How Successful Is Divorce Mediation?

On average, of all couples entering mediation, about 50 percent conclude with a final, written agreement resolving all the major issues of their divorce. Your chances of reaching this degree of success in mediation will depend on many factors, including the attitudes and abilities of you and your spouse, the particular issues in your separation, and the skill of your mediator.

In the recent California study, 50 percent reached final agreement on all issues, 8 percent reached agreement on some issues, and 15 percent resolved some matters though they did not complete mediation.[18] (Some of these withdrew because they decided not to proceed with their divorce. Said one couple: "We decided that we really wanted to redirect our energies into rebuilding our marriage instead of terminating it." Said another: "I rate your service very highly and credit the process with saving our marriage.")

Only about 26 percent of couples in the California study were unable to resolve anything through mediation, and, on average, these couples discontinued mediation after just four sessions.

Among the majority of couples in the California study who did reach agreement on some or all issues, the researchers found that women in mediation "were more satisfied with their property, custody, and spousal support agreements" than women in adversarial divorces, and that men and women in mediation "were significantly more satisfied with both the process and the various outcomes than adversarial men and women."

Why Do Some Couples Not Complete Mediation?

The California study found that people who terminated mediation, excluding those couples who reconciled, often fell into two groups. In the first group were men and women who came to feel overwhelmed by the process of mediation and felt they lacked the personal abilities and strength to adequately represent themselves. "Many women do feel empowered by mediation," note researchers Kelly, Gigy, and Hausman, "but those who feel overwhelmed and lacking a sense of empowerment tend to terminate mediation before an agreement is reached."[19] In the second group were those who just could not stand being with their spouses, because—even in mediation—they found their spouses to be too unreasonable, untrustworthy, and angry.

Significantly, over half of those who terminated still said they were neutral or satisfied with mediation. Said one couple: "Although we didn't continue, I do feel the mediator helped my spouse to be more open to a more equitable and realistic solution. We then managed to come to an agreement through our attorneys without needing to go to court."[20]

How to Get Started

Either you or your spouse, or both of you together, can begin the mediation process. Usually, one spouse is more interested in using mediation than the other, and it is that spouse who makes the first contact with the mediator. On the telephone or in an initial free consultation, the mediator will explain his or her services, fees, and particular approach or philosophy. Some mediators, however, will give only limited information to one spouse; they prefer to give information to both spouses together to avoid even the appearance of bias. Some mediators have brochures about their practice that they will send you to review at home.

You can begin mediation at any stage of the separation and divorce process—generally, the earlier the better. If you are already working with a lawyer, explain to the lawyer that you want to try mediation but will continue to retain him or her to consult with during mediation and also to review the Memorandum of Understanding afterwards.

Some lawyers will be glad to work with you on this basis and may even refer you to a mediator. On the other hand, some who have limited understanding of mediation may distrust it or, perhaps, see it as a threat. "Attorneys have not been enthusiastic about a practice that most of them do not offer," note Robert E. Emery and Melissa M. Wyer.[21] If your lawyer is one who opposes mediation on principle, get another lawyer to work with, because you will need your lawyer to be supportive and helpful during the mediation process.

How to Find a Mediator

People who are good at divorce mediation usually concentrate in that field and do not handle more general types of disputes, such as consumer, business, or neighborhood matters. Today, in the United States, there are between 2000 and 3000 active mediators who specialize in divorce.

Most divorce mediators work independently or in small practices. Therefore, in locating divorce mediators you will most often be looking for sole practitioners rather than a large mediation center or service.

Perhaps the easiest way to find a list of divorce mediators is simply to look in the telephone directory under "mediation" or "divorce." The Academy of Family Mediators, the largest professional association of divorce mediators, has encouraged its members to petition local telephone companies to include these headings in their yellow page listings. Some do, and some do not.

Other people in your community who may be able to give you the names of divorce mediators include:

- the staff of your public mediation center
- matrimonial lawyers
- the staff at the family services office
- clergy
- therapists
- employee assistance personnel at large corporations
- friends and relatives who have used a mediator

In addition, several national and many statewide organizations maintain lists of divorce mediators and may be able to provide you names of practitioners in your community (see Appendix D).

Questions to Ask a Prospective Mediator

You will want to be sure not only that the mediator you select is professionally competent, but that his or her style and philosophy of mediation are compatible with your own. When you find a mediator you think you would like to work with, ask for names of lawyers who have reviewed memoranda drafted for other couples; the lawyers are in a good position to give you an opinion on the mediator's technical competence.

Of course you will want to ask prospective mediators about fees, but beyond that, there are other issues of qualification, philosophy, and style you should review with them, either on the phone or at the first meeting. Following are eight issues you may want to explore:

1. *Professional Background*

Most divorce mediators have a professional background in some other discipline, such as law, social work, mental health, education, or the clergy. You may feel more comfortable with a mediator from one of these backgrounds than from another.

2. *Training and Qualifications*

Only a handful of states set minimum qualifications for divorce mediators (for example, California, Florida, Minnesota, Michigan), and in most cases these apply only to mediators practicing in court-connected programs, where child custody and visitation are mediated by order of a judge or under state law. In most other cases, there are no minimum qualifications or training requirements set by law for divorce mediators who practice on their own.

Most novice mediators have at least completed a three to five day training program offered by a private training service or a non-profit public mediation center. The training covers conflict resolution theory, state divorce law, laws and issues of custody, support, asset distribution, taxation, and the pyschological issues of separation, divorce, and child development. Some training programs also involve supervised observation of actual divorce mediations.

More experienced mediators will also have taken continuing education seminars on particular issues, such as taxation or child custody issues.

3. *Experience*

Divorce mediation is a relatively young field, and mediator experience varies widely. One survey found a majority of mediators had less than two years' experience; many had handled fewer than 12 cases. The most experienced 25 percent of mediators had worked between three to fourteen years and had handled from 34–400 cases. [22]

4. *Professional Accreditation*

Your mediator will not be "licensed" or "certified" by the government, as is a psychiatrist or lawyer. In the absence of state licensing requirements, your mediator's membership in, or accreditation by, various professional organizations may be some indication of his or her qualifications and ability.

The leading professional organization of divorce mediators is the Academy of Family Mediators, founded in 1981. Membership in the academy does not guarantee the quality of a mediator's work. It does show, however, that the mediator meets the academy's qualifying standards for its various classes of membership. The academy maintains four membership classes:

Affiliate: Anyone may become an affiliate member

Associate: This class requires master's degree in relevant area, plus 40 hours specialized training; or undergraduate degree, two to four years' experience, plus 40 hours of training.

Senior Member: This member meets qualifications for Associate member and has completed at least 15 mediations, 10 hours of additional consultation with an experienced mediator, and has submitted six Memoranda of Understanding for review.

Fellow: A Fellow must have been Senior Member for at least five years, and be reviewed by the Academy's Fellows Committee.

The Academy publishes a directory, organized by state, containing the names, addresses, and telephone numbers of its members. Similarly, the American Association of Family Counselors and Mediators, a national association of family, school, and community mediators, also publishes a directory of its members who meet minimum qualifications of education, training, and experience. For information on ordering either directory, see Appendix D.

5. *Attorney Representation*

Some mediators may advise couples to hire just one lawyer merely to "translate" the Memorandum of Understanding into "legalese" for filing with the court. This is inadequate. One lawyer cannot look out for the rights of both husband and wife, because in many cases their rights will be in conflict. A mediator who does not require you and your spouse each to have your own lawyer is not watching out for your best interests. Ask prospective mediators whether they require both spouses to retain their own lawyers.

6. *Willingness to Intervene*

As noted, a "power imbalance" between mediating spouses does pose the risk that one spouse may strike a deal that is not in his or her best interests, or in the interests of the children. If you think it is possible during the course of mediation that you would find yourself in this situation, then you will probably want to select a mediator willing to follow the advisory of the American Bar Association and intervene to prevent an unfair agreement. Ask prospective mediators to explain their position on the issue of mediator-intervention, and to describe under what circumstances they would reject a proposed agreement they personally believed to be unfair.

7. *Private Caucuses*

When mediation is used for disputes other than divorce, it is common for the mediator to meet privately first with one disputant, and then the other, to discuss in confidence that party's bottom line or new ideas for settlement options. In divorce mediation, however, some couples find this objectionable, because of the greater degree of mistrust that often exists between the spouses. Other couples find caucusing useful. Consider your position on this and then ask prospective mediators if they use the caucus.

8. *Meeting with Children*

Some mediators like to devote a half-session or whole session to meeting privately with children above eight to ten years of age. Explains mediator Jack Heister:

> When the parenting part of the negotiations is finished, I like to meet with the kids alone to affirm to them that they are loved, that their parents are working hard to arrive at a good parenting plan, to describe the mediation process their parents are going through, and then to go over the plan to elicit their response. If they have problems with any part of it, I'll take these back to the parents, and they often will

modify it. This is empowering for the kids; it lets them become part of the process.

Other mediators, however, prefer not to have the children involved. If you feel strongly about this one way or the other, find out if your prospective mediator's position on this issue is compatible with your own.

AT A GLANCE

Issues to Consider in Choosing a Divorce Mediator

1. Professional background
2. Training and qualifications
3. Experience
4. Professional accreditation
5. Position on attorney representation for each spouse
6. Willingness to intervene to reject unfair agreement
7. Position on use of private caucuses
8. Position on meeting privately with children

Dealing with the Reluctant Spouse

It is common for one spouse to be more willing than the other to try mediation. If you are trying to get mediation started but your spouse is reluctant, some mediators will agree—if you ask—to call your spouse and discuss mediation with them and answer questions. Other mediators will not do this, because they feel a private conversation with either spouse compromises their neutrality.

One tactic you could try is simply to agree to pay the full cost of the first mediation session yourself. This may be enough to get your spouse to attend so that he or she can meet the prospective mediator and learn firsthand how mediation works.

The Stages of Mediation

As with other types of mediation, divorce mediation proceeds through stages. If you decide to try mediation for your divorce, you can expect the sessions to follow the general scheme outlined below, although procedures used by particular mediators may vary.

Stage One: Intake and Commitment

In the first session, the mediator will explain the procedures he or she will follow, the rules of confidentiality, the fees, as well as issues of legal representation, caucusing, and meeting with children. This is the time to ask questions, and to decide whether you can trust and feel comfortable with this mediator and want him or her to mediate your divorce.

John Haynes has written that during the first session he sometimes tells a couple:

> "I will share these options (for settlement) with you, but I will never tell you what to do—because, you see, I won't have to live with your choices; you will. Therefore, I believe you should always make the decisions. Now, there will be times when you will wonder why you ever used mediation. You will want me to give you the answers, and you will say to yourselves that, if you had taken the litigation route, your attorney would have told you what or what not to do. And, when that happens, you will probably get angry with me and wish you had never come to see me. However, that too will pass, and you will negotiate your own mutually acceptable agreement."[23]

Stage Two: Fact-Finding

At the end of your first mediation session, the mediator will give you financial worksheets on which you will need to list all your assets, such as bank accounts, stocks, bonds, real estate, partnerships, pension funds, and business interests. You may be asked to submit—and you should request that your spouse submit—payroll records, checkbooks, pension plan summaries, and three years' worth of past federal and state tax returns.

If substantial assets are involved, such as a family business or a company pension plan, you may want to have your attorney, or an accountant, review your spouse's financial records to be sure everything has been disclosed and to interpret financial data.

Review and analysis of this information typically occupies the second and part of the third mediation sessions.

Stage Three: Identifying the Issues

Around the third session, after all the financial cards have been laid on the table, the couple and the mediator begin to focus on the issues in dispute. On some issues, such as who will have primary custody of the children, the couple may already be in agreement. But as to the extent of visitation and amount of child support, the couple may be far apart. Some property issues may also emerge that are going to need a lot of negotiation: Should the cost of the husband's professional degree be considered marital property? Who should get the home computer?

The mediator, often using a large flip-chart, will write down all the issues the couple needs to negotiate and then order them according to which ones will be discussed first and which saved for later.

Stage Four: Negotiation

For the next five or more sessions, the couple will address—in sequence—the issues in dispute. As each issue is discussed, the mediator will help the couple think of ways to resolve it ("option-generating") that they may not have thought of on their own. Often, separating couples, because of their anger and emotional fatigue, are unable to see options for settling disputes beyond a few obvious choices. One of the mediator's most important contributions at this stage will be to help the couple take a fresh look at the issues, in order to think of new and creative options for settlement.

In reality, "sequential" negotiation does not work well. Most couples view their settlement plan as a package, so that while they may begin by discussing one issue at a time, by the fourth or fifth session they are probably considering several issues at once, as they begin trading off one thing for another in order to arrive at a fair settlement package.

Stage Five: Agreement, Drafting the Memo, Closing

When negotiations have concluded, the mediator will draft the proposed Memorandum of Understanding, reviewing each part with the couple to be sure the wording accurately reflects their agreement. Both spouses are given copies for their lawyers separately to review. Some mediators end their services there; others hold one session in reserve in case the couple needs to discuss questions raised by their lawyers.

The final session with the mediator, whether it comes before or after the lawyer's review, may include a small "closing ceremony" to mark the successful end of the couple's hard work at cooperative negotiation. The "ceremony" may involve a glass of wine for everyone and a simple toast to the future. Some mediators may suggest the children attend, in order to help them gain a sense of emotional closure and finality.

One couple arranged to surprise the mediator with a treat at the last session. The wife brought a cake and the husband brought champagne. They toasted themselves and their mediator for a job well done.

CHAPTER
11

*B*usiness *Mediation*

In 1987, the owner of a pizza franchise in Hawaii rented space in a shopping plaza for a new restaurant. While renovating, he found asbestos in the ceiling, a discovery which delayed the restaurant's opening for nearly a year. He asked the plaza to pay him 70,000 dollars for damages and lost income, but the plaza refused, saying he had rented the space "as is."

Weeks of negotiation left the two sides thousands of dollars apart, at which point the restaurant owner suggested mediation. The plaza owner agreed.

On the second day of mediation, during private caucus, the mediator asked the plaza owner to think of alternatives to paying the restaurant more money. The plaza owner mentioned that the restaurant's marketing strategy was aimed at children under 12, and then hit on a new idea: he could buy gift certificates from the restaurant and distribute them to real estate agents and other clients who had children. Purchase of the certificates would transfer cash to the restaurant and help build its business; distributing the certificates would create good will for the plaza. The restaurant owner agreed to the proposal, ending the dispute.[1]

As author Jerald Auerbach has observed, merchants and businesspeople have for centuries "been among the most outspoken proponents of nonlegal dispute settlement." They have strived "to elude lawyers and courts and to retain control over their dis-agreements."[2] Early in this century, it was the business community that pushed for laws to allow out-of-court arbitration. Today, businesspeople are among those most eagerly embracing mediation and other forms of alternative dispute resolution (ADR), including:

- mini-trials
- "rent-a-judge"
- arbitration
- in-house mediation programs

Joseph T. McLaughlin, a partner with the law firm of Shearman & Sterling, has written that U.S. corporations "spend up to 80 billion dollars a year on legal expenses, approximately one quarter of which is related to litigation."[3]
Says McLaughlin:

Not only is litigation costly to parties in terms of attorney's fees, it is often a great drain on executive time and energy.

Long-standing customer relationships, often a company's most valuable commodity, can be harmed or destroyed by litigation.

In sum, litigation often drains a corporation's most valuable resources—money, time, relationships, public image, and the energies of its employees.[4]

It is not surprising, therefore, that, as noted earlier, more than 400 major businesses have signed the Center for Public Resources's ADR pledge, committing themselves to try mediation or another ADR technique before filing a lawsuit.
The pledge states:

Alternative Dispute Resolution Pledge

We recognize that for many business disputes there is a less expensive, more effective method for resolution than the traditional lawsuit. Alternative dispute resolution (ADR) techniques . . . often can spare businesses the high cost and wear and tear of litigation.

In recognition of the foregoing, we subscribe to the following statement of principle. In the event of a business dispute between our corporation and another corporation which has made or will then make a similar statement, we are prepared to explore . . . resolution of the dispute through negotiation or ADR techniques.[5]

Recently, according to the Center, 60 companies that signed the ADR pledge announced a two-year savings of nearly 50 million dollars in legal fees and costs. "We've reduced our litigation docket by two-thirds, and we've had fantastic savings in legal fees," Clifford L. Whitehill, senior vice president and general counsel of General Mills, Inc., told the *New York Times*. "Unlike litigation, these alternatives resolve our disputes quickly so we can get on with business."[6]

What is surprising, however, is that, while the very largest American corporations—those best able to afford litigation—have embraced mediation, smaller businesses have not.

"It's absolutely true that the large companies, particularly service companies, are the ones taking advantage of ADR," says Don Reder, founder and president of Dispute Resolution, Inc., a private dispute resolution firm in Hartford, Connecticut. "The large corporations have embraced ADR because they have such a large body of disputes. They can track on computers exactly how much management time and legal time they expend with ADR vs. litigation, and then figure how much they might save by using ADR.

"But the guy who runs a small machine shop and feels he's getting screwed by a supplier is hardly on the cutting edge of litigation technology. He'll give the case to his lawyer, probably a general practitioner, who proceeds in the usual way with litigation."

Which Business Disputes Can Be Mediated?

The following types of business disputes often are taken to mediation:

1. Contract disputes
2. Consumer complaints
3. Personal injury complaints
4. Product liability complaints
5. Construction disputes
6. Disputes arising from mergers and acquisitions
7. Employer vs. employee disputes
8. Disputes between employees
9. Disputes between partners
10. Disputes between family members in a family business

Several of these are discussed more fully below.

Breach of Contract

Contract disputes successfully resolved through mediation involve all varieties of business pursuits, including construction, computer sales and leasing, home remodeling, office products supply, etc.

CASE IN POINT: The developer of an office tower contracted with a construction firm to apply marble paneling to the outside of the building. Within a year, however, the panels began to fall off whenever there were high winds. The developer sued the contractor, but city officials, fearing danger to the public if the panels were not soon repaired, persuaded both sides to try mediation. A California-based dispute resolution firm was hired to provide mediation, and the dispute was successfully resolved.

Employment Disputes

These cases include disputes between employers and employees as well as disputes among employees. Mediation can be especially effective because of its ability to address the interpersonal conflicts involved in these matters. (Labor contracts that set out grievance procedures may preempt the use of mediation.)

CASE IN POINT: Six security guards who worked the night shift at a manufacturing plant were so entangled in personality disputes that absenteeism was high and the quality of security services suffered. At the suggestion of the men's supervisor, the company retained a local public mediation center to provide conflict training for the men in two successive weekend sessions. As a result, the level of personal antagonism on the job declined enough so that no layoffs were needed.

Family Business Disputes

Lewis D. Solomon and Janet Stern Solomon have written: "It is notorious that no feuds are so venomous as those within families, and a closed corporation is often a Petri dish for the cultivation of every known strain of human vindictiveness, greed, and chicanery."[7] Due to the interpersonal conflict inherent in family business disputes, these matters—as well as partnership dissolutions—are among the business cases most frequently handled by private dispute resolution firms. "We do a lot of business divorces," confirms William Hartgering, vice-president of Endispute, Inc., of Chicago.

CASE IN POINT: The widows of two brothers who before World War II had founded what eventually became a large chain of auto service centers in New England, were shocked when a nephew revealed to them that one of the brothers had used corporate funds to develop a private real estate business on the side. The revelation threatened to tear apart the extended family of siblings and cousins who owned shares in the enterprise. To avoid a wrenching and potentially public battle among the family, the two women retained a private dispute resolution firm in Boston to help the family resolve the conflict, if possible, and if not, then to help structure a sale or liquidation of the company that would be fair to all sides.

Personal Injury

Insurance companies are today among the largest users of ADR techniques. In 1988, for example, the Travelers Corporation sent nearly 5500 personal injury and commercial claims to mediation or arbitration, an eightfold increase over that of 1984.[8] The company reports that out of 15,000 cases submitted over five years, 7000 were resolved, at average cost savings of 1000 dollars per case and seven months in time saved.[9]

CASE IN POINT: The owner of a grocery store received a demand for personal injury damages following an incident in which a 30-year-old customer cut her hand on the jagged edge of a pole in the parking lot. The store's insurance company contacted the customer's lawyer to propose mediation through the American Arbitration Association. The customer's attorney accepted. The insurance company agreed that the store was negligent in not fixing the unsafe condition, but its initial offer to the customer of 1500 dollars was far below the amount demanded. In less than a half-day hearing, both sides agreed that a 7500-dollar settlement was fair.[10]

When Is Mediation Appropriate?

As a businessperson, your interests will normally best be served if you can resolve a dispute quickly and privately through direct negotiation. It is only when negotiation holds little promise, or when you have tried it without success, that you should consider mediation.

The factors to consider in deciding whether to mediate are essentially the same as those discussed in Chapter 2 for regular mediation.

Mediation may be indicated, for example:

• When no legal remedy is available (such as a personality dispute between partners or employees).

- When you want to keep down legal costs (legal fees would be too high compared to amount in dispute).
- When you want to avoid delays (you need to resolve a dispute with suppliers quickly so that manufacturing can resume before inventory is depleted).
- When you want to avoid publicity (a customer complaint about product quality or safety, if litigated, would generate bad publicity).
- When you want to preserve a business relationship (you and a supplier disagree over pricing but if a fair pricing formula could be found it will be advantageous to both to continue doing business).

Litigation, on the other hand, may be indicated:

- When you need to establish a legal precedent (the validity of a patent which your company holds).
- When you need to publicly prove the truth (a customer's complaint about product quality or safety has received wide attention in the press and only a jury verdict in your favor can reestablish your product's good name).
- When your company's legal rights have been infringed and you stand a good chance of reaping a large judgment in court (another firm has infringed your company's patent rights and you stand to collect substantial damages in federal court).
- When your opponent is unable or unwilling to participate in mediation.
- When serious crimes are involved in the dispute.

The Mediation Process

In other chapters, we have closely examined the mediation process. In this section, we will consider only those aspects of business mediation that differ from regular mediation.

Selecting a Mediation Service

Nonprofit Services

Though nonprofit public mediation centers often hear consumer complaints brought against businesses, many centers are not accustomed to hearing cases between two businesses and may not have mediators on their panels trained to hear complex business disputes. It would not hurt to check with your local mediation center, however; because if they can provide you with a suitable mediator, this would be the least expensive place to take your dispute.

One nonprofit service capable of hearing any size business dispute is the American Arbitration Association. The AAA has, in recent years, expanded beyond its middle name to offer a full range of commercial mediation services through its 32 local and regional offices.

Private Dispute Resolution Services

The growing demand for business mediation has itself spawned a new type of business: private dispute resolution services. These are for-profit businesses that market mediation and other ADR services to business clients.

"We're seeing a real explosion in demand in the last couple of years," says William D. Logue of Dispute Resolution, Inc. "In 1988, we handled 1250 cases, up nearly 40 percent over the previous year. For 1989, we are projecting 1800 to 2000 cases." Dispute Resolution, Inc., founded in 1981, was one of the early entrants in this field. The firm handles commercial disputes ranging in size from 5000 to 3 million dollars.

Today, there are about a dozen national dispute resolution firms capable of providing mediators to business clients in any part of the country. If the firms do not have an office where you live, for example, they will arrange for one of their mediators to travel to your community on the day a hearing is scheduled.

Other dispute firms operate at a local or regional level. For example:

In Chicago, Resolve Dispute Management, Inc., has mediated cases involving construction disputes, management and control of closely-held businesses, and partnership dissolutions.

In the upper midwest, the Minneapolis-based Americord, Inc., handles breach of contract, wrongful death, and other commercial disputes. Cases range from about 50,000 to 2 million dollars.

In Beachwood, Ohio, the dispute management firm of Weiss and Eisenhardt mediates commercial cases for individuals and businesses throughout the greater Cleveland area.

Most private firms offer a range of dispute resolution services of which mediation is the most common. "We see mediation as the door to all other ADR services," explains Barbara Ashley Phillips, president of American Intermediation Services, Inc., a national firm based in San Francisco. "Yes, we do mini-trials. Yes, we do arbitration. Yes, we do rent-a-judge. But deciding which of these other services to use is best done within the context of mediation." (In June 1989, American Intermediation Service became a wholly-owned subsidiary of Judicate, Inc., a national dispute resolution firm specializing in private judging, or "rent-a-judge.")

In general, businesses use private dispute resolution firms on an "as needed" basis. When a dispute arises and you want to try mediation, you contract with that firm to mediate that particular case. An interesting variation, however, is being tried by Mediation Arbitration International, Inc., of Fort Lauderdale, Florida. That firm bills itself as a "private membership organization" for professionals, small- and medium-sized businesses, large corporations, and trade associations. In exchange for an annual fee, the firm provides customized mediation and arbitration clauses for a member's business contracts, provides training in ADR techniques, and expedites handling of mediation hearings.

Names, addresses, and telephone numbers of many national, regional, and local private dispute resolution firms can be found in Appendix B.

Fees

To retain a national dispute resolution firm for a typical commercial matter will cost you a minimum fee of 350 to 1500 dollars per party, depending on the firm, the amount in dispute, the complexity of the case, and the number and location of parties involved. For the minimum fee, a firm usually will work to get all necessary parties to submit to mediation and then conduct a half-day hearing. For complex cases, some firms have charged fees up to 20,000 dollars and more.

If you use a smaller, local firm, minimum fees would start at about 250 dollars per party—again, depending on amount in dispute and number and location of the parties.

How to Begin Mediation

One way to get your business's disputes to mediation is by putting a clause into your contracts that commits the parties to try mediation before going to court. These are similar to arbitration clauses which have been used for years in business contracts. Following is a sample mediation contract recommended by the American Arbitration Association:

> If a dispute arises out of or relates to this contract, or the breach thereof, and if said dispute cannot be settled through negotiation, the parties agree first to try in good faith to settle the dispute by mediation under the Commercial Mediation Rules of the American Arbitration Association [or to participate in mediation with some other mediation service] before resorting to arbitration, litigation, or some other dispute resolution procedure.[11]

Whether or not you use a mediation clause in your business contracts, you and your opponent will need to complete and sign a Submission to Mediation form identifying the issues in dispute and the remedy you are seeking. This is the same procedure as is used in regular mediation and was discussed earlier in Chapter 4.

Binding vs. Nonbinding

As a businessperson, you will probably be even more concerned than most participants in mediation that the agreement you reach be final and binding so that you can get the dispute behind you and get on with your business. When completing the submission form, be sure to indicate that you intend any agreement that emerges from mediation to be final and binding.

Getting the Other Side to the Table

Your opponent probably will be unfamiliar with mediation and will need to be educated about it and then persuaded to try it. You can do the educating and persuading yourself, or have your lawyer do it for you, but you can avoid this burden entirely (and avoid appearing weak by seeming too eager to mediate) by letting your dispute service do it for you. Most of the services claim a success rate of 75 to 90 percent in getting the other side to the table.

"Our job is to get folks to participate in ADR," says Don Reder, founder and president of Dispute Resolution, Inc. "We understand the 20 to 30 objections normally raised to using ADR and we consider it our job to turn that initial 'no' to a 'yes.' We are not just administrators of ADR, we are very proactive folks who are going to go in there and get this case settled. We do it by showing the reluctant party's attorney how ADR will benefit their client."

Barbara Ashley Phillips, president of American Intermediation Service, Inc., agrees that getting the opposing side to the table is best handled by the mediation provider, not by the parties.

"It is counterproductive for one side to try to get the other party to agree to mediate," she explains. "If one party proposes, the other opposes. It is best to let us do it. Our success rate is 85 percent in these matters."

Phillips' firm charges the initiating party in multiparty cases an average of 500 to 1500 dollars to cover the firm's costs in getting the other side to the table and helping the parties prepare for the mediation.

"Mediation firms are supremely well-positioned to get the parties to the table," says Phillips. "Lawyers may say, 'The other side will never agree to talk.' Well, guess what? They're wrong. A significant number of times when lawyers say that, we'll get the other party to the table.

"The perception of the lawyer is that the other side will not talk, and the other side may in fact have said that. But we don't take that as final, we take it as an initial position and work from there. Tenacity has a lot to do with success."

Training and Selection of Your Mediator

Mediators who handle business cases under contract with private dispute firms are paid anywhere from 500 to 2500 dollars a day. For this kind of fee, you will have the services of someone especially trained to mediate business disputes and with experience in the particular subject area of your dispute.

The person chosen to mediate your case is likely to be a lawyer or business executive who has been specifically trained, by means of classroom lecture and apprenticeship, to mediate business disputes. Typically, the dispute service will send you a list of possible mediators all of whom have experience and knowledge of the subject area of your dispute. You will be asked to review the list and cross off the names of any mediators who, on the basis of biographical information supplied, appear to have a conflict of interest due to business, social, or family ties with you or your opponent.

Parties at Table Need Authority to Settle

Since no one involved in a business dispute wants to waste time at an unproductive hearing, it is generally a rule in business mediation that both sides must be represented by parties with authority to settle. If you are in charge of your own business, you can attend the hearing, or you can send your attorney to represent you. However, as mediation allows businesspersons to keep control of their company's disputes, it makes sense for the executive to participate directly.

Keeping it Brief

With an eye on the clock, your business mediator will try to get your dispute to the hearing table and conduct the hearing with minimum delay.

For example, before the hearing begins, business mediators may study the background of a dispute by reviewing briefs submitted by each side's lawyers, reading court papers if one side has already filed a lawsuit, and visiting both parties' places of business to review records and interview personnel. All of this is meant to get them up to speed, so that when the hearing starts, the two sides can begin discussing the issues in dispute.

Telephone Mediation Possible

If it will be impossible for you and your opponent to attend a face-to-face mediation hearing, business mediators sometimes are able to forego one of the fundamental requirements of regular mediation: a face-to-face meeting between the disputants. Instead, some

will allow their mediators to conduct hearings by
ephone, either caucusing by phone first with one
other, or using conference calls with all disputants

Other ADR Procedures

Business mediation hearings generally follow the same procedures
as used in regular mediation. These have been examined in earlier
chapters and need not be repeated here. What follows are brief
descriptions of three other ADR techniques: the mini-trial, private
judging, and an innovative program of in-house mediation.

Mini-Trial

Since its invention in a 1977 patent dispute between TRW, Inc.,
and Telecredit, Inc., the mini-trial has emerged as one of the most
popular forms of alternative dispute resolution, particularly among
large corporations and government agencies. The U.S. Army Corp
of Engineers, for example, has used the device to resolve claims
of more than 56 million dollars.[12]

The mini-trial allows top managers from both disputing companies to say, in effect, "let's hear your best case, you hear our
best case, and then we'll sit down and see if we can settle this
thing." Most of the national dispute resolution firms are experienced in conducting mini-trials.

The Players

The players needed for a mini-trial include a top manager from
each side who has authority to settle, each side's lawyers, and a

neutral advisor, supplied by the dispute firm, to conduct the hearing. The neutral advisor should be someone who is knowledgeable in the subject matter in dispute and also in the legal aspects of the case. Often, dispute firms provide a retired judge or law professor to fill this role.

The "Trial"

Mini-trials, like mediations, have distinct stages. These are outlined briefly below:

Stage One: Agreement to Use Mini-Trial. Parties must agree on rules and procedures. These are provided by the dispute service.

Stage Two: Case Preparation. Strict time limits (usually just a few weeks) are set, during which period both sides' lawyers may gather needed documents, witnesses, etc., and get ready for their presentations. They may use documents already obtained in preparation for real trial, or they may request access to opponent's documents in preparation for the mini-trial.

Stage Three: Informal Hearing. As the mini-trial opens, lawyers for each side are given the chance within strict time limits—usually half a day—to present their best case before executives from both sides and the neutral advisor. No transcript of the hearing is produced and rules of evidence are not enforced; anything can be presented and usually no objections are permitted.

The neutral advisor's role is not to be a judge but to make sure the rules are followed. Everything is confidential and nothing said or shown in the hearing can be used later if the case should go to a real trial. After the lawyers' presentations, the executives and the neutral advisor may ask questions.

Stage Four: Neutral Advisor Gives Opinion. The neutral advisor now gives a nonbinding advisory opinion to the executives, outlining his or her reaction to the strengths and weaknesses of each side's case and giving an opinion as to how a judge might decide the case if it went to court.

Stage Five: Top Managers Discuss Settlement. The company executives with decision-making authority now retire to a private room and, away from their lawyers and subordinates, attempt to negotiate a settlement between themselves based on the information and opinions presented at the hearing.

The best type of dispute for a mini-trial is one that concerns a factual matter—not a legal matter. If the relevant law is well-settled, and only the facts are in dispute, then it is easier for the neutral advisor and executives to form an opinion on how a real court might decide the case.

As noted, the mini-trial is strictly a confidential proceeding. The neutral advisor is never allowed to testify for or against either side, should the case go to trial. Indeed, even the fact that a mini-trial is held is normally considered confidential by the disputants.

Private Judging (Rent-a-Judge)

Like Federal Express, dispute firms that offer private judging have found a lucrative niche by taking over a service once exclusively provided by government.

As noted earlier, when actress Valerie Harper and Lorimar Productions filed breach-of-contract suits against each other over Harper's role in the TV series *Valerie*, the two sides agreed to have the case heard privately under the auspices of Judicate, Inc. The two sides, which together paid court fees of 15,000 dollars per week (including 250 dollars per hour for the services of a former Judge of the Los Angeles Superior Court), figure they saved about four years over the time it would have taken to resolve the case in public courts.[13]

In many states, citizens can petition the courts to appoint a "referee" to judge their dispute and issue findings that will have the effect of a court judgment. Therefore, instead of going to a real court, you can go to a private court where you pay for the service and agree in advance that the decision will be final and binding. Most dispute services offering private judging employ retired state and federal judges who preside in private courts for 150 to 300 dollars per hour. Judicate, the largest in the field, has about 500 judges on its roster, and in 1988 handled 1347 disputes in more than three dozen states.

The benefits of private judging include not only the speed with which a case can be heard, but also the ability to select a judge with expertise in the subject area of dispute. The privacy of the proceeding is another attractive advantage.

In-House Mediation

Some businesses facing a potentially large volume of disputes that can be mediated have found it advantageous to establish mediation programs run by their own staffs. One innovative in-house program, as described by Judy C. Cohn and Adam J. Conti was that developed in Atlanta by A. L. Williams and Associates, Inc., a life insurance and financial investment firm.[14]

A. L. Williams conducts its business through a network of more than 140,000 independent agents in all 50 states. At times, disputes between headquarters and independent agents led to lawsuits. After one such court case resulted in a jury award in favor of an agent, the company in 1985 formed an in-house dispute resolution office to try to resolve such cases without litigation.

The office was staffed by seven full-time mediators trained by the Justice Center of Atlanta. Upon receiving a complaint from agents or managers, the mediation staff would investigate the case and attempt conciliation. If the investigating mediator was unable to affect a settlement, the case was assigned to another mediator for a formal hearing. Mediation hearings could be conducted by telephone or in person, either at headquarters or at a field office.

By 1988, more than 2000 disputes had been resolved. "Cooperation between managers and agents has improved, enhancing the enthusiasm of A. L. Williams representatives for the organization and contributing substantially toward its success," write Cohn and Conti. They believe the system developed at A. L. Williams could work with other large franchise, insurance, or real estate operations. And though A. L. Williams' sales agents are independent contractors, not employees, the system could be adapted to employer-employee relationships "provided it has the full support of top management and the trust of employees and that it is permitted to operate independently." Indeed, since her experience at A. L. Williams, Cohn has founded her own firm, American Mediation Resources, Inc., based in Atlanta, which specializes in setting up in-house mediation programs for businesses.

Although a large employee population would be needed to justify a separate in-house mediation department, in smaller firms responsibility for mediation could be assigned as part of an employee's duties. "In even the smallest organizations," write Cohn and Conti, "external mediators can be used on a contract or an ad hoc basis."[15]

Private judging, mini-trials, and in-house mediation programs are just a few alternative dispute resolution techniques that can, as the ADR pledge states, "spare businesses the high cost and wear and tear of litigation."

CHAPTER 12

Mediating Community Disputes

In 1987, an Atlanta company made an anonymous 100,000-dollar gift to help a Baptist church expand its night shelter for the homeless. Neighborhood residents opposed the expansion plan, however, and this well-intentioned gift triggered a community-wide dispute that threatened to entangle the church, the city of Atlanta, and area residents in years of hatred, mistrust, and litigation.

Disputes over issues of public policy, such as how and where to provide shelter for the homeless, are common today. What is uncommon about the Atlanta dispute is that instead of years of battling in the newspapers and the courts by competing interest groups, this dispute was resolved in just eight hours, through mediation.

This chapter will examine how you can use mediation to help resolve disputes that may affect large numbers of people in your community.

The Shelter Controversy

The 100,000-dollar gift was to enable the Christian Council of Metropolitan Atlanta to increase the population at the shelter from

60 to 300 people and to accomodate not only women and children but also men. Unfortunately, the Christian Council did not advise residents of surrounding neighborhoods of its plans. Rumors began to circulate about the planned expansion of the shelter. By the time the Christian Council was ready to request a Special Use permit from the city zoning board to expand the shelter, the neighbors were well-prepared to mount a forceful effort to block it.

Joseph Beasley, a representative of the United Baptist Church, where the shelter was located, said his church was prepared for some dissent from neighbors who did not want the shelter to expand, "[but] we weren't prepared for the level of opposition. Between the Board of the Christian Council and the neighborhood group, there really was a hostile environment."[1]

Church and neighborhood representatives considered asking various people with political standing in Atlanta to mediate the dispute, but as the names were suggested one side or the other dismissed them because they distrusted that person's ability to be neutral.

Finally, a city official asked Edith Primm, executive director of the Atlanta Justice Center, to mediate. The Justice Center is one of the oldest and largest public mediation centers in the country. With an annual budget of more than 400,000 dollars, the nonprofit Center mediates about 1200 cases a year. Primm agreed to mediate, on condition that all groups with an interest in the matter be invited to participate.

Marathon Mediation

The Justice Center had one major problem immediately: it learned of the case on May 3rd; on May 14th, the Zoning Board was scheduled to hear the request for the Special Use permit. Primm decided to bring the various groups together for one marathon mediation hearing that might result in an agreement before the Zoning Board's deadline.

The hearing was held on a Saturday at the Justice Center. Gathered around the table were four representatives from the affected neighborhoods, three from the Christian Council, one from the Baptist Convention, and three from city government. Primm began by explaining the purpose and ground rules of the mediation, and then began what she expected would be a five- or six-hour hearing. After opening statements, Primm caucused with each group, then reconvened for joint discussions, all the time outlining and summarizing the negotiation process—with colored markers, on a flip-chart—so that participants could visually follow their progress toward agreement.

After an exhausting eight hours—more than two beyond what she had scheduled—Primm announced an agreement: a nine-point plan signed by each group representative. The plan would allow for phased expansion of the shelter over time, including up to 10 adult males if each is part of a nuclear family living at the shelter; 24-hour staffing including a full-time director on premises; offering job-training skills for all adult residents; quarterly reports to the mayor; and a new managing board, with at least 20 percent of its membership from surrounding neighborhoods.

The agreement was presented to the Zoning Board as the recommendation of all the groups involved in the mediation. The Zoning Board hearing room was filled with more than 70 people, many of whom thought a confrontation was inevitable. Instead, in less than ten minutes, the Board approved and adopted the plan outlined in the mediation agreement. In the following weeks, some neighbors who had not been present at the mediation suggested minor changes to fine-tune the plan; some of these changes were adopted.

In Atlanta, a dispute that could have dragged on for years, doing neither the city, nor the church, nor the neighbors, nor, indeed, the homeless, any good, was instead resolved in one day in a way that satisfied all concerned. As one participant said, "Neither side wanted to give in, but everybody came out with something. All wounds weren't healed, but everyone was heard."

Which Community Disputes Can Be Mediated?

Any disputes in your community where competing interest groups are involved and where the law does not dictate a solution, may be good candidates for mediation. In terms of subject matter, the disputes may involve, for example, economic, social, political, or environmental matters. Disputes are often like those in Atlanta where residents of a neighborhood feel their way of life threatened by some outside activity. The threatening activity can be the expansion of a shelter for the homeless, the opening of a new landfill, or construction of a highway or an office park.

No Memorial Day Parade

Some community disputes are idealogical. In 1984, in Rochester, New York, for example, a dispute developed when peace activists, marching alongside veterans in the city's annual Memorial Day Parade, unfurled banners and signs concerning the number of gay soldiers killed in Vietnam and opposing economic programs of the Reagan administration. Offended by the display, the veterans voted to march in no more parades unless the peace groups were kept away. The following Memorial Day, the veterans did not march; some peace activists marched alone, but few citizens came to watch.

Rochester Mayor Thomas Ryan called Andrew Thomas, executive director of the Center for Dispute Settlement, Inc. The Center, founded in 1972, was one of the first, and is still one of the largest, public mediation centers in the country. "I'm not sure what to do," the mayor told Thomas. "Can you help me out on this one?"

Thomas agreed to try to mediate. Four representatives of the Peace and Justice Coordinating Group, two from the Veterans' Memorial Executive Council, and one from the veteran's national office agreed to participate. All during the fall, winter, and spring, Thomas met in separate and joint sessions with the groups in hopes of finding a solution in time for the next year's Memorial Day Parade.

The veterans refused to march in the same parade with the peace activists, whom they viewed as not commemorating the dead but as promoting political issues, including gay rights. They suggested the peace activists stage their own parade on a different day during the three-day Memorial Day weekend. But the peace groups, knowing from experience they could not draw a crowd by themselves, insisted on marching with the veterans.

At one point, the veterans claimed that they had a contract with the city to organize each year's parade and the city was obligated to pay them 8500 dollars for the service. The peace group said they would bring in legal briefs from the American Civil Liberties Union proving that if there was such a contract with the city, it was unconstitutional. The veterans produced their own briefs supporting their theory. Exasperated, Thomas told both groups if they wanted a legal fight they could go to court; in mediation, their purpose was not to fight about the law but to find a solution.

The following April, Thomas called a press conference to announce a clever, if not amicable, agreement to the Memorial Day mess. Under the plan worked out in mediation, the peace activists would hold a separate parade that would start 100 yards behind the end of the veterans' parade. The city of Rochester would share parade funds between both groups and, importantly, city officials would remain in the reviewing stands until both parades had passed. Two parades would march on Memorial Day, but for practical purposes—and in the eyes of the public—they would appear as one.

Some Trust Needed

As Edith Primm, of the Atlanta Justice Center, observes, mediation of community disputes—no matter what the subject matter—does require some minimal level of trust between the parties. She offers as an example a dispute between a pastor and his church where the pastor had run off with church funds. "Where moral outrage is so great and trust has been shattered, mediation may be impossible because there is no trust between the parties to build on."

Motivating the Parties to Mediate

Whether mediation can work to solve a given community dispute will depend not so much on the subject of the dispute as on the willingness of the parties involved to mediate. If one side thinks it can get all it wants in court or at city hall, it will not be motivated to try mediation where it probably would have to settle for less than 100 percent.

It's nice to think of all sides to a community dispute agreeing to sit down to work out their problems "for the common good." This might seem realistic in theory, but community disputes involve politics and power, and few parties will agree to compromise without a strong motivation to do so.

Saul Alinsky, who in the 1950s and 60s successfully organized labor, black, and other community groups around the country, once addressed this issue in an interview with journalist Edwin Newman. Alinsky told Newman:

> It's the old business . . . that people only do the right things for the wrong reasons. This is the way the world has always been. . . . You always think of tactics in those terms.
>
> There's some guys up at Harvard—professors—who say there are two approaches in America. One is the negative conflict approach of Alinsky. The other is the cooperative search for the common good. Can you imagine: I'm a labor organizer; you're an employer, so I come in to you and I say, "Now, look, I don't want to go around and organize your people, and I don't want to be one of those Alinsky negativisitic conflict guys. Why don't you and I, in our cooperative search for the common good, sign a contract?"
>
> What are you going to do? You're going to call Bellevue [hospital] and have me picked up, aren't you?[2]

One hopes, of course, that as the idea of resolving public disputes through formal mediation becomes more widely accepted, parties to community disputes will, in a spirit of cooperation, agree to mediate. But, until that time comes, just what is it that might motivate the various players in your community dispute to try mediation?

Motivation: Lawsuits

Lawsuits can be good motivators. When residents of Friendship Heights, a Maryland suburb of Washington, D.C., learned that three developers each planned to build multistory office buildings nearby, they immediately filed lawsuits challenging the projects. Months or even years of delays for the developers were possible. While the cases were pending in an appeals court, five people representing the three developers and five representing various neighborhood groups, plus their attorneys, agreed to try mediation at the Center for Dispute Settlement of Washington, D.C., a public mediation center.

"For the neighbors," recalls mediator Brenda Irons-LeCesne, "litigation was the leverage. That was all they had to hold off the developers." Nine weeks and 22 mediation sessions later, an agreement was reached. It called for a reduction in the size of each project and relocation of one of the projects farther away from a residential street. A lawyer for the neighborhood groups called the agreement "a small masterpiece in damage control for the residents."[3]

Motivation: Deadlines

Deadlines can help motivate parties to mediate, too. In the case discussed above, the D.C. City Council had set a date just two months in the future, when it would decide whether to close some public roads required for the proposed construction. This deadline encouraged the neighbors and the developers to work hard at mediation before road closings created even more public controversy and perhaps put the dispute beyond their control.

Motivation: Bad Press

Another motivator is the potential for bad publicity. Even without a lawsuit or a road closing, if one party to a dispute poses a potential threat to another party's public reputation—by picketing and demonstrations, for example, or by release of sensitive documents to the press—that may be enough to motivate a reluctant party to come to mediation.

Choosing a Mediator

If you are involved in a community dispute for which you think mediation might offer a solution, one of your first tasks will be to locate a suitable person to be the mediator. The choice is important not only because that person will conduct the mediation but because he or she will have to help persuade reluctant parties to agree to participate. And without participation of all concerned parties, there will be no mediation.

Local Leader?

Often, the first impulse of those inexperienced in community mediation will be to suggest that a respected local civic leader—a politician or prominent businessperson, for example—be asked to mediate. After all, the thinking goes, if Henry Kissinger can shuttle around the mideast "mediating" among various warring countries, surely our own president of the Chamber of Commerce can do the same for our small, local controversy.

This is a tempting idea, and occasionally it may work if, by luck, the person selected happens to have all the right personal qualities and the requisite skills—and the available time—to do the job. This is exactly what happened in 1973 when New York City faced neighborhood protests over the city's plans to build a large public housing project in the middle-class Forest Hills section of Queens. With the dispute gaining nationwide attention and with no settlement in sight, Mayor John Lindsay asked Queens lawyer Mario Cuomo (now governor of New York State) to mediate. Cuomo accepted the job and eventually succeeded in helping resolve the conflict. He, however, never actually brought the disputing parties together for formal, face-to-face mediation; Cuomo approached the role more as a fact-finder and shuttle-diplomat.[4]

Still, the odds of picking a Mario Cuomo are slim. Too often, respected but untrained local civic leaders invited to mediate will find that they are in over their heads, once they are engaged in prolonged hearings on a multi-party, multi-issue dispute.

There are people trained to do this kind of work. If you have the opportunity to use them, it makes good sense to do so.

Using Local Mediators

Depending on how large and complex your dispute is, your best choice for mediator may be someone as close as your local public mediation center. Though most mediators at local centers are accustomed to handling the routine neighborhood, landlord/tenant, or consumer dispute, there may be several mediators on the local panel who have had training or experience in multi-party cases and who could effectively handle your community dispute.

Linda Singer, director of the Center for Dispute Settlement in Washington, D.C., states, "Mediators at local nonprofit dispute centers are often an overlooked resource when the community decides it wants a mediator for a major local dispute." Nevertheless, she cautions that the mediator chosen should have training or experience in multi-party disputes in order to handle a complex matter.

Using an Outside Mediator

Sometimes local disputes can become so complex and contentious that no local mediator will have the expertise needed to handle the matter or the confidence of all parties concerned. In such cases, you may want to consider obtaining an outside mediator by means of several national and regional firms that specialize in community disputes.

The Texas Highway Dispute

For example, residents of Fort Worth, Texas, found themselves in just such a complex dispute in 1979. The Texas Department of Highways and Public Transportation announced a 56 million-dollar project to widen from four to eight lanes a mile-and-a-half stretch of Interstate 30, running through downtown Fort Worth. A group of citizens calling themselves I-CARE (Interested Citizens Advocating Responsible Expansion) opposed the project because they said the expansion would damage nearby historic buildings and a city park. I-CARE urged an alternative plan that would run the highway under the existing street level, although they acknowledged this would create major traffic problems during construction.

Prominent Fort Worth citizens lined up on either side of the dispute, with I-CARE preservationists led by Robert M. and Anne T. Bass against central business district merchants backed by oilman H. E. "Eddie" Chile and others.[5]

In 1983, I-CARE filed suit in federal court against the State of Texas claiming that regulations had not been properly followed in developing the project. The preservationists lost after a five-week trial, but two years later a U.S. appeals court overturned the decision.

By the end of 1985—six years after the road improvement was announced—the project was still at a standstill. City leaders were desperate for a solution. It was at that point that they asked for help from James Laue. At the time, Laue was president of the Conflict Clinic, a nonprofit dispute resolution center established in 1983 and now located in Fairfax, Virginia. In response to the city's call, Laue flew to Fort Worth, met with the various parties battling over the highway issue, and agreed to mediate.

Laue and his associate Sharon Burde spent the first four months interviewing the various players in the Fort Worth controversy, and then helped to pull together a group of 14 representatives of the various factions, called the "I-30 Working Group" to participate in the mediation. By February, 1986, the group began holding regular meetings at the Texas and Southwestern Cattle Raisers Foundation on the edge of Fort Worth.[6]

"There were a bunch of people in the room with big personalities, mine included," I-CARE attorney Jonathon Nelson told the Fort Worth *Star Telegram*. "But we checked our egos at the door and stuck to the facts."

After nearly two years of fact-finding and negotiation, the *Star Telegram* could report:

> Twenty-two months ago, nobody believed the bitter battle over the Interstate 30 overhead in downtown Fort Worth would ever end.
>
> The heroes in achieving a peaceful solution are a national

mediator, James Laue, and members of a mediation group who left their egos at the door.[7]

What Laue and the Working Group discovered around the mediation table was that neither of the positions originally taken by the pro-highway people or the preservationists was the only possible solution. Instead, working together they found an alternate plan, whereby a new road could be built on a railway corridor without disrupting traffic or infringing on historical areas.

"Dr. Laue did an excellent job," said Forth Worth City Manager Douglas Harman. "He had good credentials, credibility, and experience. He got the warring parties together so that we could talk, and we did so behind closed doors and let the realities of the situation be recognized. It is essential that the mediator have a good personality and get on with the participants. This was true in Laue's case."

Nelson, the attorney for I-CARE, agreed. "The issue would never have been settled in court had Laue not been around. I am totally in favor of mediation: a true believer. Any kind of alternative dispute resolution is preferable to the courthouse in terms of time, money, and resolution [of the conflict]."[8]

In addition to the Fort Worth highway case, Conflict Clinic mediators have also helped resolve disputes between Iowa farmers and banks (establishing the Iowa Farmer-Creditor Mediation Service), between several states concerning use of the Missouri River, and between musicians and management of the St. Louis Symphony Orchestra, to name just a few.

Other organizations that specialize in resolving community-wide disputes are listed in Appendix E. (Many of the private dispute resolution services described in Chapter 11 as specializing in business disputes will also handle community disputes.)

Fees

The fee for mediating your community dispute will vary, depending on what person or service provides the mediation, how many parties are involved, and how complex the issues are.

If you are able to use the services of your local public mediation center, there may be no fee, or only a modest fee. For Andrew Thomas's year-long service in mediating the Memorial Day Parade dispute in Rochester, New York, the Center for Dispute Settlement charged the city a flat fee of 5000 dollars. For Edith Primm's work in mediating the homeless shelter dispute in Atlanta, the Atlanta Justice Center charged no fee. Primm explains that her organization—which is funded in part by the city of Atlanta—mediates community disputes within Georgia at no charge. Out-of-state clients are charged based on the complexity of a case, but never by the hour. "The mediator should not be invested in how long the case takes or if a settlement is achieved," she explains.

The cost of using a national mediation service, even one that is nonprofit, is likely to be more substantial. National services that handle community disputes may charge a flat fee per case or assess fees based on the services of their mediators, for which they charge from 300 to 2000 dollars per day, plus out-of-pocket costs such as travel. The Conflict Clinic mediator's fees range from 400 to 800 dollars per day, according to William R. Potapchuk, associate director.

For James Laue's work, and that of his associate, in mediating the Fort Worth highway case over a period of two years, the Clinic charged 100,000 dollars. The bill was shared by the city of Fort Worth, the Texas highway department, and the Washington-based National Institute for Dispute Resolution, an organization that promotes use of mediation. The parties found it money well-spent.

"No one is turned down because of inability to pay," says Potapchuk of the Conflict Clinic. "If the parties to a dispute cannot afford our services, we will search for funding on their behalf." Possible funding sources include foundations, business corporations, and national mediation advocates such as the National Institute for Dispute Resolution.

Who Pays the Fee?

With multi-party community disputes, the issue of who pays the mediator is one that needs to be addressed early. Often, one or more parties to a community dispute is a governmental body, such as your city or county, or a state agency, and will pick up the whole tab out of public funds. In other cases, however, each of the parties will be expected to pay a share of the cost. Sometimes, this arrangement will threaten to scuttle mediation even before it begins, if an important party to the dispute, such as a neighborhood association or nonprofit group, cannot afford its share of the mediator's fee.

If you face a problem of how to pay for your group's seat at the mediation table, a local business corporation, civic group, or foundation might be a source of funds for you, if this source can be made to see how the whole community would benefit by having the dispute resolved peacefully through mediation.

If you cannot find local funds, then consider some state and national funding sources. The National Institute for Dispute Resolution (NIDR) in Washington, D.C., for example, has in recent years made grants to help cover mediation expenses of parties in a variety of public policy disputes, including a Chicago real estate discrimination case, a dispute between insurance carriers and AIDS patients, and a Federal Trade Commission negotiation involving the auto industry and consumer groups. Going a step further, NIDR plans to establish a 450,000-dollar Fund for Public Interest Mediation "to underwrite the expenses of those parties who must be at the mediation table but cannot afford the cost of getting there," according to NIDR president Madeleine Crohn.

At the state level, NIDR has successfully encouraged several states to set up their own mediation offices to identify public policy disputes that arise within the state and to provide funds to help cover the cost of mediation. Explains Madeleine Crohn, "In public policy disputes, with the exception of the labor-management field, there is no rule, no mechanism, no procedure for taking the dispute to mediation. Where these kinds of cases have gone to mediation, it has often been through the entrepreneurship or initiative of the mediator's themselves or because the parties were already familiar with mediation. What we're concerned with is establishing a trigger mechanism and an infrastructure so that turning to mediation will not be just a haphazard experience."

To date, statewide offices have been set up in Hawaii, New Jersey, Massachusetts, and Minnesota. They have handled a variety of cases, including farmer-lender disputes in Minnesota and toxic waste disposal disputes in New Jersey. (Information on how to contact the four state offices can be found in Appendix E.)

Who Comes to the Table?

If your community dispute is to have a fair chance of being mediated successfully, you must make sure that all parties to the dispute have the chance to participate. The general rule is to be inclusive, that is, any group affected by the dispute should be represented in the mediation. Lawrence Susskind and Connie Ozawa, who studied the Forest Hills housing dispute, have noted: "the more comprehensive the effort to take account of competing interests, the more stable will be the final agreement (since involved parties are less likely to block the implementation of an agreement they helped to draft)."[9]

Finding all the groups that should be at the table may take some work. Normally, a few groups are obvious and vocal as a dispute develops, and they, of course, should participate. But there may be other groups, not so readily visible, who should also participate and who, if they are not involved, may have the ability to undercut an agreement reached without them.

The mediator and the core members of the mediation group must work to find and bring to the table any nonobvious interest groups. They can do this by informing the community, through the press, that the dispute is going to be mediated and that all interested groups are welcome to participate.

In some cases, you may find a group of community residents who have a stake in the outcome of mediation but do not have an organization to represent them. If the unrepresented interest group were, for example, pet owners, then you could ask the local humane society to represent them.

Once the participating groups are identified, they should each appoint representatives to participate in the mediation. Representatives should be those who can communicate well, who are willing to work cooperatively and patiently with opponents, and who can be trusted to protect the confidentiality of the mediation hearing.

The "rule of inclusiveness" sometimes can lead to another problem: too many chairs at the table. Exactly how many participants is too many will depend on the mediator and the nature of the dispute. Russell Train, former administrator of the Environmental Protection Agency, mediated a case in 1979 involving a plan by Consolidated Edison Company of New York to build a power plant at the base of Storm King Mountain, 40 miles north of New York City. The case involved three environmental groups, four public agencies, and five utility companies. Joining Train at the mediation table were 28 people. Even much smaller, local disputes can involve many parties. In the Atlanta homeless shelter case, mediator Edith Primm had 12 people at the session. "I was 'maxxed' at the church mediation," she recalls. "There is a size beyond which it is too unwieldly to handle."

If you find that your mediation group is growing too big, groups with similar concerns can be asked to share a single representative.

Authority to Represent Group Essential

Representatives of each group must have clear authority to speak for their group in mediation. It is a good idea to get this authority in writing so that everyone at the table can be assured that the others are legitimate spokespeople, and no one will worry that being a participant is a waste of time.

If possible, representatives should also have authority to bind their groups. This way, an agreement worked out in mediation can be final and not conditioned upon representatives going back to their groups and "selling" them on it. In a study of 132 environmental disputes submitted to mediation, when the parties at the table had formal decision-making authority, they were able to reach an agreement in 82 percent of the cases. When the agreements took the form of recommendations to a decision-making body that did not participate in the hearing, the parties reached agreement only 73 percent of the time.[10] Says Edith Primm of the Atlanta Justice Center, "Your group needs to elect you and give you authority to make a deal."

If someone at the mediation table appears authorized to make a deal but the actual authority is unclear, the consequences can be serious. An example of this occurred in 1966 in Rochester, New York, when Eastman Kodak Company was locked in a hostile dispute with local blacks and their supporters over minority hiring practices. Black leaders, frustrated by what they considered Kodak's intransigence, threatened to "make Rochester the Selma of the North" (referring to the civil rights marches in Selma, Alabama, the previous year).[11] The threats were called off only after a two-day negotiation at a motel between black leaders and a Kodak assistant vice-president produced a written agreement committing Kodak to a stepped-up program of job-training. The black group immediately announced the agreement to the press. Two days later, however, Kodak released a statement saying "the person who signed the papers did not have the authority to make an agreement" and that Kodak would not honor it. The effect was disastrous. Black leaders, who said they had been told by Kodak's president that the vice-president with whom they met had authority to represent the company, accused Kodak of bad-faith bargaining. All talks broke down, and the dispute between Kodak and black residents of Rochester continued to escalate.[12]

Dealing with the Press

Most community disputes are matters of intense public interest. Whether a shopping plaza should be built on land zoned for residential use, or whether power boats should be allowed on the bay, the local press will want to cover the story. "Conflict makes good copy," as reporters say, and so—by definition—a dispute over community issues is of interest to the press.

Consequently, even though all participants in mediation agree to resolve a dispute quietly and privately, the local press may continue to view it as of public concern and try to report what is happening in mediation. This problem becomes especially hard to deal with when there are many parties and the hearings last for weeks or months. Leaks to the press quickly can destroy the trust needed for successful mediation.

To deal with this issue, you need to get a firm agreement, preferably in writing, from all participants that absolutely no one will speak to the press during the course of the mediation. If you want, the mediator can be authorized to make occasional public statements as agreed to by all the parties.

"The mediation has to be a protected forum," says Edith Primm. "I tell the parties, 'If you go to the press and tell them what's going on in the mediation, the chances of getting a settlement are next to none.' It's their choice," she continues, "I can't stop a person from being a jackass or a jerk."

When this rule of privacy is violated, mediation can be disrupted. For example, in the Memorial Day Parade dispute, mediator Andrew Thomas set a ground rule at the start of mediation that no participant would speak to the press and that all press contacts would be through the Public Affairs Office of the City of Rochester. "We did have a leak from city hall," Thomas recalls. "Someone in the city told the press about something going on in the mediation. That was bad enough, but what was worse was that we didn't find out the source of the leak right away, and before we did, the veterans group went to the press themselves because they assumed the leak had come from the Peace and Justice people. It took a little while to put everything in order again and regain the trust that was lost."

Fact-Finding

Many community disputes are based not on complex issues of policy, but on facts and projections: how much traffic *will* a new shopping mall generate in our neighborhood? How far from the bay *will* noise from speedboats be audible?

Often, disputing groups come to the mediation table armed with their own set of "facts" derived from experts sympathetic to their position. This is what Susskind and Ozawa refer to as "the battle of the print-outs."[13] To avoid such a battle, it is helpful for representatives of disputing groups to form fact-finding committees and jointly retain independent experts they all respect and whose data they can believe.

Assuring Compliance with Your Agreement

If you are able to reach an agreement of your community dispute through mediation, there are several steps to take to help ensure it will be followed by all concerned. First, unless the participants have firm, written authority to bind their groups, they should go back to their groups and obtain approval of the agreement. This can be done by referendum or through informal meeting. Then, releasing the text of your agreement to the press, after all approval has been received, is a good way to have all participants commit themselves publicly to abide by its terms.

Susskind and Ozawa suggest that the agreement be structured so that required actions are scheduled in alternating fashion, that is, first one side does A and then the other side does B, and then the first side does C, etc. This alternating sequence helps to assure mutual performance.[14]

The question of how to make an agreement legally binding can be handled in various ways. Like agreements in other disputes (see Chapter 7), the agreement in your community dispute can be drafted with the formalities of a legal contract so that, if necessary, it can be enforced in court. Or, as in the Atlanta case discussed earlier, the terms of an agreement—in that case, rules for the operation of a homeless shelter—can be adopted by the legislature and, thus, become law.

Is the Public Left in the Dark?

When community disputes are settled through closed-door mediation, is the public disserved? Some critics have made this charge. To create trust and protect confidentiality, mediation of public disputes are conducted in private. However, the results become public and ultimately have to meet public approval.

"Obviously," says Edith Primm of the Atlanta Justice Center, "the final product of mediation must stand the light of day of public scrutiny. If it does not, the agreement will never hold up."

Community mediation is not the settling of public disputes in private, it is the use of privacy and the skill of the mediator to settle disputes for the benefit of, and ultimate approval of, the public.

Mediating Environmental Disputes

During the last decade, the mediation of environmental disputes has become an important specialty within the broader field of public policy mediation.

Litigation continues to play an important role in resolving environmental disputes. However, the parties most often involved in these cases—environmental groups, private corporations, and government agencies—increasingly have come to acknowledge that litigation, with its focus on relatively narrow issues, is not always the best way for society to work out a consensus on complex environmental questions. These may include how much development should be allowed near national parks, who should be responsible for protecting water quality in a lake bordering several states, and what recreation, if any, should be allowed on wildlife refuges.

FOR EXAMPLE: In the fall of 1985, environmentalists challenged the Minnesota Division of Forestry's practice of spraying herbicides from airplanes over old forests to make room for new trees such as pines and firs. The Sierra Club, People Against Chemical Contamination, and about 50 individuals petitioned the state to study the environmental effect of the spraying, which they said could harm human health, wildlife, forest ecosystems, and the quality of the groundwater.[15]

The state's Department of Natural Resources responded with a report in December, 1985, but the environmentalists charged it was flawed and insufficient. Faced with potential lawsuits, the department turned to the Minnesota Office of Dispute Resolution to see if the dispute could be resolved through mediation. Roger Williams, director of the office, helped locate several mediators with environmental mediation experience.

In February, 1987, both sides agreed to retain Leah Patton of the Seattle-based Mediation Institute to mediate the dispute. The Sierra Club and others set aside plans to sue the state agency, and the state deferred its plans to issue an environmental impact analysis. Representatives of the forestry, chemical, and agricultural industries also agreed to participate in mediation.

During the next four months, the parties held eight full-day mediation sessions. At a two-day retreat ending June 5, an agreement was drafted and signed.

The 12-page agreement calls on the department to protect public health, wildlife, water, and fisheries by reducing the level and impact of herbicide spraying through changes in the way it conducts its tree-regeneration program. It appoints the Minnesota Office of Dispute Resolution to chair a Forest Herbicide Committee to evaluate compliance with the agreement. And it commits all parties to use their best efforts to reach important targets by 1993—such as reducing by 50 percent the number of acres treated with aerial herbicides.

The actual agreement in the above case is reproduced in Appendix F.

Gail Bingham, director of the Program on Environmental Disputes of the Conservation Foundation in Washington, D.C., and author of *Resolving Environmental Disputes*, has described the types of environmental disputes most often submitted to mediation. These are:

Land-use: including neighborhood and housing issues, commercial and urban development, parks and recreation, preservation of agricultural land.

Natural resource management: including fisheries resources, mining, timber management, and wilderness areas.

Water resources: including water supply and quality, flood protection, and thermal effects of power plants.

Energy: including siting small-scale hydroelectric plants, and conversion of power-plant fuel from oil to coal.

Air quality: including application of national air quality and acid rain legislation.

Toxics: including regulation of chemicals, plans to remove asbestos from schools, pesticide policy, and hazardous materials cleanup.[16]

Mediation of environmental disputes has enjoyed a success rate comparable to that of general mediation. In a study of 132 environmental matters in which the parties' objective was to reach an agreement (as opposed to just improving communication), Bingham reports that agreements were reached in 103, or 78 percent, of the cases.[17]

If you find yourself involved in a community dispute that includes environmental issues, you may wish to contact one of the regional or national organizations specializing in this field. They can inform you of similar disputes resolved through mediation or, if you desire, can provide a mediator from their staff, or refer you to an independent mediator who specializes in environmental cases. Fee arrangements for such services will be similar to those of other private dispute resolution firms handling community or business disputes, discussed earlier in this chapter and in Chapter 11. Information on how to contact environmental mediation services will be found in Appendix E.

CHAPTER 13

How to Become a Mediator

"Blessed are the peacemakers"

—Matt. 5:9

If you find you like mediation and think you might make a good mediator yourself, this is the time to get in on the ground floor of this new profession.

As noted earlier, the number of people working as mediators in the United States has increased from just a few thousand a decade ago to about 22,000 today. Most serve as volunteers at public mediation centers; others work for a fee, full- or part-time, in specialized areas such as divorce, business, public policy, or environmental mediation. Though mediator ranks are growing and the profession developing, the situation here is nothing like in China, where there are about a million mediators, some of whom are elected to their positions.

In this country, mediators elect themselves. Though everyone who would mediate must complete a training program, the field is still young and eager to welcome to its ranks anyone who, as David Strawn, chairman of the Florida Supreme Court's Mediation and Arbitration Rules Committee, has said, has the skills of an "intuitive peacemaker."[1]

In this chapter we consider briefly how to become a mediator, either as a volunteer or a paid professional. Actually, this distinction

somewhat misleading, because as we will see, most professionals
gin as volunteers.

Volunteer Opportunities

At the Community Dispute Settlement Program of Delaware County,
Pennsylvania, "volunteers are the backbone" of the program, writes
mediator Anne Richan. There, trained volunteers of varied ages
and backgrounds do all the mediation.

> Approximately thirty men and women ranging from the
> early twenties to over eighty come to the [center] from the
> ranks of teachers, social workers, business people, home-
> makers, administrators, attorneys, carpenters, contractors,
> students, and retirees.[2]

Professor Susan J. Rogers of the John Jay College of Criminal
Justice in New York City recently conducted a pilot study of 50
mediators in New York State. She asked them why they volun-
teered to serve as mediators at their local public mediation centers.
The leading reasons they gave were:

- to help others
- to improve my community
- for personal growth

About one-quarter of the volunteers said they were also preparing
for a possible career in mediation.
   Asked what they like about the work, they replied:

- they enjoy helping the community
- they like the camaraderie with fellow mediators
- the work is challenging and stimulating
- mediating helps "broaden their understanding of people from
  different backgrounds"[3]

Qualifications

What does it take to be a mediator? It does not take a college degree, although statistics show most mediators are college graduates. Neither does it take a background in a particular profession, although many mediators do have backgrounds in law, teaching, and the social sciences.

What it takes is simply the skills to do the job. Some people seem to be born with these skills—the "intuitive peacemakers." Others, by years of experience as managers, educators, counselors, and even (or especially) as parents, develop the skills. Many of these skills were discussed in Chapter 3. They include the ability to listen effectively, to see issues on multiple levels, to persuade without coercing, criticize without demeaning, and to see possible solutions where none were seen before.

Consequently, most public mediation centers set no particular qualifications for people who want to try to become mediators (except, perhaps, a minimum age of 18 and the absence of a criminal record). If you can complete the training program and demonstrate—in the course of an extended apprenticeship—an ability to mediate successfully, the centers will be glad to have you as a mediator.

Getting Trained

Most public mediation centers offer training programs once or twice a year. Anyone may sign up. The training is usually conducted by staff of the local center or by professional trainers hired by the center. Fees to take the training program usually are minimal.

As discussed in Chapter 3, the training consists of about 40 hours of classroom time including lectures and role-plays, and then an extended period of apprenticeship. The classroom portion will usually run for five days in a single week or sometimes be spread over two or three weekends. The apprenticeship lasts longer, usually a couple of months. There needs to be time for you to observe several actual mediation hearings, then co-mediate a few cases with an experienced mediator, and then handle a few cases on your own while being observed. Those who complete the course successfully will be certified by the local center.

To find out when the next training program is scheduled in your community, contact the local public mediation center.

Demand for Mediators

A center's need for new mediators may vary from time to time. Sometimes, a center may have more mediators than cases to hear; at other times, the center may be in short supply of mediators. Every center is delighted, however, to add a skilled person to its list, or panel, of mediators.

Centers are doubly glad to find new mediators with special backgrounds or skills that will help the center meet the needs of disputants. For example, if you have a background in engineering, or construction, or early childhood behavior, or if you speak Spanish or Chinese, this might help the center match you to a case in which these abilities are needed.

Need for Older Mediators

One "specialty" that mediation centers are interested in is age; many centers would like to add more older people to their panels.

The American Bar Association's Standing Committee on Dispute Resolution has identified several "compelling benefits" of having older people serve as mediators. These include:

• Older persons draw on a wealth of life and professional experience which can lend expertise and credibility to them as mediators.

• Older persons may be able to communicate more effectively and gain the trust of their peers more readily than can younger mediators.

• Retired people may be available to mediate on a flexible schedule, including the evening and daytime.

• Older persons trained as mediators gain valuable skills in conflict resolution, which are useful in their own lives.[4]

In 1988, a Congressional forum was held in Washington, D.C., to explore how older people can help mediation grow by becoming mediators (and, in turn, how increased use of mediation can benefit older people). It has often been noted that in other cultures, particularly nonindustrialized societies, older people traditionally play the role of dispute resolver.[5] "I believe that older persons are an 'untapped' and 'overlooked' resource as mediators," writes Arthur Flemming, former Secretary, U.S. Department of Health, Education, and Welfare.[6] If you are an older person, your local public mediation center may be eager to train you as a mediator.

Time Commitment

Public mediation centers generally require no firm time commitment from their volunteers. On average, mediators probably hear one case a month, but some may hear two or three cases and others may go for many months without hearing a case. This all depends on the number of disputes submitted to mediation, the number of mediators available, and the mediator's own schedule.

Professional Opportunities

The number of opportunities for full- or part-time work as a paid mediator is small, but growing. Still, you will need to be something of a self-starter to find your way.

"The way this field is structured," says Barbara Ashley Phillips, president of American Intermediation Service, "we don't have any career track that says you can become a mediator by doing such and such. This is very disappointing." Phillips' firm gets plenty of job applications but uses only about a dozen mediators (and not all of them full-time) to handle its case load.

Another national firm, Endispute, reports a similar situation. "We get applications all the time," says vice-president William Hartgering, "Everyone wants to be a mediator. But like most national services, we use a very small number of mediators and those we do use, besides full-time staff, are on an as-needed basis."

Getting Started

So how do you start making a living as a mediator?

"Go to your local public mediation center," Hartgering advises, "and get yourself trained. Most local centers have very good training programs. That's how I got started." He continues, "Then get some experience doing volunteer mediation and see if you like it and are any good at it. Then, if you want to go on from there, the next step is very hard. You need to go out and set up your own practice as a private mediator. Some people go into the divorce area; others go into the business area."

Hartgering acknowledges that setting up your own mediation practice will not be easy. "Starting up a mediation practice is much harder than starting a legal practice or a medical practice," he says, "because people still don't understand what it is you are offering and you've got to get hired by both sides."

Starting a Business Mediation Practice

Mary S. Alton, president of the Mediation Alternative in St. Paul, Minnesota, may be typical of the sole practitioner who specializes in business mediation. Her practice focuses on non-union employment discrimination and wrongful termination cases, business "divorces," and contract negotiations.

A large part of her practice, and the bread and butter of many private mediators, are cases involving insurance companies. As discussed earlier, many insurance companies find that disputed claims related to personal injury and property damage often can be settled through mediation at considerable savings of time and legal fees. Consequently, developing steady referrals from insurance carriers can be an important part of private mediation practice.

Starting a Divorce Mediation Practice

Those who choose to specialize in divorce mediation may have a somewhat easier time getting established, because the general public is more familiar with the service. As noted earlier, between 2000 to 3000 people today are active as divorce mediators.

As with the business mediator, the easiest and least expensive way to start is by being trained at your local public mediation center. After that, most divorce mediators set up a private practice, either alone or in partnership with a few others. Membership in the Academy of Family Mediators, the Society of Professionals in Dispute Resolution, or other groups listed in Appendix D, will help establish your credentials for the legal community and for your clients. Most referrals will come from lawyers, clergy, social service agencies, and word of mouth.

Building a Practice

As a private mediator, whether in the business or divorce fields, you will also want to contact some of the relevant national or regional dispute services listed in Appendix B to see if you can be placed on the roster of mediators to whom they will refer cases that happen to involve parties living in your community.

"Private practice is hard," acknowledges Hartgering, "but it is the only way to go as the profession is now structured. And people are doing it. They are building independent mediation practices around the country."

"Still," he cautions, "don't leave your day job right away."

Private Training Services

In addition to training through your local public mediation center, several private firms now specialize in mediator training. Their courses cover both business mediation and divorce mediation, as well as other specialty fields like public policy and environmental disputes. These programs generally run for 40 hours over a five-day period. Fees average about 500 dollars. These programs may be more rigorous than the training you would get at most local centers. Some mediators, once they get some experience and decide to pursue the field seriously, take these private training courses as a way of building on the initial training they received at their local centers.

Private training services are listed in Appendix G. You can write any company for a schedule of training sessions during the coming year. Many services hold classes in major cities around the country on a rotating basis.

Becoming a Peacemaker

We began this book by quoting from notes Abraham Lincoln made for a lecture on law he intended to give to a group of lawyers. Lincoln wrote: "Discourage litigation. Persuade your neighbors to compromise whenever you can. Point out to them how the nominal winner is often a real loser—in fees, expenses, and waste of time."[7]

The very next sentence in Lincoln's notes is also of interest. He wrote: "As a peacemaker, the lawyer has a superior opportunity of being a good man. There will still be business enough."[8]

Today, the opportunity to be a peacemaker is open to everyone. If you have the desire and the skill, becoming a mediator will give you that chance. And there is no shortage of disputes. For mediators and for lawyers alike, there still should be "business enough."

Notes

Chapter 1: Why Mediate?

1. Philip Van Doren Stern, ed., *The Writings and Speeches of Abraham Lincoln*, Crown, New York, 1961, p. 15.

2. Joseph T. McLaughlin, "Resolving Disputes in the Financial Community: Alternatives to Litigation," *Arbitration Journal*, vol. 41, September 1986, p. 18.

3. *Final Report of the Board of Directors*, Connecticut ADR Project, Inc., Hartford, Conn., 1988, p. 1.

4. *New York Times*, November 23, 1981, p. C-2.

5. *Alternative Dispute Resolution Report*, Bureau of National Affairs, Washington, D.C., 1988, p. 311 (hereafter cited as *ADR Report*).

6. David M. Trubek et al., "The Costs of Ordinary Litigation," *U.C.L.A. Law Review*, vol. 31, 1983, p. 121.

7. Joe R. Greenhill, "State of the Judiciary Message," quoted in Judy Kurth Dougherty, "Family Mediation—What Does It Mean for Lawyers?", *Texas Bar Journal*, 51, p. 31.

8. Quoted by Warren E. Burger in "Isn't There a Better Way?" *Annual Report on the State of the Judiciary*, Society of Professionals in Dispute Resolution, Washington, D.C., 1982, Occasional Paper no. 82-2, unpaginated.

9. Steven N. Robinson and George R. A. Doumar, "Is It Better to Enter a Tiger's Mouth than a Court of Law?", *Dickinson Journal of International Law*, 5, p. 252, n. 37.

10. Kenneth Cloke, "Politics and Values in Mediation: The Chinese Experience," *Mediation Quarterly*, no. 17, 1987, p. 69.

11. Jerold S. Auerbach, *Justice Without Law?*, Oxford University Press, New York, 1983, p. 25.

12. R. F. Cook, J. A. Roehl, and D. Sheppard, "Neighborhood Justice Centers Field Test: Final Evaluation Report, Executive Summary," Government Printing Office, Washington, D.C., 1980, p. 7.

13. Ibid., pp. 67–68.

14. *Dispute Resolution Act, Statutes at Large* 94, sec. 17 (1980), *U.S. Code*, vol. 28, sec. 2(a)(5).

15. Daniel McGillis, *Community Dispute Resolution Programs and Public Policy*, U.S. Department of Justice, Washington, D.C., 1986, p. 7.

16. *Dispute Resolution Program Directory*, Special Committee on Dispute Resolution, American Bar Association, Washington, D.C., 1987.

17. "Keeping the Power: The Topography of Conflict Resolution," videotape produced by the Community Boards of San Francisco, 1986.

18. Craig McEwen and Richard Maiman, "Small Claims Mediation in Maine: An Empirical Assessment," *Maine Law Review*, vol. 33, 1981, p. 237.

19. Ibid., p. 264.

20. McGillis, p. 68, citing R. Davis, M. Tichane, and D. Grayson, *Mediation and Arbitration as Alternatives to Criminal Prosecution in Felony Arrest Cases*, Vera Institute of Justice, New York, 1980.

21. "Harassment Cases Center of Disputes," *The Daily Record*, Rochester, N.Y., March 24, 1987, p. 1.

22. Anne Richan, "Developing and Funding Community Dispute Settlement Programs," *Mediation Quarterly*, no. 5, 1984, p. 86.

23. David E. Matz, "Why Disputes Don't Go to Mediation," *Mediation Quarterly*, no. 17, 1987, p. 4.

24. Auerbach, *Justice Without Law?*, p. viii.

25. Paul Wahrhaftig, "Nonprofessional Conflict Resolution," in Joseph E. Palenski and Harold M. Launer (eds.), *Mediation Contexts and Challenges*, Charles C. Thomas, Springfield, Ill., 1986, p. 47.

(The notion of "wrestling back control" can be taken too far. In 1984, to avoid litigation—and to attract a great deal of publicity—rock star, Cyndi Lauper, and her former advisor, Captain Lou Albano, hired women wrestlers to fight it out in a 15-minute match at Madison Square Garden. *National Law Journal*, August 8, 1984, p.47.)

26. *Annual Report of the Institute for Civil Justice, 1988–1989*, The RAND Corp., Santa Monica, Cal., 1989, p. 46.

27. Pat Samples, "Sidestepping the Court System," *USAir Magazine*, November 1987, p. 12.

28. Kenneth Cloke and Angus Strachan, "Mediation and Prepaid Legal Plans," *Mediation Quarterly*, no. 18, 1987, p. 94.

29. Mario M. Cuomo, "The Truth of the 'Middle Way,' " *Arbitration Journal*, vol. 39, September 1984, p. 4, citing remark by Justice Holmes.

30. Sam Howe Verhovek, "Pact Reached in Collapse of Building," *New York Times*, November 16, 1988, p. B-2. An account of this case also appears in *ADR Report*, vol. 2, December 8, 1988, p. 419.

31. Warren Burger, "Our Vicious Legal Spiral," *Judges Journal*, vol. 16, fall 1977, pp. 22, 49, quoted, in part, in Nancy H. Rogers and Richard A. Salem, *A Student's Guide to Mediation and the Law*, Matthew Bender & Co., New York, 1987, p. 41, n. 5.

32. Jay Folberg and Alison Taylor, *Mediation*, Jossey-Bass, San Francisco, 1984, p. 251.

33. *ADR Report*, vol. 2, August 4, 1988, p. 268.

34. *Wall Street Journal*, October 6, 1988, p. B7.

35. *ADR Report*, vol. 2, August 18, 1988, p. 287.

Chapter 2: Which Disputes Should You Mediate?

1. Nancy H. Rogers and Richard A. Salem, *A Student's Guide to Mediation and the Law*, Matthew Bender, New York, 1987, pp. 41–59.

2. *ADR Report*, vol. 2, June 9, 1988, p. 209.

3. Jack Ethridge, "Mending Fences: Mediation in the Community," in Levin, *et al.* (eds.) *Dispute Resolution Devices in a Democratic Society*. (Final Report of the 1985 Chief Justice Earl Warren Conference on Advocacy in the United States). The Roscoe Pound-American Trial Lawyers Foundation, Washington, D.C., 1985, p. 76.

4. Larry Ray with Anne L. Clare, "The Multi-Door Courthouse Idea, Building the Courthouse of the Future . . . Today," 1 *Ohio State Journal of Dispute Resolution*, vol. 1, 1985, pp. 15–16.

5. David M. Trubek et al., "The Costs of Ordinary Litigation," *U.C.L.A. Law Review*, vol. 31, 1983, p. 91.

6. Ibid., p. 90.

7. Joe R. Greenhill, "State of the Judiciary Message," quoted in Judy Kurth Dougherty, "Family Mediation—What Does It Mean for Lawyers?", *Texas Bar Journal*, vol. 51, no. 1, January 1988, p. 31.

8. Robert Coulson, "Remarks to the Fifteenth Anniversary Luncheon of the Center for Dispute Settlement," Rochester, N.Y., September 27, 1988.

9. "Settlement Weeks Stress Mediation, Not Litigation," *Bar Leader*, American Bar Association, Chicago, Ill., November–December, 1988, p. 31.

10. *Annual Report of the Community Dispute Resolution Centers Program, 1987–1988*, N.Y. State Office of Court Administration, Albany, N.Y., 1988, p. 3.

11. *Community Mediation in Massachusetts, 1975–1985*, Administrative Office of the District Court, Salem, Mass., 1986, app. E, p. 183.

12. *ADR Report*, vol. 2, April 28, 1988, p. 168.

13. Craig McEwen and Richard Maiman, "Small Claims Mediation in Maine: An Empirical Assessment," *Maine Law Review*, vol. 33, 1981, p. 237.

Chapter 3: What Your Mediator Does

1. Jerome T. Barrett, "The Psychology of a Mediator," Society of Professionals in Dispute Resolution, Washingtron, D.C., 1983, occasional paper no. 83-1, unpaginated.

2. "Mediation Centers Reach Sixty Counties," *New York Mediator*, Community Dispute Resolution Centers Program, Fall/Winter 1987–1988, no. 2, p. 1.

3. *Community Mediation in Massachusetts, 1975–1985*, Administrative Office of the District Court, Salem, Mass., 1986, p. 29.

4. Ibid., p. 21.

5. Susan J. Rogers, "The Dynamics of Conflict Behavior in a Mediated Dispute," *Mediation Quarterly*, no. 18, 1987, p. 67.

6. Ibid.

7. Jeanne M. Brett, Rita Drieghe, and Debra L. Shapiro, "Mediator Style and Mediation Effectiveness," *Negotiation Journal*, vol. 2, July 1986, p. 277.

8. *ADR Report*, vol. 2, July 7, 1988, p. 246.

9. "Ethical Standards of Professional Responsibility," Society of Professionals in Dispute Resolution, Washington, D.C., 1986, sec. 3.

10. Ibid.

11. *Texas Civil Practice and Remedies Code Annotated*, Vernon, Tex., 1986, Sec. 154.053, (b).

12. Ibid., Sec. 154.073, (b).

13. *ADR Report*, vol. 1, September 17, 1987, p. 213.

Chapter 4: How to Start Your Case

1. Daniel McGillis, *Community Dispute Resolution Programs and Public Policy*, U.S. Department of Justice, Washington, D.C., 1986, p. 91.

2. *Dispute Resolution Program Directory*, Special Committee on Dispute Resolution, American Bar Association, Washington, D.C., 1987, introduction.

3. McGillis, p. 84, n. 7.

4. *Time*, August 29, 1988, p. 50.

5. Neil B. McGillicuddy, Gary L. Welton, and Dean G. Pruitt, "Third-Party Intervention: A Field Experiment Comparing Three Different Models," *Journal of Personality and Social Psychology*, no. 1, 1987, p. 104.

6. See, e.g., R. F. Cook, J. A. Roehl, and D. Sheppard, *Neighborhood Justice Centers Field Test: Final Evaluation Report, Executive Summary*, Government Printing Office, Washington, D.C., 1980, p. 8; and *Annual Report*, 1987–1988, Community Dispute Resolution Centers Program, Albany, N.Y., p. 75.

7. Maria R. Volpe and Charles Bahn, "Resistance to Mediation: Understanding and Handling It," *Negotiation Journal*, no. 3, 1987, p. 302.

8. Anne Richan, "Developing and Funding Community Dispute Settlement Programs," *Mediation Quarterly*, no. 5, 1984, p. 81.

9. S. Merry and S. Silbey, "What Do Plaintiffs Want? Reexamining the Concept of Dispute," *The Justice System Journal*, no. 9, 1984, p. 153. Cited by David E. Matz, "Why Disputes Don't Go to Mediation," *Mediation Quarterly*, no. 17, 1987, p. 4.

10. *ADR Report*, vol. 2, June 9, 1988, p. 209.

11. McGillis, p. 47.

12. Ibid., p. 44.

Chapter 5: Preparing Your Case

1. Linda Hack, "Model Legislation," *Mediation Quarterly*, no. 18, 1987, p. 16.

Chapter 6: Inside the Hearing Room

1. Nancy H. Rogers and Richard A. Salem, *A Student's Guide to Mediation and the Law*, Matthew Bender, New York, 1987, p. 13.
2. Christopher Honeyman, "Five Elements of Mediation," *Negotiation Journal*, vol. 4, no. 2, April 1988, p. 153.
3. Vivian Einstein, *Conflict Resolution*, West Publishing Co., St. Paul, Minn., 1985, p. 73.
4. Anne Richan, "Developing and Funding Community Dispute Settlement Programs, *Mediation Quarterly*, no. 5, 1984, p. 79.

Chapter 7: Writing an Agreement That Works

1. Ernie Odom, "The Mediation Hearing: A Primer," in Joseph E. Palenski and Harold M. Launer (eds.), *Mediation: Contexts and Challenges*, Charles C. Thomas, Springfield, Ill., 1986, p. 13 (emphasis added).
2. Henry Weihofen, *Legal Writing Style*, West Publishing Co., St. Paul, Minn., 1980, p. 64.
3. *Minnesota Civil Mediation Act*, Sec. 572.35, (1).
4. Odom, p. 14.
5. Christopher W. Moore, *The Mediation Process*, Jossey-Bass, San Francisco, 1986, p. 260.

Chapter 8: If No Agreement Is Reached: The Arbitration Option

1. Craig McEwen and Richard Maiman, "Small Claims Mediation in Maine: An Empirical Assessment," *Maine Law Review*, vol. 33, 1981, p. 264.
2. David D. Siegel, *Handbook on New York Practice*, West Publishing Co., St. Paul, Minn., 1978, p. 827.
3. Amy Bermar, "Resolving Disputes Without the Courts," *Boston Globe*, July 21, 1988, p. 43.
4. "A Commercial Arbitration Guide for Business People," American Arbitration Association, New York, 1985, p. 11.
5. "Commercial Arbitration Rules," American Arbitration Association, New York, 1985, p. 13.
6. "A Guide for Commercial Arbitrators," American Arbitration Association, New York, 1985, p. 16.

Chapter 9: Case Completed: Assuring Your Satisfaction

1. Cathleen Cover Payne, "Enforceability of Mediated Agreements," *Ohio State Journal on Dispute Resolution*, vol. 1, 1986, p. 386, n. 12.

Chapter 10: Divorce Mediation

1. Joan B. Kelly and Lynn Gigy, "Divorce Mediation: Characteristics of Clients and Outcomes," in K. Kressel and D. Pruitt, (eds.), *Mediation Research: The Process and Effectiveness of Third-Party Intervention*, (Jossey-Bass, San Francisco, 1989), p. 11, (hereafter cited as Kelly and Gigy, "Characteristics").

2. Ibid., p. 6; and Joan B. Kelly, Lynn Gigy, and Sheryl Hausman, "Mediated and Adversarial Divorce: Initial Findings from a Longitudinal Study," in *Divorce Mediation*, Jay Folberg and Ann Milne (eds.), Guilford Press, New York, 1988, pp. 457, 460, (hereafter cited as Kelly, Gigy, and Hausman, "Initial Findings").

3. Kelly and Gigy, "Characteristics," p. 10.

4. John Haynes, "Mediated Negotiations: The Function of the Intake," *Mediation Quarterly*, no. 6, 1984, p. 10.

5. Katheryn M. Dutenhaver, "Qualifications of Family Mediators," *Mediation Quarterly*, no. 19, 1988, p. 3, n. 6.

6. Haynes, p. 12.

7. Judith S. Wallerstein, "Children After Divorce," *New York Times Magazine*, January 22, 1989, p. 20.

8. *ADR Report*, vol. 2, September 1, 1988, p. 304.

9. Kelly, Gigy, and Hausman, "Initial Findings," p. 461.

10. Ibid., p. 465.

11. *ADR Report*, vol. 2, September 1, 1988, p. 305.

12. Howard Yahm, "Divorce Mediation: A Psychoanalytic Perspective," *Mediation Quarterly*, no. 6, 1984, p. 62.

13. Karen L. Schneider and Myles J. Schneider, *Divorce Mediation*, Acropolis Books, Washington, D.C., 1984.

14. Kelly and Gigy, "Characteristics," p. 25.

15. Kelly, Gigy, and Hausman, "Initial Findings," pp. 463, 467.

16. "Standards of Practice for Lawyer Mediators in Family Disputes," *Summary of the Actions of the House of Delegates, Reports of Sections 22–23*, American Bar Association, Chicago, 1984, Standard V.

17. Joseph P. Folger and Sydney E. Bernard, "Divorce Mediation: When Mediations Challenge the Divorcing Parties," *Mediation Quarterly*, no. 10, 1985, p. 19.

18. Kelly and Gigy, "Characteristics," pp. 17, 19, 20, 26.

19. Kelly, Gigy, and Hausman, "Initial Findings," p. 470.

20. Kelly and Gigy, "Characteristics," pp. 17, 18.

21. Robert E. Emery and Melissa M. Wyer, "Divorce Mediation," *American Psychologist*, May 1987, p. 477.

22. Folger and Bernard, p. 10.

23. John Haynes, p. 11.

Chapter 11: Business Mediation

1. *Arbitration Times*, summer/fall 1987, p. 2.

2. Jerold S. Auerbach, *Justice Without Law?*, Oxford University Press, New York, 1983, p. 5.

3. Joseph T. McLaughlin, "Resolving Disputes in the Financial Community: Alternatives to Litigation," *Arbitration Journal*, vol. 41, September, 1986, p. 19, citing James F. Henry, "Use of Minitrial Seeks to Ease Burden of Corporate Litigation," *Washington Post*, October 13, 1985, p. D-4.

4. Ibid., pp. 19, 20.

5. James F. Henry and Jethro K. Lieberman, *The Manager's Guide to Resolving Legal Disputes*, Harper & Row, New York, 1985, p. 154.

6. *New York Times*, February 17, 1989, p. B5.

7. Lewis D. Solomon and Janet Stern Solomon, "Using Alternative Dispute Resolution Techniques to Settle Conflicts Among Shareholders of Closely Held Corporations," *Wake Forest Law Review*, vol. 22, spring 1987, p. 105.

8. *New York Times*, p. B5.

9. *ADR Report*, vol. 2, September 1, 1988, p. 300.

10. Robert Coulson, *Business Mediation: What You Need to Know*, American Arbitration Association, New York, 1988, p. 59–60.

11. Ibid., p. 77.

12. Lester Edelman and Frank Carr, "The Mini-Trial: An Alternative Dispute Resolution Procedure," *Arbitration Journal*, vol. 42, March 1987, p. 14. The discussion of mini-trial procedures in the text is based in part on this article.

13. "Tell It to the Rent-a-Judge," *Time*, August 29, 1988, p. 50.

14. Adam J. Conti and Judy C. Cohn, "An Internal Corporate Mediation Program," *Employment Relations Today*, Spring 1988, p. 56.

15. Ibid., pp. 60, 61.

Chapter 12: Mediating Community Disputes

1. *ADR Report*, vol. 1, October 15, 1987, p. 253. The discussion of this case in the text is based on this article by Edith B. Primm.

2. Edwin Newman, "Interview with Saul Alinsky," *Speaking Freely*, Station WXXI, June 16, 1972.

3. *ADR Report*, vol. 1, April 30, 1987, p. 22.

4. Lawrence Susskind and Connie Ozawa, "Mediating Public Disputes: Obstacles and Possibilities," *Journal of Social Issues*, no. 2, 1985, p. 153.

5. *Fort Worth Star Telegram*, December 19, 1987, p. 21.

6. *ADR Report*, vol. 2, October 27, 1988, p. 381. The discussion of this case in the text is based largely on this account.

7. *Fort Worth Star Telegram*, pp. 21, 22.

8. *ADR Report*, vol. 2, October 27, 1988, p. 383.

9. Susskind and Ozawa, p. 157.

10. Gail Bingham, *Resolving Environmental Disputes*, The Conservation Foundation, Washington, D.C., 1986, p. xxi.

11. P. David Finks, *The Radical Vision of Saul Alinsky*, Paulist Press, New York, 1984, p. 206,

12. Ibid., pp. 208, 221.

13. Susskind and Ozawa, p. 149.

14. Ibid., p. 158.

15. "Resolving Minnesota's Forestry Dispute," *Dispute Resolution Forum*, National Institute for Dispute Resolution, Washington, D.C., December, 1987, p. 10. The discussion of this case in the text is based largely on this account.

16. Bingham, p. xviii.

17. Ibid., p. xxi.

Chapter 13: How to Become a Mediator

1. *ADR Report*, vol. 2, March 31, 1988, p. 110.

2. Anne Richan, "Developing and Funding Community Dispute Settlement Programs," *Mediation Quarterly*, no. 5, 1984, p. 84.

3. Susan J. Rogers, "Research on Volunteer Mediators," unpublished. Dr. Rogers is now conducting a more extensive study of mediators in 10 centers in New York State. The study, funded by the State Justice Institute, will cover 350 mediators and explore factors that affect the retention and productivity of community mediators.

4. *Mediation: The Coming of Age*, American Bar Association Standing Committee on Dispute Resolution, Washington, D.C., 1988, p. 21.

5. Daniel McGillis, *Community Dispute Resolution Programs and Public Policy*, U.S. Department of Justice, Washington, D.C., 1986, p. 35.

6. *Mediation: The Coming of Age*, p. 21.

7. Philip Van Doren Stern, ed., *The Writings and Speeches of Abraham Lincoln*, Crown, New York, 1961, p. 15.

8. Ibid.

Selected Bibliography

Alper, Benedict S. and Nichols, Lawrence T. *Beyond the Courtroom*. Lexington, Mass.: D.C. Heath and Co., 1981.

Auerbach, Jerold S. *Justice Without Law?* New York: Oxford University Press, 1983.

Bingham, Gail. *Resolving Environmental Disputes*. Washington, D.C.: The Conservation Foundation, 1986.

Blades, Joan. *Mediate Your Divorce*. Englewood Cliffs, N.J.: Prentice-Hall, 1985.

Coogler, O.J. *Structured Mediation in Divorce Settlement*. Lexington, Mass.: Lexington Books, 1978.

Coulson, Robert. *Business Mediation: What You Need to Know*. New York: American Arbitration Association, 1988.

Einstein, Vivian. *Conflict Resolution*. St. Paul, Minn.: West Pub. Co., 1985.

Evarts, W. Richard; Grenstone, James L.; Kirkpatrick, Gary J.; and Leviton, Sharon C. *Winning Through Accommodation*. Dubuque, Iowa: Kendall/Hunt, 1983.

Finks, P. David. *The Radical Vision of Saul Alinsky*. New York: Paulist Press, 1984.

Folberg, Jay, and Taylor, Alison. *Mediation*. San Francisco: Jossey-Bass, 1984.

Folberg, Jay, and Milne, Ann, eds. *Divorce Mediation*. New York: Guilford Press, 1988.

Goldberg, Stephen B.; Green, Eric D.; and Sander, Frank E. A. *Dispute Resolution*. Boston: Little, Brown and Co., 1985.

Haynes, John M. *Divorce Mediation*. New York: Springer Pub. Co., 1981.

Henry, James F., and Lieberman, Jethro, K. *The Manager's Guide to Resolving Legal Disputes*. New York: Harper & Row, 1985.

Knebel, Fletcher, and Clay, Gerald S. *Before You Sue*. New York: William Morrow, 1987.

Krantz, Martin. *Getting Apart Together*. San Luis Obispo, Calif.: Impact, 1987.

Kressel, K., and Pruitt, D., eds. *Mediation Research: The Process and Effectiveness of Third-Party Intervention*. San Francisco: Jossey-Bass, 1989.

Lieberman, Jethro. *The Litigious Society*. New York: Basic Books, 1981.

McGillis, Daniel. *Community Dispute Resolution Programs and Public Policy*. Washington, D.C.: U.S. Department of Justice, 1986.

Moore, Christopher W. *The Mediation Process*. San Francisco: Jossey-Bass, 1986.

Palenski, Joseph E., and Launer, Harold M. edt. *Mediation Contexts and Challenges*. Springfield, Ill.: Charles C. Thomas, 1986.

Rogers, Nancy H., and Salem, Richard A. *A Student's Guide to Mediation and the Law*. New York: Matthew Bender, 1987.

Schneider, Karen L., and Schneider, Myles J. *Divorce Mediation*. Washington, D.C.: Acropolis Books, 1984.

Special Committee on Dispute Resolution. *Dispute Resolution Program Directory*. Washington, D.C.: American Bar Association, 1986.

Stern, Philip Van Doren, ed. *The Writings and Speeches of Abraham Lincoln*. New York: Crown, 1961.

Ury, William L.; Brett, Jeanne M.; and Goldberg, Stephen B. *Getting Disputes Resolved*. San Francisco: Jossey-Bass, 1988.

PART
FOUR

Appendixes

APPENDIX
A

Guide to Public Mediation Centers

The following list is based in part on information compiled by the Standing Committee on Dispute Resolution of the American Bar Association.

Alaska

Peninsula Mediation
PO Box 1044
Homer, AK 99602

Arizona

Community Mediation
  Program
423 North Tucson Blvd.
Tucson, AZ 85716
(602) 323-1706

Community Mediation
  Program of Our Town
  Family Center
PO Box 26504
Tucson, AZ 85726

Arkansas

Humanist as Mediator/
  Arbitrator
University of Arkansas at Little
  Rock
33rd and University
Little Rock, AR 72204
(501) 569-3000

Small Claims Program
Little Rock Municipal Court
Markham and Spring Sts.
102 Pulaski County
  Courthouse
Little Rock, AR 72201
(501) 372-8510

California

Berkeley Dispute Resolution
   Service
1771 Alcatraz Ave.
Berkeley, CA 94703

Arts Arbitration and Mediation
   Services
California Lawyers for the Arts
315 West Ninth St.
Los Angeles, CA 90015
(213) 747-9453

Hearing Officer Program
D.A.'s Office
320 West Temple, Rm. 780-23
Los Angeles, CA 90012
(213) 974-7401

Los Angeles City Attorney
   Program
1700 City Hall East
200 North Main Street
Los Angeles, CA 90012
(213) 485-5471

Dispute Resolution Center of
   the Eastern Sierra, Inc.
Old Mammoth Mall, Suite 213
PO Box 2535
Mammoth Lakes, CA 93546

Family Court Services of the
   Superior Court
928 Main St.
Martinez, CA 94553
(415) 372-2681

Mountain View Tenant/
   Landlord Service
650 Castro

Mountain View, CA 94041
(415) 856-4062

Rental Housing Mediation
   Task Force
Human Relations Commission
City of Palo Alto
PO Box 10250
Palo Alto, CA 94303
(415) 329-2375

Community Dispute
   Resolution Center
330 South Oak Knoll Ave.
Pasadena, CA 91101
(818) 793-7174

Sacramento Neighborhood
   Mediation Center
PO Box 5275
Sacramento, CA 95817
(916) 739-7069

Community Mediation
   Programs
San Diego Law Center
Alcala Park
San Diego, CA 92110
(619) 260-4815

Golden Hill Mediation Center
1004-24th St.
San Diego, CA 92102
(619) 238-1022

Arts Arbitration and
   Mediation Services
California Lawyers for the Arts
Fort Mason Center, B-300
San Francisco, CA 94123
(415) 775-7715

The Community Board
  Program
149 Ninth St.
San Francisco, CA 94103
(415) 552-1250

Community Dispute Services
American Arbitration
  Association
445 Bush St.
San Francisco, CA 94108
(415) 434-2200

Neighborhood Mediation and
  Conciliation Services
70 West Hedding St.
San José, CA 95110
(408) 299-2206

San Mateo Neighborhood
  Boards Program
Peninsula Conflict Resolution
  Center
177 Bovet Rd.
San Mateo, CA 94402

Mediation Services
Administration Bldg.
Civic Center, Rm. 243
San Rafael, CA 94903

Program for Consumer Affairs
701 Ocean St., Rm. 240
Santa Cruz, CA 95060
(408) 425-2054

Neighborhood Justice Center
1320-C Santa Monica Mall
Santa Monica, CA 90401
(213) 451-8192

Community Boards Program of
  the Monterey Peninsula
PO Box 1538
Seaside, CA 93955
(408) 394-1992

Colorado

CDR Associates
100 Arapahoe
Boulder, CO 80302
(303) 442-7367
(800) MEDIATE

Neighborhood Justice Center
Office of the District Attorney
326 South Tejon
Colorado Springs, CO 80907
(303) 520-6016

Center for Dispute Resolution
1900 Wazee St.
Denver, CO 80202
(303) 295-2244

Connecticut

Fair Haven Neighborhood
Mediation Program
126 Grand Ave.
New Haven, CT 06513
(203) 787-9586

Delaware

Wilmington Citizen's Dispute
  Settlement Center
800 N. French St.
Wilmington, DE 19801
(302) 571-4200

District of Columbia

Center for Dispute Settlement
1666 Connecticut Ave., NW
Washington, DC 20009
(202) 265-9572

DC Citizen's Complaint and
  Mediation Center
Superior Court Bldg. A
Fifth and F Sts., NW
Washington, DC 20001
(202) 724-8215

14th Street Inter-Agency
  Community Services Center
3031-14th St., NW
Washington, DC 20010
(202) 673-6989

Florida

Citizen Dispute Settlement
  Program
250 N. Wilson Ave.
Bartow, FL 33830
(813) 533-0731

Citizen Dispute Settlement
516 S.E. Fifth Court
Fort Lauderdale, FL 33301
(305) 765-5724

Citizen Dispute Settlement
1700 Monroe St.
Fort Myers, FL 33901
(813) 335-2885

Citizen Dispute Settlement
PO Box 1437
Gainesville, FL 32602
(904) 374-3675

Citizen Dispute Settlement
330 East Bay St.
Jacksonville, FL 32202
(904) 633-6643

Citizen Dispute Settlement
Melbourne Courthouse
50 S. Neiman Ave.
Melbourne, FL 32901
(305) 727-9712

Citizen Dispute Settlement
1500 N.W. 12th St., Rm. 708
Miami, FL 33125
(305) 547-7885

Community Conflict Resolution
  Service
Joseph Caleb Community
  Center
5400 N.W. 22nd Ave.
Miami, FL 33142
(305) 638-6735

Arbitration and Mediation
Collier County Gov't Center
Building A
Naples, FL 33962
(813) 774-8704

Orange County Bar Association
Citizen Dispute Settlement
801 N. Orange Ave.
Orlando, FL 32801
(305) 423-5732

Citizen Dispute Settlement
150 Fifth St., North, Rm. 166
St. Petersburg, FL 33701
(813) 825-1796

Twelfth Circuit Citizen
Dispute Settlement Program
PO Box 48927
Sarasota, FL 34230

Citizen Dispute Settlement
407 East Street
Tampa, FL 33602
(813) 272-5642

Citizen Dispute Settlement
307 N. Dixie Highway
West Palm Beach, FL 33401
(305) 837-3283

Georgia

Justice Center of Atlanta
976 Edgewood Ave., N.E.
Atlanta, GA 30307
(404) 523-8236

Hawaii

Ku'Ikahi YMCA Mediation
Center
300 West Lanikaula St.
Hilo, HI 96720
(808) 935-7844

Neighborhood Justice Center
of Honolulu
200 North Vineyard
Honolulu, HI 96817
(808) 521-6767

Kauai Economic Opportunity
Mediation Board
PO Box 1027
Lihue, HI 96766
(808) 245-7305

Mediation Services of Maui,
Inc.
95 Mahalani St.
Wailuku, HI 96793
(808) 244-5744

Illinois

Neighborhood Justice of
Chicago
53 West Jackson
Chicago, IL 60604
(312) 939-7383

Indiana

Community Justice Center
PO Box 149
Anderson, IN 46015
(317) 649-7341

Community Mediation
609 S. E. Second St.
Evansville, IN 47713
(812) 423-3681

St. Joseph County Night
Prosecutor
County-City Bldg., 10th Fl
South Bend, IN 46601
(219) 284-9201

Iowa

Committee on Criminal Justice
Mediation Program
304 Lynn Ave.
Ames, IA 50010
(515) 292-3820

Community Dispute
Settlement Center
445 First St., S.W.
Cedar Rapids, IA 52404
(319) 398-3693

Polk County Attorney's
Neighborhood Mediation
Center
12th and University
Des Moines, IA 50314
(515) 286-3057

Webster County Mediation
Center
Courthouse
701 Central
Fort Dodge, IA 50501
(515) 955-2773

North Iowa Dispute
Settlement Center
Cerro Gordo County
Courthouse
220 North Washington
Mason City, IA 50401
(515) 421-3119

Sieda Dispute Settlement
Service
226 West Main
Ottumwa, IA 52501
(515) 682-8741

Kansas

Project Early Dispute
Settlement
465 South Parker
Olathe, KS 66061
(913) 764-8585

Kansas Mediation Service
3600 S.W. Burlingame Rd.
Topeka, KS 66611
(913) 267-5622

Kentucky

Kenton-Campbell Pretrial
Office
Kenton Municipal Bldg.
Third and Court Sts.
Covington, KY 41011
(606) 292-6517

Fayette Mediation Program
136 Walnut St.
Lexington, KY 40507
(606) 233-4085

Pretrial Services
514 West Liberty St.
Louisville, KY 40202
(502) 588-4142

Louisiana

State Consumer Protection
Office
PO Box 94455
Capitol Station
Baton Rouge, LA 70804
(504) 925-4401

Maine

Court Mediation Service
PO Box 66 D.T.S.
Portland, ME 04112
(207) 879-4700

Maryland

College Park Community
  Mediation Center
4511 Knox Rd.
College Park, MD 20740
(301) 277-5591

Montgomery County Office of
  Consumer Affairs
100 Maryland Ave.
Rockville, MD 20852
(202) 251-7373

Massachusetts

Mediation Project
University of Massachusetts
425 Amity St.
Amherst, MA 01002
(413) 545-2462

Athol-Orange Community
  Mediation Program
100 Main St.
Athol, MA 01331
(617) 249-4422

Face-to-Face Mediation
  Program
Dep't of Attorney General
131 Tremont St.
Boston, MA 02111

Mediation Clinic
Downtown Center, Law
  Center
University of Massachusetts—
  Boston
Boston, MA 02125
(617) 956-1088

Cambridge Dispute Settlement
  Center
One West St.
Cambridge, MA 02139
(617) 876-5376

Edgartown Mediation Program
Box 1284
Edgartown, MA 02539
(617) 627-8228

Framingham Court Mediation
  Services
600 Concord St.
Framingham, MA 01701
(617) 872-9495

North Essex Mediators
25 Locust St.
Haverhill, MA 01830
(617) 373-1971

Alternative Dispute Resolution
  Program for Greater Lowell
167 Dutton St.
Lowell, MA 01852
(617) 459-0551

Community Mediation Service
19 Sutton St.
Lynn, MA 01901
(617) 598-4874

Quincy District Court
  Mediation Services
One Dennis F. Ryan Parkway
Quincy, MA 02169
(617) 471-1650

Salem Mediation Program
First District Court of Essex
65 Washington St.
Salem, MA 01970
(617) 745-4165

Somerville Mediation Program
One Summer St.
Somerville, MA 02143
(617) 776-5931

Dispute Resolution Project
31 Elm St.
Springfield, MA 01103
(413) 787-6480

Community Mediation Center
340 Main St.
Worcester, MA 01608
(617) 754-5322

Michigan
Dispute Resolution Center of
    Washtenaw County
4133 Washtenaw Rd.
Ann Arbor, MI 48107
(313) 971-6054

Volunteer Mediation Program
Detroit Human Rights Dept.
150 Michigan Ave.
Detroit, MI 48226
(313) 224-4950

"Justice Without Walls"
Human Relations Commission
1101 South Saginaw
Flint, MI 48502
(313) 766-7195

Citizen's Dispute Settlement
    Program
40700 Romeo Plank Rd.
Mt. Clemens, MI 48044
(313) 286-8010

Minnesota
Northland Mediation Service
802 Torrey Bldg.
Duluth, MN 55802
(218) 723-4003

West Suburban Mediation
    Center
32 Tenth Ave., S.
Hopkins, MN 55343
(612) 933-0005

Citizen's Dispute Settlement
    Program
A-1700 Hennepin County
    Govt. Center
Minneapolis, MN 55487
(612) 348-7496

Hawthorn Area Neighborhood
    Dispute Service
2507 Fremont Ave., N.
Minneapolis, MN 55411
(612) 529-6440

Dispute Resolution Center
265 Oneida St.
St. Paul, MN 55102
(612) 290-0790

Mediation Center for Dispute
    Resolution
1821 University Ave.
St. Paul, MN 55104
(612) 644-1453

Missouri

Mediation Program Housing
  Information Center
7546 Troost
Kansas City, MO 64131
(816) 523-6700

Dispute Resolution Program
University of Missouri—St.
  Louis
8100 Natural Bridge
St. Louis, MO 63121
(314) 553-6040

Nebraska

Douglas County Conciliation
  Court
Hall of Justice
Omaha, NE 68183
(402) 444-7168

Nevada

Division of Consumer Affairs
2501 East Sahara Ave.
Las Vegas, NV 89104
(702) 386-5293

New Hampshire

New Hampshire Mediation
  Program
33 Stickney Ave.
Concord, NH 03301
(603) 224-8043

New Jersey

Community Justice Institute
1201 Bacharach Blvd.
Atlantic City, NJ 08401
(609) 345-7267

Bergen County Municipal
  Dispute Program
133 River St.
Hackensack, NJ 07601
(201) 646-3592

Family and Neighborhood
  Dispute Settlement Project
Murdoch Hall
114 Clifton Place
Jersey City, NJ 07306
(201) 451-3404

Comprehensive Justice Center
Burlington Co. Courts Facility
49 Rancocas Rd.
Mt. Holly, NJ 08060
(609) 261-5160

Citizens Dispute Settlement
  Program
129 Church St.
New Brunswick, NJ 08093
(201) 745-3886

Community Dispute
  Resolution Project
Essex County Bar Assoc.
Gateway One, 16th Fl
Newark, NJ 07102
(201) 622-6207

Mercer County Mediation Unit
650 South Broad St.
Trenton, NJ 08650
(609) 989-6081

New Mexico

Mediation Center
1500 Walter St., SE
Albuquerque, NM 87102
(505) 843-9410

New York

Albany Mediation Program
PO Box 9140
Albany, NY 12209
(518) 436-4958

Dispute Settlement Center of
  Orleans County
Orleans County Adm. Bldg.
Route 31
Albion, NY 14411
(716) 589-5673

Dispute Settlement Center of
  Genesee County
Main St.
Batavia, NY 14020
(716) 343-8180

ACCORD, Inc.
The Cutler House
834 Front St.
Binghamton, NY 13901
(607) 724-5153

Brooklyn Mediation Center
210 Joralemon St.
Brooklyn, NY 11201
(718) 834-6671

Dispute Settlement Center
346 Delaware Ave.
Buffalo, NY 14203
(716) 856-7180

Resolve—A Center for
  Dispute Settlement
Stoneleigh Housing, Inc.
120 East Center St.
Canastota, NY 13032
(315) 697-3809

Dispute Settlement Center of
  Allegany and Wyoming
  Counties
PO Box 577
Caneadea, NY 14717
(716) 373-5133

Northern New York Center for
  Conflict Resolution
PO Box 70
Canton, NY 13617
(315) 386-4677

Putnam County Mediation
  Program
PO Box 776
Carmel, NY 10512
(914) 225-9555

Common Ground
PO Box 329
Catskill, NY 12414
(518) 943-9205

Community Mediation Center
356 Middle Country Rd.
Coram, NY 11727
(516) 736-2626

Neighborhood Justice Project
  of the Southern Tier
147 East Second St.
Corning, NY 14830
(607) 936-8807

Cortland County Resolve—A
  Center for Dispute
  Settlement
Charles M. Drum Center
111 Port Watson St.
Cortland, NY 13045
(607) 753-6952

Delaware County Dispute
Resolution Center
72 Main St.
Delhi, NY 13753
(607) 746-6392

Northern New York Center for
Conflict Resolution
Essex County Center
North County Community
College
Elizabethtown, NY 12932
(518) 873-9910

Neighborhood Justice Project
451 East Market St.
Elmira, NY 14901
(607) 734-3338

Tri-County Center for Dispute
Resolution
39 East Main St.
Fonda, NY 12068
(518) 853-4611

Nassau County Community
Dispute Center
585 Stewart Ave.
Garden City, NY 11530
(516) 222-1660

Center for Dispute Settlement
4241 Lakeville Rd.
Geneseo, NY 14454
(716) 243-4410

Center for Dispute Resolution
One Franklin Square
Geneva, NY 14456
(315) 789-0364

Washington County Mediation
Services
5 North St.
Granville, NY 12832
(518) 642-1237

Community Dispute
Resolution Program
c/o Catholic Family and
Community Services
216 Henry St.
Herkimer, NY 13350
(315) 866-4268

Common Ground
PO Box 1
Hudson, NY 12534
(518) 828-4611

Community Dispute
Resolution Center
124 The Commons
Ithaca, NY 14850
(607) 273-9347

Community Mediation
Services
89-64 163rd St.
Jamaica, NY 11432
(718) 523-6868

Dispute Settlement Center of
Chautauqua County
Jamestown Municipal Bldg.
300 East Third St.
Jamestown, NY 14701
(716) 664-4223

Queens Mediation Center
119-45 Union Turnpike
Kew Gardens, NY 11375
(718) 793-1900

Dispute Settlement Center of
  Niagara County
1 Locks Plaza
Lockport, NY 14094
(716) 439-6684

Lewis Mediation Service
5402 Dayan St.
Lowville, NY 13637
(315) 376-7991

Center for Dispute Settlement
26 Church St.
Lyons, NY 14489
(315) 946-9300

Northern New York Center for
  Conflict Resolution
55 West, PO Box 270
Malone, NY 12953
(518) 483-5470

Orange County Mediation
  Project
57 North St.
Middletown, NY 10940
(914) 342-6807

Mediation Alternative Project
100 East Old Country Rd.
Mineola, NY 11051
(516) 741-5580

Mediation Services of Sullivan
  County
PO Box 947
Monticello, NY 12701
(914) 794-3377

Rockland Mediation Center
151 South Main St.
New City, NY 10956
(914) 634-5729

Mediation Services of Ulster
  County
PO Box 726
New Paltz, NY 12561
(914) 691-6944

Institute for Mediation and
  Conflict Resolution
Dispute Resolution Center
425 West 144th St.
New York, NY 10031
(212) 690-5700

Institute for Mediation and
  Conflict Resolution
Manhattan Office
Summons Part of Criminal
  Court
346 Broadway
New York, NY 10007
(212) 766-4230

Institute for Mediation and
  Conflict Resolution
Bronx Office
215 East 161st St.
New York, NY 10451
(212) 590-2380

Community Mediation Project
Washington Heights—Inwood
  Coalition
652 West 187th St.
New York, NY 10033
(212) 781-6722

Dispute Resolution Center for
  Chenango County
Norwich Center Office Plaza
27 West Main St.
Norwich, NY 13815
(607) 336-5442

Dispute Settlement Center of
Cattaraugus County
110 West State St.
Olean, NY 14760
(716) 373-5133

Agree—A Center for Dispute
Settlement
9 South Main St.
Oneonta, NY 13820
(607) 432-5484

Resolve—A Center for
Dispute Settlement
198 West First St.
Oswego, NY 13126
(315) 342-3092

ACCORD
55 North Ave.
Owego, NY 13827
(607) 687-4864

Northern New York Center for
Conflict Resolution
Clinton County Center
Ward Hall, Room 212A
SUNY at Plattsburg
Plattsburg, NY 12901
(518) 564-2327

Community Dispute
Resolution Center
327 Mill St.
Poughkeepsie, NY 12601
(914) 471-7213

Center for Dispute Settlement
87 N. Clinton Ave.
Rochester, NY 14604
(716) 546-5110

Community Dispute
Settlement Program
Law, Order, and Justice
Center
161 Jay St.
Schenectady, NY 12305
(518) 346-1281

Dispute Settlement Program
Moreau Community Center
144 Main St.
South Glens Falls, NY 12801
(518) 793-7015

Staten Island Community
Dispute Resolution Center
130 Stuyvesant Place
Staten Island, NY 10301
(718) 720-9410

Resolve—A Center for
Dispute Settlement
210 East Fayette St.
Lafayette Bldg., 7th Fl.
Syracuse, NY 13202
(315) 471-4676

Dispute Resolution Center
Onondaga County Civic
Center
12th Floor
Syracuse, NY 13202
(315) 425-3053

Community Dispute
Settlement Program
35 State St.
Troy, NY 12180
(518) 274-5920

Community Dispute
  Resolution Program
214 Rutger St.
Utica, NY 13501
(315) 797-6473

Adirondack Mediation Services
c/o Warren County Family
  Court
Warren County Municipal
  Center
Warrensburg, NY 12845
(518) 761-6401

Community Dispute
  Resolution Center
PO Box 899
Watertown, NY 13601
(315) 782-4900

Neighborhood Justice Project
111 9th St.
Watkins Glen, NY 14891
(607) 535-4757

Cayuga County Dispute
  Resolution Center
9021 North Seneca St.
Weedsport, NY 13166
(315) 834-6881

Westchester Mediation Center
201 Palisade Ave.
Yonkers, NY 10703
(914) 963-6500

North Carolina
The Mediation Center
189 College St.
Asheville, NC 28801
(704) 251-6089

Transylvania County Dispute
  Settlement Center
PO Box 1153
Brevard, NC 28712
(704) 884-3614

Orange County Dispute
  Settlement Center
302 Weaver St.
Carrboro, NC 27510
(919) 929-8800

UNC Dispute Settlement
  Center
Assistant Dean of Students
01 Steele Bldg 050A
Chapel Hill, NC 27514
(919) 966-4041

Dispute Settlement Program
817 E. Trade St.
Charlotte, NC 28202
(704) 336-2424

Polk County Dispute
  Settlement Center
PO Box 865
Columbus, NC 28722
(704) 863-2973

Dispute Settlement Center of
  Durham
PO Box 2321
Durham, NC 27702
(919) 683-1978

Cumberland County Dispute
  Resolution Center
310 Green St.
Fayetteville, NC 28301
(919) 486-9465

Goldsboro/Wayne Dispute
    Settlement Center
1309 East Walnut St.
Goldsboro, NC 27530
(919) 735-6121

Alamance County Dispute
    Settlement Center
PO Box 982
Graham, NC 27253
(919) 227-9808

Guilford County Dispute
    Settlement Center
1105 E. Wendover Ave.
Greensboro, NC 27405
(919) 273-5667

Henderson County Dispute
    Settlement Center
140 Fourth Ave. West
Hendersonville, NC 28793
(704) 697-7055

Robeson County Dispute
    Resolution Center
207 E. 14th St.
Lumberton, NC 28358
(919) 488-0354

Chatham County Dispute
    Settlement Center
PO Box 1151
Pittsboro, NC 27312
(919) 542-4075

Mediation Services of Wake,
    Inc.
Box 1462
Raleigh, NC 27602
(919) 821-1296

Piedmont Mediation Center
PO Box 169
Statesville, NC 28677
(704) 873-7624

Neighborhood Justice Center
PO Box 436
Winston-Salem, NC 27102
(919) 724-2870

Ohio

Private Complaint Program
Hamilton County Justice
    Center
1000 Sycamore St.
Cincinnati, OH 45202
(513) 763-5130

Mediation Program
Office of the Prosecutor
1200 Ontario St.
Cleveland, OH 44113
(216) 664-4800

Community Youth Mediation
    Program
3000 Bridge Ave.
Cleveland, OH 44113
(216) 771-7297

Night Prosecutor's Program
Municipal Court Bldg.
375 South High St.
Columbus, OH 43215
(614) 222-7483

Small Claims Division
Franklin County Municipal
    Court
375 South High St.
Columbus, OH 43215
(614) 222-7381

Night Prosecutor's Program
Safety Bldg.
335 West Third St.
Dayton, OH 45402
(513) 443-4400

Newark Night Prosecutor
    Program
Law Director, City of Newark
40 West Main St.
Newark, OH 43055

Citizens Dispute Settlement
    Program
555 North Erie St.
Toledo, OH 43624
(419) 245-1951

Oklahoma

Oklahoma City Dispute
    Mediation Service
1613 North Broadway
Oklahoma City, OK 73103
(405) 236-0413

Citizen Complaint Center,
    Multi-Door Project
1446 S. Boston St.
Tulsa, OK 74119
(918) 584-5243

Early Settlement—A Pre-
    Court Hearing Program
600 Civic Center
Tulsa, OK 74103
(918) 592-7786

Oregon

Community Mediation Board
PO Box 11222
Eugene, OR 97440
(503) 683-5574

Neighborhood Mediation
    Center
4815 N.E. Seventh
Portland, OR 97211
(503) 243-7320

Pennsylvania

Community Dispute
    Settlement
Program of Delaware County
884-B Main St.
Darby, PA 19023
(215) 532-2375

Bucks County Mediation
    Service
William Penn Center
9300 New Falls Rd.
Fallsington, PA 19054
(215) 295-8154

Mediation Center
900 East King St.
Lancaster, PA 17603
(717) 397-1137

Dispute Resolution Program
Commission on Human
    Relations
601 City Hall Annex
Philadelphia, PA 19107
(215) 686-2872

Mediation Program
Good Shepherd Neighborhood
  House
5356 Chew Ave.
Philadelphia, PA 19138
(215) 843-5413

Small Claims Mediation
  Program
Philadelphia Municipal Court
City Hall Annex
Philadelphia, PA 19107
(215) 686-2974

Eastern Pennsylvania
  Mediation Service
105 W. Chestnut St.
Souderton, PA 18964
(215) 721-1813

Puerto Rico

Dispute Resolution Center
San Juan Judicial Center
PO Box 887, Hato Rey Station
San Juan, Puerto Rico 00919
(809) 763-4813

Tennessee

Baptist Center Dispute
  Program
1230 West Scott St.
Knoxville, TN 37921
(615) 525-9068

Citizen's Dispute Office
Pretrial Services
201 Poplar Ave.
Memphis, TN 38103
(901) 576-2520

Texas

Dispute Mediation Service of
  Dallas
3310 Live Oak
Dallas, TX 75204
(214) 821-4380

Dispute Resolution Services of
  Tarrant County
1300 Summit St.
Fort Worth, TX 76102
(817) 877-4554

Dispute Resolution Centers
Criminal Courts Bldg.
301 San Jacinto
Houston, TX 77001
(713) 221-8274

Bexar County Mediation
  Center
212 Stumberg
San Antonio, TX 78204
(512) 220-2128

Utah

Rental Dispute Mediation
637 East 400 South
Salt Lake City, UT 84102
(801) 328-8891

Vermont

Burlington Mediation Center
135 College St.
Burlington, VT 05401
(802) 864-0904

Dispute Resolution Clinic
659 Elm St.
Montpelier, VT 05602
(802) 229-0516

Virginia

Community Mediation Center
280 Green St.
Harrisonburg, VA 22801
(703) 434-0059

Dispute Resolution Center
701 East Franklin St.
Richmond, VA 23219
(804) 343-7355

Washington

Northwest Mediation Service
405-144th Ave., S.E.
Bellevue, WA 98004

Dispute Resolution Center of
  Snohomish County
PO Box 839
Everett, WA 98206
(206) 339-1335

Dispute Resolution Center of
  Seattle-King County
PO Box 21148
Seattle, WA 98111
(206) 329-3944

Wisconsin

Try Mediation, Inc.
721 Oxford Ave.
Eau Claire, WI 54703
(715) 839-6995

Milwaukee Mediation Center
436 West Wisconsin Ave.
Milwaukee, WI 53203
(414) 271-2512

Dispute Settlement Center of
Racine County
730 Wisconsin Ave.
Racine, WI 53403
(414) 636-3277

Waukesha County Mediation
  Program
414 West Moreland Blvd.
Waukesha, WI 53188
(414) 544-5431

APPENDIX
B

Guide to Private Dispute Resolution Services

Many of the services listed below are private, for-profit firms that specialize in business-related disputes.

Agreement, Inc.
18 Border Road
Needham, MA 02192
(617) 444-2346

American Arbitration
   Association
140 West 51st St.
New York, NY 10020
(212) 484-4000
(Regional offices in 32 cities.)

American Intermediation
   Service
One Montgomery St., Suite
   2100
San Francisco, CA 94104
(415) 788-6253
(Other locations in Los
   Angeles, CA; Riverside,

CT; Chicago, IL; and
   Philadelphia, PA.)

American Mediation
   Resources, Inc.
PO Box 71314
Marietta, GA 30007
(404) 256-3409

Americord, Inc.
Suite 375 Renaissance Square
512 Nicollet Mall
Minneapolis, MN 55402
(614) 344-1999

Arbitration Forums, Inc.
200 White Plains Rd.
Tarrytown, NY 10591
(914) 332-4770
(800) 426-8889

Arbitration Mediation
International, Inc.
Radice Corporate Center
1000 Corporate Drive
Fort Lauderdale, FL 33334
(305) 938-9100

CDR Associates
100 Arapahoe
Boulder, CO 80302
(303) 442-7367
(800) MEDIATE

Center for Dispute Settlement
1666 Connecticut Ave., NW
Washington, DC 20009
(202) 265-9572

Center for Public Resources
680 Fifth Ave.
New York, NY 10019
(212) 541-9830

Construction Mediation, Inc.
PO Box 181
Huntington, NY 11743
(516) 271-7697

Dispute Resolution, Inc.
Suite 508
179 Allyn Street
Hartford, CT 06103
(203) 724-0861

Endispute, Inc.
1820 Jefferson Place, N.W.
Washington, DC 20036
(202) 429-8782
(Other locations in Chicago,
   IL; New York, NY; and
   Cambridge, MA.)

David S. Foster
PO Box 52389
Lafayette, LA 70505
(318) 232-9313

Judicate, Inc.
1608 Walnut St.
Philadelphia, PA 19103
(215) 546-6200
(800) 631-9900

Judicial Arbitration &
   Mediation Services, Inc.
500 N. State College Blvd.
Orange, CA 92668
(714) 939-1300
(Other locations in San Diego,
   San Bernardino, Los
   Angeles, Sacramento,
   Fresno, and San Francisco,
   CA.)

Judicial Conference Mediators
5860 S. Wood Sorrel Dr.
Littleton, CO 80123
(303) 798-7244

Kansas Mediation Service
3600 S.W. Burlingame Rd.
Topeka, KS 66611
(913) 267-5622

Lemmon Mediation Institute
5248 Boyd Ave.
Oakland, CA 94618
(415) 547-8089

The Mediation Alternative
23 Empire Drive
St. Paul, MN 55103
(612) 223-8662

The Mediation Group
47 Eliot St.
Brookline, MA 02167
(617) 277-9232

National Center Associates
3924 N. 32nd St.
Tacoma, WA 98407
(206) 759-3039

Resolve Dispute Management,
    Inc.
Seven East Huron
Chicago, IL 60611
(312) 943-7477

Settlement Consultants
    International, Inc.
14330 Midway Rd., Suite 108
Dallas, TX 75244
(214) 661-3771

United States Arbitration and
    Mediation, Inc.
525 Westland Bldg.
100 S. King St.
Seattle, WA 98104
(206) 467-0794

(Other locations in Phoenix,
AZ; Little Rock, AR; Los
Angeles and San Francisco,
CA; Denver, CO; Miami/
Ft. Lauderdale, FL;
Atlanta, GA; Honolulu, HI;
Boise, ID; Chicago, IL.;
Indianapolis, IN; Des
Moines, IA; Louisville, KY;
New Orleans, LA; Boston,
MA; Detroit, MI; St. Louis
and Kansas City, MO;
Missoula, MT; Omaha, NE;
Rochester, NY; Columbus,
OH; Philadelphia, PA;
Columbia, SC; Dallas and
Houston, TX; Salt Lake
City, UT; Milwaukee, WI;
and Casper, WY.)

Weiss & Eisenhardt
23200 Chagrin Blvd.
Beachwood, OH 44122
(216) 292-8171

Sample Memorandum of Understanding

MONA MILLER
Arbitrator • Mediator
2201 East Avenue
Rochester, N.Y. 14610
716-271-1042

Memorandum of Understanding

Jim. R. and Debbie R. have been married for thirteen years. They have reached the following tentative agreements during mediation sessions. Their intent is to incorporate these decisions, after review by their respective attorneys, into a legal separation agreement.

Financial:

Debts: Jim and Debbie have outstanding marital debts with these outstanding balances as of April, 1988:

Credit cards

(Acct. #1)	$1,398.00
(Acct. #2)	404.00
(Acct. #3)	70.00
(Acct. #4)	2,031.00
Line of credit at commercial bank	1,609.00
Department store charge account	500.00
	$6,012.00

Debt Repayment: Jim agrees to assume two-thirds of the marital debts, while Debbie will pay one-third. Accordingly, Jim will assume the debt on Credit Cards #1, #2, #3, the commercial bank loan, and the department store debt, as listed above. Debbie will assume Credit Card #4.

Support:

1. Income & Budgets

The present combined gross income of the Rs is $770.00 monthly gross for Debbie and $2,400.00 monthly gross for Jim. They have developed budgets based on Debbie remaining in the house with the children and Jim renting an apartment within close proximity. They realize the financial difficulties of maintaining separate households and consequently have reevaluated living expenses and also see the need for each to make an effort to increase future income. Debbie is increasing her work hours now and plans to work full-time after a reasonable period of adjustment for herself and a period of maturing for the children.

2. *Child Support*

Jim agrees to pay child support in the amount of $300.00 monthly, per child. Support for each child will continue until that child is 21 or until an emancipation event occurs, whichever comes first.

3. *Spousal Maintenance*

Jim and Debbie agree that their wish to maintain quality care for the children and a period of transition for Debbie are factors in determining this formula.

Jim agrees to pay Debbie $220.00 per month for two years from the time of this Agreement at which time the amount will be decreased to $200.00 monthly for year three, then $175.00 monthly for year four and $150.00 monthly for year five. Spousal maintenance terminates at the end of five years.

4. *Income Tax Return*

Jim and Debbie will file a joint tax return for 1986. The tax refund, expected to be about $800.00, will be split between them.

5. *Legal Fees*

The legal fees will be paid out of the proceeds of the refinancing of the house.

6. *Wills*

Jim and Debbie waive the rights to one another's estate.

Property:

1. *Autos*

Debbie will keep the 1983 Ford and will make the payments on it. Jim has a company car.

2. *Personal Property*

Jim and Debbie have agreed to an equitable division of marital household property.

3. *Marital Residence*

The house will be refinanced resulting in a single mortgage of $42,000. Debbie will be responsible for paying the mortgage. Jim and Debbie agree that Debbie will remain in the house with the children until the younger one is 21 or emancipated, whichever comes first. If the house is sold, at any time before that event, they agree to divide the net proceeds after the costs of sale are subtracted, and compensation is made to Jim for half the costs of any major repairs to the house for which he has paid.

At the time the last child is 21 or emancipated, Debbie may either buy out Jim's interest, based on an agreed-upon realtor's appraisal of the market value at that time, or they may sell the house and use the same formula for distribution of the proceeds.

Children:

1. *Custody*

Debbie and Jim agree that their values and practices are similar regarding the raising of their children, Seth, age 10 and David, age 8. They have concluded that joint legal custody is appropriate for them and beneficial to their continued dual responsibilities to their children.

The children's primary physical residence will be with Debbie in the marital residence.

2. *Visitation*

Jim and Debbie wish to ease the change in their children's lives for the first two years by retaining as much of the custom and tradition of family outings as is practicable. They recognize that arrangements for time with the children will need to be flexible on occasion to accomplish this goal, and they also recognize that these outings will involve one or the other parent and not usually both of them. If either of the children or either parent wishes to change customs, Jim and Debbie agree to negotiate such changes.

On a *weekly* basis, Jim will have the children overnight from Tuesday at 5 p.m. to Wednesday a.m. and take them to school.

On alternate weekends, Jim will have the children from Friday at 5 p.m. to Sunday at 6 p.m.

In addition, Jim and Debbie agree that one evening every four weeks, arranged in advance, one child will remain with Debbie and one will be with Jim, so that each child has some individual time with a parent.

Holidays will be alternated by year with Jim having the children for Memorial Day this year, and alternating thereafter. Holidays include: Thanksgiving, Christmas, New Year's Day, Easter, Memorial Day, July 4th, and Labor Day.

Birthdays of the children will be celebrated by arranging some time for each parent on that day.

School recess time will follow the normal daily schedule.

Summer vacation time of one week minimum and two weeks maximum will be available to each parent annually. Trips out of town will be made known to the other parent in advance.

All of these arrangements are made with Jim and Debbie's full awareness of the importance of making these decisions jointly as parents and recognizing one another's right to be involved. They also realize that, as the children grow, they will need to continue communicating in order to adapt to their children's changing needs.

3.   Health Care

Jim will continue to carry the children on his health insurance plan and will be responsible for nonreimbursed medical and dental bills up to $250.00 annually. Any amount over $250.00 will be divided between them.

4.   Life Insurance

Jim agrees to maintain adequate life insurance policies for the protection of the children.

5. *College Education*

Jim and Debbie agree that each will contribute to college education for the children according to his or her means.

May 12, 1988

_____

MONA MILLER
Mediator

APPENDIX
D

Resources for Divorce Mediation

The organizations listed below will provide, without charge, names of divorce mediators in your community. Those listed under "National Resources" maintain rosters of mediators nationwide; those listed under "State Resources" maintain rosters for the states or regions where they are located.

NATIONAL RESOURCES

Academy of Family Mediators
PO Box 10501
Eugene, OR 97440
(503) 345-1205

American Association of
  Family Counselors and
  Mediators
5225 Route 347, Suite 26
Port Jefferson Station, NY
  11776
(516) 551-5796

Association of Family and
  Conciliation Courts

329 West Wilson St.
Madison, WI 53703
(608) 251-4001

National Center for
  Mediation Education
2083 West St., Suite 3-C
Annapolis, MD 21401
(301) 261-8445

Society of Professionals in
  Dispute Resolution
1730 Rhode Island Ave., NW
Washington, DC 20036
(202) 833-2188

STATE RESOURCES

Arizona

Mediation Association of
Southern Arizona
1540 North Tucson Blvd.
Tucson, AZ 85716

California

Northern California Council
for Mediation
2501 Park Blvd.
Palo Alto, CA 94306

Southern California Mediation
Network
169 Pier Ave.
Santa Monica, CA 90405

Colorado

Colorado Council on Mediators
and Mediation Organizations
c/o AAA
1775 Sherman
Denver, CO 80203
(303) 629-9414

Connecticut

Connecticut Council on
Divorce/Family Mediators
410 Asylum St.
Hartford, CT 06103

Florida

Florida Association of
Professional Family
Mediators
4400 Bayou Blvd.
Pensacola, FL 32504
(904) 474-0338

Georgia

Mediation Association of
Georgia
150 E. Ponce De Leon Ave.
Decatur, GA 30030
(404) 378-3238

Idaho

Idaho Mediation Assoc.
750 Warm Springs Ave.
Boise, ID 83712
(208) 343-4164

Illinois

Conflict Resolution Associates
702 Bloomington Road
Champaign, IL 61820
(309) 452-2722

Indiana

Mediation Association of
Central Indiana
8802 North Meridian
Indianapolis, IN 46260

Louisiana

Family Mediation Council of
Louisiana
500 Dufossat St.
New Orleans, LA 70115
(504) 897-6600

Maryland

Baltimore Council of
Divorce/Family Mediators
Five Light St.
Baltimore, MD 21202

Massachusetts

Mass. Council on Family
  Mediation
264 Beacon St.
Boston, MA 02116

Michigan

Michigan Council for Family
  and Divorce Mediation
405 N. Main St.
Ann Arbor, MI 48104
(313) 358-1250

Michigan Inter-Prof.
  Association on Marriage,
  Divorce & Family
15669 Buckingham
Birmingham, MI 48009

Minnesota

Minn. Council of Family
  Mediation
815 McKusick Rd., Circle N
Stillwater, MN 55082

Missouri

Midwestern Association of
  Divorce/Family Mediators
80000 Bonhomme
St. Louis, MO 63105

New Hampshire

N. H. Mediators Association
  33 Stickney Ave.
Concord, NH 03301

New Jersey

Family Mediation Association
  of Delaware Valley
263 S. Park Dr.
Westmont, NJ 08108
(609) 854-3600

New Jersey Council for
  Divorce & Family Mediation
PO Box 6211
Bridgewater, NJ 08807

New Jersey Council on
  Divorce Mediation
88 Park St.
Montclair, NJ 07042
(201) 744-4901

New York

New York State Council on
  Divorce Mediation
300 Garden City Plaza
Garden City, NY 11530
(516) 294-5827

Divorce Mediation Council of
  New York
127 West 79th St.
New York, NY 10024
(212) 362-3324

Oregon

Oregon Mediation Association
PO Box 2952
Portland, OR 97208
(503) 285-6340

The Mediation Center
1158 High St.
Eugene, OR 97401
(503) 345-1456

Pennsylvania

Family & Divorce Mediation
  Council of Central Penn.
650 N. Twelfth St.
Lemoyne, PA 17043

Family Mediation Association
  of the Delaware Valley
Box 15934
Philadelphia, PA 19103
(215) 545-4227

Family Mediation Council
7101 Hamilton Ave.
Pittsburgh, PA 15208
(413) 371-8040

Rhode Island

Divorce Mediation Council of
  Rhode Island
69 Glenwood Ave.
Pawtucket, RI 02860
(401) 728-3044

Texas

Mediation Network of Greater
  Houston
1200 Blalock
Houston, TX 77055

Vermont

Vermont Mediation Association
5 The Green
Woodstock, VT 05091
(802) 253-8547

Virginia

Richmond Mediation Network
  c/o Psychological and
  Counseling Resources
6901 Patterson Ave.
Richmond, VA 23226
(804) 288-7227

Wisconsin

Wisconsin Association of
  Divorce Mediators
PO Box 11612
Milwaukee, WI 53211
(414) 963-2135

APPENDIX
E

*R*esources for Community
& *Environmental Mediation*

The following organizations have experience in handling disputes involving community-wide, public policy issues. The "E" denotes organizations specializing in environmental disputes.

American Arbitration
  Association
140 West 51st St.
New York, NY 10020
(212) 484-4000
(The AAA maintains 32
  regional offices in cities
  across the country.)

Center for Dispute Settlement
1666 Connecticut Ave., NW
Washington, DC 20009
(202) 265-9572

CDR Associates
100 Arapahoe
Boulder, CO 80302
(303) 442-7367
(800) MEDIATE

Clean Sites, Inc. (E)
1199 N. Fairfax St.
Alexandria, VA 22314
(703) 683-8522

Conflict Clinic
George Mason University
4400 University Drive
Fairfax, VA 22030
(703) 764-6225

Conservation Foundation (E)
1250 Twenty-Fourth St., NW
Washington, DC 20037
(202) 293-4800

Environmental Conflict Project
(E)
2036 Dana Bldg.
School of Natural Resources
University of Michigan
Ann Arbor, MI 48109
(313) 764-1511

Environmental Mediation
International (E)
Suite 1000
1775 Pennsylvania Ave., NW
Washington, DC 20006
(202) 457-0457

Hawaii:
Judiciary Program on
Alternative Dispute
Resolution
Office of Administrative
Director of the Courts
PO Box 2560
Honolulu, HI 96804
(808) 548-3080

ICF, Inc.
9300 Lee Highway
Fairfax, VA 22031
(703) 934-3000

Institute for Mediation and
Conflict Resolution
99 Hudson St.
New York, NY 10013
(212) 966-3660

Justice Center of Atlanta
976 Edgewood Ave., N.E.
Atlanta, GA 30307
(404) 523-8236

Keystone Center
PO Box 606
Keystone, CO 80435
(303) 468-5822

Massachusetts:
Mediation Service
Executive Office for
Administration and Finance
Statehouse, Room 373
Boston, MA 02133
(617) 727-2224

Minnesota:
Office of Dispute Resolution
State Planning Agency
658 Cedar St.
St. Paul, MN 55155
(612) 296-2633

National Center Associates,
Inc.
3924 N. 32nd St.
Tacoma, WA 98407
(206) 759-3039

National Institute for Dispute
Resolution
1901 L St., NW, Suite 600
Washington, DC 20036
(202) 466-4764

New England Environmental
Mediation Center (E)
123 Main St.
Gloucester, MA 01930
(508) 283-1153

New Jersey:
Center for Public Dispute
   Resolution
Dept. of the Public Advocate
CN 850-25 Market Street
Trenton, NJ 08625
(609) 292-1770

Western Network (E)
1215 Paseo de Peralta
Santa Fe, NM 87501
(505) 982-9805

APPENDIX F

Sample Environmental Mediation Agreement

I. Preamble

The undersigned (the "Parties") enter into this Memorandum of Agreement (the "Agreement") as a result of the mediation process which began in January, 1987.

The Parties to this Agreement recognize that:

A. The Forest Resource Management Act of 1982 directs the Department of Natural Resources (the "Department") to manage state forest resources according to multiple use and sustained yield principles to ensure a healthy, dynamic forest for the benefit of all citizens; and

B. The Department uses herbicides as a management tool for conifer regeneration; and

C. There is a public concern over potential risks associated with herbicide use; and

D. The Department's forest management program necessarily reflects a continual weighing of public and private interests that is designed to strike a practical and responsible balance among such competing considerations as economic costs, public concerns, scientific evidence, professional field expertise, and internal organizational realities; and

E. The provisions of this Agreement have been tailored, to the fullest extent possible, to respond to public concerns raised by the constituencies to which the Department is responsible. The Agreement embodies an approach to the aerial application of herbicides for conifer regeneration that is at once practical, prudent, and consistent with the Department's standards of professional forest management.

II. Guidelines for Herbicide Applications for Vegetation Management

A. The Department, in order to redirect aerial application activities, will make the following changes in its conifer regeneration program:

1. Emphasize more effective vegetation management activities during site preparation in order to reduce the need for aerial application of herbicides for conifer release.

2. Revise regeneration standards to facilitate ground treatment, but without adversely affecting long-term growth and yield.

3. In cooperation with other groups and agencies, conduct vendor workshops and develop materials designed to increase contractors' capability and competence to engage in aerial and ground treatment by both chemical and nonchemical means.

4. Seek review by the Minnesota Department of Agriculture of label interpretations to provide the Department with greater flexibility in the safe application of herbicides.

5. Obtain through purchase, lease, or other means additional equipment to increase the Department's capability to engage in ground or aerial treatment. Work with private vendors to design and have manufactured more efficient and effective equipment.

6. Conduct, with the cooperation of the other Parties, practical research concerning the effects of non-release of plantations.

B. In order to protect wildlife resources from the broadcast application of herbicides for conifer regeneration and to enhance wildlife habitat during vegetation management activities, the Department will:

1. Increase the use of nonchemical methods to reduce chemical application on wildlife forage.

2. Emphasize effective site preparation to avoid the need for release.

3. Submit the proposed treatment sites for timely review and comment by the Department's Fish and Wildlife Division.

4. On sites of 20 acres or more, not replant plantation spot failures or chemically retreat missed areas of up to five acres.

5. In consultation with the Department of Agriculture Apiary Office, the Department shall notify registered apiary operators of broadcast applications which may be of concern.

C. In order to protect human health in its broadcast application of herbicides for conifer regeneration, the Department will:

1. Notify, at least 3 days in advance of application, all resident landowners within one-quarter mile of a broadcast treatment site of the proposed application.

2. Unless a lesser distance is requested by the property owner, refrain from undertaking (a) aerial applications within 500 feet of an occupied permanent dwelling, and (b) broadcast application within 300

feet of an occupied permanent dwelling or within 100 feet of a private property line.

3. Post roads and designated recreational trails, where they enter application sites, with notices stating the name of the herbicide, a brief site description, the purpose of application, the date of application, the appropriate reentry date according to the product label, a phone number for obtaining further information, and a statement not to eat berries or other forest vegetation on the site. In addition, a copy of the container label shall be posted at the main entrance to the application site.

D. In order to protect water and fisheries resources from the broadcast application of herbicides for conifer regeneration, the Department will:

1. Maintain a minimum 100-foot buffer strip between surface water, including type 3, 4, and 5 wetlands, and broadcast herbicide treatment sites, unless the herbicide is labeled for ditchbank or aquatic use.

2. Cooperate with current and future efforts by the Pollution Control Agency, the Environmental Quality Board, the Department of Health, the Department of Agriculture, and others to monitor and evaluate the effect of herbicide use on ground and surface water.

E. In order to protect endangered and threatened species and species of special concern from the application of herbicides for conifer regeneration, the Department will:

1. Train forestry field personnel who conduct surveys to identify those species.

2. Combine the Heritage Program and the forest inventory data bases.

F. The Department will not aerially apply herbicides in State Parks for conifer regeneration.

G. By 1990, the Department shall utilize only herbicides that have been either (i) registered since November,

1978, or (ii) conditionally reregistered but which are not under special review by the United States Environmental Protection Agency.

III. Public Awareness

A. The Department shall publish in the EQB Monitor, or other publication of statewide circulation, no later than March 1 of each year, a listing, by county, of the proposed acreages to be treated by aerial application of herbicides, the chemicals to be used and the total number of treatment sites.

B. The Department shall place in its library the text of Operational Order 59, "Use of Pesticides on DNR Administered Lands," or any subsequent order, directive, or other policy guidelines that will govern the Department's herbicide application program.

C. At each regional office, the Department shall maintain a herbicide information file that will be made available for inspection and copying upon request by members of the general public. In building such a file, the Department shall subscribe to and circulate to Department staff at each of its regional offices newsletters from the following organizations: the National Coalition for Alternatives to Pesticides, the National Coalition Against the Misuse of Pesticides, Oregonians for Food and Shelter ("Thirty Day Briefing"), and Minnesota Pesticide Information and Education (PIE). When the Department distributes information to the public, it shall attempt to do so in an impartial and balanced manner.

D. A Forest Herbicide Committee is hereby created to review and evaluate the actions which the Parties have taken to carry out the provisions of this Memorandum of Agreement. The Committee shall have nine members, constituted as follows:

3 members selected by the Conservation Coalition
3 members selected by the Industry Coalition

3 members selected by the Commissioner of Natural Resources, including one employee of the Fish and Wildlife Division.

1. The initial members of the Committee shall be the following individuals:

   a. For the Conservation Coalition:

   > Nelson French
   > Gary Payne
   > Richard Rapson

   b. For the Industry Coalition:

   > Terry Ambroz
   > Bruce Barker
   > Archie Chelseth

   c. For the Department: (to be determined)

   _____

   _____

   _____

2. The Minnesota Environmental Quality Board, the Minnesota Pollution Control Agency, the Minnesota Department of Agriculture, and the Minnesota Department of Health shall each be invited to appoint a representative to participate as ex-officio members of the Committee.

3. The Committee shall be chaired and coordinated by the Director of the Office of Dispute Resolution of the Minnesota State Planning Agency.

4. The Committee shall be convened in August of each year to review and evaluate the progress and map out their administrative and legislative strategy for carrying out the programmatic changes described in Section IV below and meeting the targets described in Section V, B, 2 below.

5. The Committee shall be convened in November of each year to review and evaluate the actions which the Department has taken to carry out the provisions of the guidelines in Section II above and the Department's progress in meeting the targets described in Section V, B, 1 below.

6. Additional meetings may be convened by the Chair at any time at the request of the Department or of any four members of the Committee.

IV. Support for Programmatic Changes

The Parties agree to commit their best efforts to secure the enactment of the following measures, which are necessary for the full implementation of the provisions of this Agreement:

A. Funding for DNR forest road and bridge betterment to improve access for forest management purposes.

B. Legislation and administrative rule changes that will permit DNR greater flexibility in contracting for vegetation management.

C. Recommendations to the Governor and Legislature that funding be provided to conduct literature reviews and appropriate cooperative research projects with the University of Minnesota Vegetation Management Cooperative and the College of Forestry, Fisheries, and Wildlife, including, but not limited to, research concerning: (1) herbicide residues in deer and other game and nongame animals in sprayed areas; (2) herbicide residues on forest vegetation eaten by humans; (3) herbicide residues in surface water and groundwater in forested areas; (4) improving the efficiency of herbicide applications; and (5) developing nonchemical alternatives for vegetation management.

V. Commitments by the Parties

A. Representatives of the Parties shall, to the extent appropriate, participate in, and/or observe the research efforts described in Section II, A, 6; Section II, D, 2; and Section IV, C above.

B. The Parties agree to commit their best efforts, both jointly and severally, to reach the following targets by November 1st of the years 1989, 1991, and 1993, respectively:

1. The total annual acreage treated by aerial application should not exceed 6000 acres by 1989, 5000 acres by 1991, and from 3500 to 3750 acres by 1993.

2. In order to carry out the terms and spirit of this Agreement, the resources and flexibility available to the Department should be the following:

   a. By 1989, policy and administrative changes stipulated in Section IV, B should be accomplished.

   b. By 1991, the following additional appropriations should be available to the Department:

      i. $1,000,000 annually for forest road and bridge betterment, in accordance with the approved forest road plan.

      ii. $100,000 annually for equipment and operations associated with vegetative management.

      iii. $250,000 annually for the research described in Section IV, C (including $60,000 annually for the Forest Management Cooperative).

      iv. A one time $30,000 appropriation for combining the forest inventory and Natural Heritage data files.

   c. By 1993, the following additional appropriations should be available to the Department:

      i. $2,000,000 annually for forest road and bridge betterment in accordance with the approved Forest Road Plan.

      ii. $150,000 annually for equipment and operations associated with vegetative management.

      iii. $500,000 annually for the research described in Section IV, C above.

C. For the purpose of determining the need for an environmental impact statement in response to the petition for an EAW that has been submitted by the Conservation Coalition and the environmental assessment worksheet prepared by the Department, the Parties agree to the following:

  1. The Conservation Coalition hereby redefines its petition to indicate that the "Project" is the Department's aerial application of herbicides for conifer regeneration during the period 1986–1993.

  2. The Department will issue a record of decision which indicates that the aerial application of herbicides for conifer regeneration during the period 1986–1993 does not have the potential for significant environmental effects as long as the targets set out in Section V, B, 1 are met, and the other provisions of this Agreement are materially accomplished.

  3. The Department's aerial application of herbicides for conifer regeneration, beginning in 1994, shall be considered a new project for the purposes of environmental review.

  4. If the targets set out in Section V, B, 1 are not met or if the other provisions of this Agreement are not materially accomplished, the following shall apply:

      a. The Project shall be deemed a new project, permitting the Parties to file a new petition under the Environmental Policy Act;

      b. No such petition or any other legal or administrative challenge by any party shall be filed, however, until the following steps are taken:

    i.   The party shall give the Department and the Chair of the Forest Herbicide Committee written notice of its intention to lodge such a challenge, stating with specificity the basis for the challenge and the desired corrective action.

   ii.   The Department shall have 60 calendar days in which to respond, to use the good offices of the Chair of the Forest Herbicide Committee, or to employ any other method to seek to resolve the dispute.

  iii.   If there has not been a resolution of the issues raised in the notification of intent within the 60 day period, the party may proceed with its challenge.

D.   The Parties understand that the spirit of this Agreement is best served by taking a positive approach, both in the media and within the communities of which the Parties are a part, to the implementation of the Agreement. The Parties agree that they will make every good faith effort to resolve any differences that may arise during the course of the agreement.

The Parties, having set their hands hereto, hereby sign and acknowledge this Agreement this 5th day of June, 1987.

RAYMOND B. HITCHCOCK Dept. of Natural Resources	TERRY AMBROZ MN PIE	NELSON FRENCH Project Environment Foundation

DON BUCKHOUT Dept. of Natural Resources	BRUCE BARKER MN Timber Producers Association	GARY PAYNE Brainerd-Area Environmentalist
S. OLIN PHILLIPS Dept. of Natural Resources	ARCHIE D. CHELSETH MN Forest Industries, Inc.	RIP RAPSON Sierra Club People Against Chemical Contamination
BRUCE ZUMBAHLEN Dept. of Natural Resources	JOHN BERG MN Farm Bureau	

APPENDIX
G

*R*esources for Mediator Training

The following organizations are among those that train people to become mediators. Many of these groups conduct training sessions in locations throughout the country.

American Association of
  Family Counselors and
  Mediators
5225 Route 347, Suite 26
Port Jefferson Station, NY
  11776
(516) 551-5796

CDR Associates
100 Arapahoe
Boulder, CO 80302
(303) 442-7367
(800) MEDIATE

Center for Dispute Settlement
1666 Connecticut Ave., NW
Washington, DC 20009
(202) 265-9572

Institute for Mediation and
  Conflict Resolution
99 Hudson St.
New York, NY 10013
(212) 966-3660

Justice Center of Atlanta
976 Edgewood Ave., N.E.
Atlanta, GA 30307
(404) 523-8236

Mediation Training Institute
  International
PO Box 6261
Wolcott, CT 06716
(203) 879-3579

National Center Associates
3924 N. 32nd St.
Tacoma, WA 98407
(206) 759-3039

National Center for Mediation
   Education
2083 West St.
Annapolis, MD 21401
(301) 261-8445

Lemmon Mediation Institute
5248 Boyd Ave.
Oakland, CA 94618
(415) 547-8089

Settlement Consultants
   International, Inc.
14330 Midway Rd., Suite 108
Dallas, TX 75244
(214) 661-3771

Index